Muck and Merlot

'Whether fork in the garden or fork at the table, Tom Doorley offers
insightful advice, passion and experience at a time when Ireland is waking
up to the importance of ingredients. That this comes with his additional
knowledge of what goes in a glass only adds to the pleasure'

Hugo Arnold

'A riveting combination of nostalgia, anecdote,
advice and hard-hitting opinion'

Darina Allen

Tom Doorley is one of Ireland's best-known commentators on food and wine. He grows his own fruit and vegetables at his home in County Cork and has been at the forefront of the organic movement in Ireland, championing small producers and purveyors of what he calls 'real' food and wine. He has presented several series for RTÉ television and has appeared most recently as resident critic on 'The Restaurant'. He is noted for his irreverent and some-times controversial writing and maintains that the only true role for bullshit is as an organic fertiliser. He has contributed to numerous international publica-tions, including *Decanter* magazine, and is wine correspondent for *The Field* in Britain. His philosophy? 'Food is too important to be surrendered to industrial mass-production and marketing ...'

MUCK
AND
MERLOT

*A book about food, wine
and muddy boots*

TOM DOORLEY

ILLUSTRATIONS by ANNE O'HARA

THE O'BRIEN PRESS
DUBLIN

First published 2004 by The O'Brien Press Ltd,
20 Victoria Road, Dublin 6, Ireland.
Tel: +353 1 4923333; Fax: +353 1 4922777
E-mail: books@obrien.ie
Website: www.obrien.ie

ISBN: 0-86278-804-8

British Library Cataloguing-in-Publication Data
Doorley, Tom
Muck and Merlot : a book about food, wine and muddy boots
1.Doorley, Tom 2.Journalists - Ireland - Biography
3.Food habits - Anecdotes 4.Gardening - Anecdotes
I.Title II.O'Hara, Anne
070.4'49641'092

1 2 3 4 5 6
04 05 06 07 08 09

Editing, typesetting, layout and design: The O'Brien Press Ltd
Illustrations: Anne O'Hara
Printing: Mackays of Chatham Ltd

Dedication

For the essential women in my life: Johann, Sarah, Georgia and Roberta, and in memory of my mother, Anita Doorley, 1921–1991.

Acknowledgements

This book would never have happened without the inspiration and encouragement of Michael O'Brien. The task of helping me to translate it from an idea into print has fallen to Íde ní Laoghaire and to Rachel Pierce. To them, and to all the team at The O'Brien Press, I want to record my warmest thanks.

I also want to mention my gratitude to those editors who, down the years, have allowed me access to their readers, especially Patsey Murphy at *The Irish Times*, Roslyn Dee at the *Sunday Tribune*, and Jonathan Young at *The Field*. Thanks to RTÉ, I have enjoyed occasional breaks from the keyboard and been allowed to venture on to the national airways. I would like to pay tribute to Kevin Dawson, Lorelei Harris and Yetti Redmond, amongst many others, for having faith in my broadcasting abilities.

Finally, I want to thank my wife, Johann, and my daughters for putting up with me in general, but in particular while I struggled to translate the ideas that lie behind this book into some sort of readable form.

Tom Doorley
Carrigeen Hill, County Cork
Midsummer's Day, 2004

CONTENTS

Seedling Days

When my parents' house was sold a few years ago, I suspect it was the garden that clinched the deal. There are thousands of modest, semi-detached places to be had throughout Dublin, but very few of them afford the opportunity of raising a few cabbages let alone a clutch of free-range children. I'm not sure what the new owners had in mind in this respect; both, I hope.

There wasn't much sense of loss as far as the house was concerned. My parents had both died some years before and their presence had gradually evaporated, leaving familiar rooms somehow unfamiliar. It was a time for marvelling at how small my old bedroom really was, and identifying the socket which, thanks to my curious nature, had come within an ace of dispatching me to the wide blue yonder, aged two-and-a-half. No, I certainly was not going to miss the house, but the garden was another matter.

Not the present garden, which – although sizeable enough by suburban standards – seemed to have shrunk. Not the overgrown flowerbeds and creaky old potting shed, cracked paving slabs and the forest of long grass. Even as I examined a mock orange bush I had planted, aged fourteen (me, not the bush), I realised that the fury of the nearby traffic had changed the place utterly. The magic was gone. What I would miss would be the remembered garden, not the actual place itself.

So, I went around the garden seeking out the few survivors from the Golden Age, plants I wanted to perpetuate elsewhere: the vast red poppies, originally grown by my mother from a packet of Woolworth's seeds, the big daisy-like *Inulas*, even the standard issue dark-red paeonies, which you can buy in any garden centre, but which were important because ... well, because they and I went back a long way. And, of course, the very special plants.

There were three. There was the lily of the valley on which my mother had lavished so much care and which remains, even now, very much *her* flower. There was the weird and foul-smelling *Dracunculus vulgaris*, originally raised by my great-grandfather in County Meath. Why he ever did so is a bit of a mystery to me. Even when at its least pungent this is not a particularly attractive plant and its striped stems have a sinister sort of look. Every few years it produces an arum lily sort of flower, which smells overpoweringly of rotting meat. You need a big garden to grow *Dracunculus*; it needs to be kept at arm's length. But grow it I would, because it is an heirloom, a triumph of nostalgia over aesthetics.

And finally there was my lavender – a vast, sprawling, hideously neglected thing, and very special. I had grown it from seed, from the RHS Wisley Garden, even before I had graduated to planting mock orange bushes. It used to be called *Lavandula spica,* but now rejoices in the somewhat less prickly name of *Lavandula angustifolia,* or old English lavender. It has a turbocharged scent – the very best perfume in that fragrant family. Anyway, the point is that I had grown it from seed; and if you have ever seen lavender seed, something that is pretty difficult to do with the naked eye, you will understand that this felt like a miracle.

Miracles, you see, are what gardening is all about. Minor miracles, of course, not the crowd-pulling sort. Creating a garden, creating even a window-box, is pretty miraculous. Nature, as more than one writer has pointed out, abhors a garden. The odds are stacked against it. But seeing a packet of seeds transformed into plants – especially edible plants – is quite breathtaking. Or, rather, it would be if we stopped to think about what is involved rather than concentrating on where to put the decking.

Time was pressing as I stood and contemplated my unloved and unlovely lavender bush which, in a sense, represented a further miracle: survival. Lavender bushes are meant to be replaced every three or four years. This monster had been in situ for thirty years. Its days were numbered even if the new owners clasped it to their bosom.

And so I lopped off a branch of my straggly lavender bush,

sprinkled it with water and wrapped it in a plastic bag before closing the door on my parents' house for the last time. I drove my pieces of significant vegetation all the way home to County Cork. Next day, I snipped the branch into cuttings, anointed their bases with rooting powder, and shoved them, without the ceremony they deserved, into the ground. Six weeks later I had sixteen little lavender plants, each with a fine tuft of roots, ready for potting up. A miracle? Certainly, but a commonplace one. And it felt really good. Vegetative propagation, which is what you do when you take cuttings, means you end up with a plant that is genetically identical to the original. So my sixteen lavender plants are the same organism as the one that originally produced a pair of virtually microscopic seedling leaves some time in the spring of 1972.

A lot of my early memories of my parents' garden are not quite horticultural. One of them concerns the exquisite sensation between my toes during my mud-pie period, which would have occurred around about the time that John F Kennedy paid that fatal visit to Dallas. Somewhat later I distinctly recall sprinting down the lawn and away from an older sister who was chasing me with a riding crop. But, on the more conventional side, there was also the scent of roses.

Our rose collection was fairly typical of the era. The late 1950s and early 1960s saw rose-breeders obsessed with their new-found ability to get yellow, red and orange into the one bloom. Never mind the fact that the effect was often garish: it was possible! More was more in those days. And so was born a whole generation of roses which have now receded in the popular memory. I suppose Piccadilly is the best-known example, and you still see it in a few catalogues. In or around 1965 it was the must-have rose, and we had it.

We also had the rather blatant Orangeade, which I thought was such a cool name for a rose that I promptly christened a much-loved teddy bear after it. And there was Super Star, not a bad rose if you like them bright red and a bit bland. The real stars of the rose collection, however, were Josephine Bruce, a fabulously scented red hybrid tea, so dark that the petals sometimes look black, and the old favourite, Ena Harkness, whose vivid red colouring and big perfume compensates for the fact that she has such a droopy head it makes her look a bit squiffy. And then there are the roses of which I remember only the name: Betty Uprichard, Sutter's Gold, Grand'mere Jenny, Peace, Orange Sensation (as I say, orange was definitely 'in' in those days).

I came from a highly religious family, and we lived in what my father liked to call 'the odour of sanctity'. By this he meant that we were entirely surrounded by religious institutions. This may sound like a neat description of Irish society in general during that era, but in our case it was actually true. Forgive me if it sounds like Tennyson's 'Charge of the Light Brigade', but we had Vincentians to the right of us, Carmelites to the left of us and Rosminians filling in any remaining gaps.

The advantage of all this, as far as my friends and I were concerned, was that the religious institutions provided vast tracts of countryside within the suburbs. We knew exactly where to enter and leave these premises and how quick or otherwise were the gardeners and farm labourers whose duties included keeping down small boys. I became intimately acquainted with tadpoles, frogs, water rats and the stinging qualities of just about every organism that attacks adventurous children.

Growing up, as I say, in the odour of sanctity, with parents who, even by the standards of the day, took religious observance very seriously indeed, I found it necessary, at a very early age, to try to imagine Heaven. (I also tried to list the contents of God's pocket, this being a kind of bedtime game; my father was somewhat taken aback when I suggested a box of matches on the basis that 'Hell might go out'.)

For some bizarre reason my version of Heaven looked remarkably like the chapel of the nearby Carmelite convent at Hampton, where the altar flowers were supplied by our friend and neighbour, Colonel Pat Collins, nephew of the more famous Michael, and a man with a rather indiscriminate but militarily thorough passion for growing roses.

When questioned about my image of Heaven – and this occurred rather more frequently than was really healthy – I was prepared to accept that the physical surroundings might, just possibly, differ in some respects from that of the chapel at Hampton, but I was quite insistent that it smelled of roses. I'm sure the Carmelites would have been pleased to hear this because their founder, St Thérèse, known as the Little Flower, is supposed to have been constantly surrounded by the scent of roses. Spooky, or what?

My parents' efforts to grow roses in the dusty, grey soil of suburban Dublin met with reasonable success. This, of course, was in the days before the average gardener knew anything about composting and organic matter was at a premium. However, there was one source of the brown gold, namely the horses which drew the Merville Dairies milk floats. There was always a modest chance that our milk delivery would coincide with an equine call of nature and my poor mother, a woman of what used to be called gentle birth, would emerge with an empty coal-scuttle and a small shovel to gather up the nutrient-laden manure with considerable deftness.

All children find their parents embarrassing and I felt that my mother's pursuit of manure rather let the side down. But my real fear was that the girl for whom I entertained a passionate but unspoken love would discover our family secret. Grace was in Froebel School with me and I thought she was the most enchanting creature that ever wore a *kindergarten* smock.

When she played in our garden I ensured that the organic matter stayed well out of sight. Being no more than six at the time, we found the towering forest of raspberry canes that occupied what seemed like acres of the garden a sufficiently diverting place for exploration and impromptu tea parties. There is something about the smell of raspberry foliage, mixed with a hint of privet flowers, that I still find curiously sexy.

It took time for me to develop my respect for dung – I'm sorry but that is the only way I can put it – but I'm sure its origins go back to the Merville Dairies era. Other families dreamed of foreign holidays, new cars, or building an extension over the garage. Mine, quite rightly, recognised the superiority of horse shit.

I thought about this a few years ago as I took delivery of nine tonnes of well-rotted farmyard manure – the somewhat inferior cow version that is sometimes euphemistically referred to as FYM – and decided that if my mother could see me now she would think I had riches beyond compare. Although what amazes me now is that I lived through a time when it was possible to scoop anything off the carriageway of Grace Park Road without being killed instantly.

Merville Dairies, in the fulness of time, became Premier Dairies and the horses were replaced with less reliable, less economical, but somewhat faster motorised milk floats, which contributed nothing to the garden. This, as far as I was concerned, amounted to very poor timing. The reason was this: confined to bed with gastric 'flu at the age of ten, I had read every children's book in the house. I started to leaf, if you will forgive the pun, through a gardening book and was suddenly seized with the notion of growing vegetable marrows. Freudian? Perhaps.

The book explained – and it remains very sound advice – that you dig a little pit, pour in a bucketful of well-rotted manure, put the soil back in and you end up with a mound of earth in which your marrow plant can sit happily, dangling its roots into the vast food supply that lies beneath. That is undoubtedly the best way to grow vegetable marrows. Mind you, I think most of us have discovered that the smaller and younger the marrow, the better. It is, perhaps, significant that we don't have a word for 'baby vegetable marrow' in English and so we call them courgettes, or zucchini. Why the latter word should irritate me when pronounced in the tones of south Dublin is a complete mystery to me. Zucchini? Forsooth!

Anyway, as manure was as rare as courgettes in the Drumcondra of the 1970s (and perhaps even further afield, I would imagine), I made do with ... er ... digging a hole, filling it up again with earth and creating a small mound in which to plant my marrow seedling. You tend to be optimistic at the age of ten.

I went in search of the correct seeds in Drummond's, which was then on St Stephen's Green in a premises which has since housed White's on the Green and, latterly, Dublin's most expensive steakhouse, Shanahan's. I can't tell you my delight at finding a packet of marrow seeds with exactly the same name as in the gardening book: Green Bush. Not a very romantic name, admittedly. Not quite Connover's Colossal, or

French Breakfast – which apply to asparagus and radishes respectively – but magic words for me. I knew I had the genuine article, the sort that was in the picture, and that, with a bit of luck, I could conjure vegetable marrows out of that grey, dusty, north Dublin soil. The dearth of manure notwithstanding.

And so it was. What my marrow plants lacked in organic material they received in oceans of water. My gardening book was couched in those scarily dogmatic terms that seem to be confined to old horticultural manuals and, possibly, the *Ne Temere* decree. 'The importance of regular and abundant watering cannot be overstated,' it thundered, *ex-cathedra*. And when I was ten years old I was used to obeying orders, as I was then under the stern tutelage of the Christian Brothers, whom, I strongly suspected, would look rather askance at growing vegetable marrows, this being, in effect, a foreign game.

Water, luck and a hot summer produced a prodigious quantity of fine marrows, which, I rapidly discovered, made rather poor eating. There was wild talk of my long-suffering mother converting the beasts into marrow-and-ginger jam but, in the event, they tended to rot away in a kind of prototypical and not quite intentional compost heap. Most, but not all.

I entered the vegetable marrow class in the Clontarf Horticultural Society's Summer Show 1969. I pondered deeply as the great day approached. Would the Clontarf pundits favour size over what passes for tenderness in the vegetable marrow world? Would they tend towards the North of England's obsession with sheer steroidal bulk? Or would they go for a marrow which, as my gardening book put it, 'yields easily to pressure from the thumbnail'?

Knowing, even at the age of ten, that Clontarf was rather short on whippets, artisan dwellings and soot mulches, I reckoned they would take the thumbnail approach, and I selected my tenderest marrow and placed it gently on the show bench. It won first prize, and I basked for months in the glory of such recognition. Even now I think it was no mean feat, especially when I recall the stuff that passed for soil in our garden. My parents had done their best to prepare me for disappointment and I suspect that they were even more surprised than I was.

The sheer adrenalin rush of competitive vegetable growing – we lived a sheltered life, you understand – may have kindled some of my interest in growing things, but there is no doubt that growing up in a garden which my parents had created, without assistance, out of a bare plot had a lot to do with it.

My mother was the plantswoman; my father, the structural person. He was an obsessional crazy-paver and, like Churchill, no mean bricklayer, which afforded some light relief, I suppose, from his duties in the Economics section of the Department of Industry and Commerce. He also collected nineteenth-century botanical books with exquisite hand-coloured prints which, in those days, did not yet fetch a king's ransom. I can't claim that Curtis's *Botanical Magazine,* or Lindley's *The Lady's Botany* were regular reading material for me, but I do remember poring over the pictures and marvelling at the instructions on how to build a stovehouse using nothing more than a vast fortune and an army of pliant workers.

My mother was constantly distracted from the garden not just by the demands of a growing family but by the self-imposed tyranny of a privet hedge which was seven feet high and seemed to be about ten miles long. It was my mother's personal Forth Bridge; once she reached the end with the hedge-clippers, it was usually time to start again from the other end. Privet sucks what life there is out of the soil, and if you have a big enough hedge it will take a lot of the enjoyment out of gardening. A sternly moral hedge if ever there was one.

Another significant influence in my formative gardening years was one of the country's least appreciated resources, the National Botanic Gardens in Glasnevin, a place I still make time to visit, however inauspicious the season.

When Glasnevin was chosen as the site for the Gardens, the River Tolka was a babbling country brook with crystal-clear water and Kingfishers catching fire in the sunlight above it. Twenty-seven acres of light loam over gravel were acquired in the closing years of the eighteenth century. A hundred years later the Keeper was to write that 'a poorer soil or one less likely to produce results could scarcely have been found'. Our Drumcondra garden, of which the same could be said, was just over a mile away.

Anyway, by the time I knew the Tolka, in the early 1960s, the river flowed through the drab badlands of industrial Finglas and picked up quite a lot of dubious material along the way. But as a small boy, it was magic.

Let me qualify that. It was magic between two very distinct

points – where it entered the National Botanic Gardens via the hallowed ground of the local convent and where it left, under the bridge at Glasnevin, just opposite the futuristic (well, we are talking 1965 here) local Roman Catholic Church. This pyramidal affair, which dominates the Rose Garden, replaced an earlier, wooden building that had been known, predictably, as 'the Woodener'. The new building is, of course, known as 'the new Woodener' despite being constructed entirely of steel and concrete.

Yes, it was magic between those two important points. The Tolka meandered, usually green and putrefying – not offensively, just interestingly – through undulating gardens which had originally been laid out when Dublin was the second city of the British Empire and honed to a respectably tatty glory in the interim.

As a small boy with a deep and perhaps worrying interest in sluices, conduits, lock gates, shores, downpipes, ballcocks and anything else to do with waterways and drains, my favourite part of the Tolka's course was where it divided the Rose Garden from the rest of the 'Botanics', as we used to call it. Even today, seeing everything from a tiresomely grown-up point of view (and from a vantage point of over six feet), the magic still lingers as I approach the Mill Race through swathes of rhododendron and conifer.

Second in importance to the river were the glasshouses with their quaintly Victorian signs which still read, 'Strictly No Perambulators'. As a child, there was an equally strict order in which the glasshouses were to be approached. There was a light *aperitif* in the form of a quick snoop around the Cacti and Succulents House – rather spare, cool and clinical. Then, on to the Fern House where you would get the first suggestion – almost homeopathically diluted – of the true smell of a Glasnevin glasshouse. It was here that I decided I would like to own a luxuriant and prehistoric *Dicksonia* tree fern, and it has taken me just over thirty years to do anything about it.

Here, too, in summer, I would marvel at the lily pond in the centre of the house, with its particular variety which has leaves shaped like huge omelette pans: flat – so to speak – as a pancake and then turned up, just on the edge, at a neatly pressed angle of ninety degrees. I now know that this is called *Victoria Regia* and that it hails from the Amazon. There is a silence in the Fern House that is wonderfully calming; I suspect a controlled trial would find visitors show a distinct drop in blood pressure after two or three minutes.

And then it would be straight on to the Palm House. Not that we kids, my neighbours and I, called it the Palm House. This vast Victorian edifice was built to accommodate all manner of palms – essentially great big tropical monocotyledons – but to children, there was only one that mattered. The banana tree. In the sticky, green-tinged mist we would stand, sweating gently, and look up. It was a long way, but if you were lucky you would be rewarded with a glimpse of green banana fingers poised to become edible. The Palm House smelled – and it still does – exactly as a tropical glasshouse should smell: distinct, mysterious, exotic, earthy, green, delicious, intriguing.

Even then, in the 1960s, it was clear that the great

curvilinear range – the long glasshouse with the bulge near the middle – was in decline. The damp and moist atmosphere demanded by the exotics which inhabited it – the most recognisable of which were, I think, camellias, tender conifers and banksias – corroded the cast- and wrought-iron construction at a rate four times faster than would happen outside. This masterpiece of ironwork, by Dublin man Richard Turner, was, we thought, going to rot away. You could see high windows broken, long rusty brown streaks on the whitewashed back wall, the cogs and levers for opening the high windows all seized up and turning slowly to iron oxide.

Turner's other glasshouse masterpieces – at Belfast and at Kew – were restored before the Glasnevin structure, and the relevant bodies in Ireland were, I think, somewhat shamed by this. After all, Turner was a Dub, and his wonderful monument at Glasnevin was rotting away. New restoration techniques were developed, high-tech paints were used and the wonderful structure has been returned to pristine condition, even down to the fact that the metal is painted the original light cream shade rather than the snow-white which we now associate with glasshouses.

The Gardens were, as I say, laid out in the 1790s by the Royal Dublin Society (RDS). The Society was established to encourage agriculture, science and industry and for almost a century it cared for the gardens at Glasnevin. In 1878, Glasnevin passed into the care of the State and became the National Botanic Gardens. The first few decades of the new regime were distinguished by the influence of zealous plant-collectors like David Moore and his son, Sir Frederick Moore, Glasnevin's most famous directors.

I have no real evidence, but I have a feeling that the National Botanic Gardens were somewhat overlooked during the first few decades immediately following Independence in 1921. It is true that the vast majority of great gardeners and plant-collectors had sprung from the ranks of the landed gentry, and during the years of Little Irelandism there was undoubtedly a notion that the 'plain people of Ireland' would have no truck with such alien pursuits as horticulture, or – God forbid! – the practice of taxonomy. One of the few plant-collecting expeditions in which Glasnevin was able to participate during these years was funded by the Earl of Rosse, who created one of the world's great gardens at Birr Castle in County Offaly during the 1940s and 1950s.

Remarkably few Dubliners know that the National Botanic Gardens exist, and those who do might be hard-put to pinpoint it on the map. And so, it is a very quiet and contemplative place on a bright morning of early summer. But I'm not sure I don't prefer it in the depths of winter when you can really see the structure of the deciduous trees, or tramp along the Tolka with a light drizzle ensuring that you have the whole place to yourself. That's how I recapture the magic.

And it tends to be in terms of magic that I think of gardens and gardening. The lacklustre culinary qualities of the vegetable marrow had impressed themselves on me by the time I hit the age of eleven, and I moved on to vegetables that were good to eat. Growing radishes put quite a burden on the rest of my family. They are probably the easiest cultivated plant to grow and germinate virtually overnight. However, a glut of the beasts taxes even the strongest of constitutions, and I was in my twenties before I discovered that they go very well with a little sea salt and a large glass of cool white wine.

Beetroot followed, I had a partially successful stab at peas and I grew a prodigious quantity of small white turnips which fuelled the family soup pot. But best of all was the shallots. The joy of shallots is that you take them, stick them in the ground, and a few months later each of them will have divided into several new shallots. This, I believed, and still do, is a very economical vegetable and also very tasty, being milder than onions and conveniently small.

Having cut my young gardening teeth in this way – which was quite a trial to my family – I soon realised that there was a whole realm of gardening beyond the veg patch. I started to grow a few old-fashioned roses, which in those days were, if you like, even more old-fashioned than they are today. I still have the original Konigin von Danemark that I planted in

Drumcondra in 1972; she is frail, but responding well to judicious pruning and the rich, slightly acid soil of County Cork. I amazed my parents when I requested La France, the world's first hybrid tea, and the stunning white damask Madame Hardy for my fifteenth birthday. They were even more amazed when I explained that they would have to come from Hillier's of Winchester.

By this stage I was not just a member of the Royal Horticultural Society of Ireland but was appointed, in a moment of misguided enthusiasm for youth, to its council. I remember very little of this peculiar experience, but I do know that I failed to change the course of horticultural history and that my main contribution to the Society lay in patrolling its summer show at the RDS, pointing out to people that if they touched the cacti they would sustain unpleasant injuries.

Small boys with an interest in gardening are rare enough at the best of times and I was given great encouragement – and lots of cuttings – by many of the RHSI members. Miss Brunner and Miss Violet McCormick, now long dead, tried in vain to interest me in alpines, the excitement of which has eluded me to this day. The late Lord Talbot de Malahide, who gave Malahide Castle to the nation, regularly showed me over his vast garden with its rare Tasmanian plants and gave me *lapsang souchong* tea, for which I developed a lasting enthusiasm. I like to imagine that my interest in his garden helped to convince him that his gift of Malahide Castle and Gardens would be appreciated by at least one very young member of the Irish nation.

I suppose it was when I hit sixteen that gardening began to take a back seat. I had discovered writing and publishing (there are some deeply embarrassing, unofficial school magazines still in existence, but I know where most of them are) and, of course, girls. I'm not sure that teenage sexuality was recognised, let alone encouraged, in Ireland in the 1970s, but it is not entirely compatible with the contemplative nature of gardening. And so, I started to contemplate my navel and a rather larger portion of the female anatomy. It took quite a while for me to rediscover the joy of growing things, but when I did, the wheel came full circle. Amongst the first crops I planted were courgettes.

Planted Out

There is something about classrooms that never fails to give me a touch of butterflies in the tummy. Even today, when I walk in to meet a new crop of pupils at Ballymaloe Cookery School, I experience a twinge of anxiety. They invariably turn out to be delightful and wide-ranging people; deeply knowledgeable food enthusiasts from Canada or Carlow, pretty teenagers who want to be chalet girls, career-changers who have discovered grub, kitchen designers, the odd bored housewife, people who have always wanted a restaurant, inscrutable and polite Japanese folk, every sort you can imagine.

My task is to teach a course that introduces them to the world of wine, with plenty of tasting, as much technical stuff as they need and, I hope, an injection of enthusiasm for the subject. And yet, as I say, the first encounter always induces a degree of anxiety in me. I suppose it's because I associate schools and classrooms with danger. I'm just being Pavlovian.

I remember taking a few lessons at Downside, the Benedictine public school in Somerset, when I was an undergraduate.

I was enjoying a few days of monastic hospitality (the food at Downside is, in the true Benedictine tradition, exceptionally good) when one of the monks suggested that I try this baptism by fire. Facing a group of impeccably behaved fourteen-year-old boys and waffling on about the Corn Laws, or something equally lapel-grabbing, I gradually came to notice, with mounting horror, that all twenty-five of the pupils had, as one, risen to their feet and were looking at me with what seemed to be a steely gaze. I had seen the film *If* not long before and decided that this must be the start of the rebellion in which all schoolmasters and other figures of authority – even rather weedy ones like me – would shortly be swinging from the nearest lampposts.

Eventually, one of them spoke. 'Er ... the Angelus, Sir ...' And, indeed, the bell of the Abbey church had sprung into action in the distance. Relief was soon replaced by mounting embarrassment. I hadn't a clue how to start the prayer – which is what my charges were waiting for me to do – nor, indeed, how to continue.

'You,' I barked, gesturing to a particularly pious-looking youth in the front row, 'be so good as to start, please.' Which he did, the others joining in, word-perfect, as I swept around to face the crucifix that hung above the blackboard so that I could repeatedly mumble the word 'rhubarb' until the end was reached.

Any teacher going into the classroom for the first time needs nerves of steel. There is something deeply unnatural about having thirty or so young people sitting at desks, in rows, and prepared to listen to what you have to say about a subject which probably doesn't interest them much anyway. I mean, who could blame them for starting a mutiny?

I have a theory that a considerable minority of teachers were miserable during their own schooldays and return to the classroom only to get some kind of revenge on Fate by being unpleasant to a new generation of young people. And I reckon I was taught by quite a few of them myself.

My schooldays could not be described as a bundle of laughs. They were emphatically not the happiest days of my life. I was sent, at first, to the Dominican convent in Eccles Street, where I was taught by a formidable lady by the name of Miss Frawley. She was a stern disciplinarian whom I soon christened 'Miss Creepy Crawley', an early manifestation of my inability to pay due respect to figures of authority. Poor Miss Crawley was not a ray of sunshine and eventually she fell seriously ill. She was replaced by a very young, exceptionally pretty and wildly enthusiastic young nun with whom I instantly fell in love.

I had a feeling, of course, that she could not possibly be a real nun. Real nuns, of which the school had an abundant supply, were old, somewhat wrinkly and you could just about glimpse their footwear – shoes that looked very close to hobnailed boots – under their crackling skirts. Our teacher may well have been similarly dressed – I guess the outfit was compulsory – but she had a gorgeous smile and a silvery laugh which she employed regularly. She organised a nature table, hatched tadpoles, built things out of cardboard boxes and *papier-mâché.* She actually seemed to like us and enjoy our company. I can't be sure, of course, but I suspect this kind of carry-on was pretty unusual in Irish schools in 1965.

If my education had continued in this vein I am sure that I, and all the rest of the class, would have ended up as very clever, well-adjusted, high-achieving people; reality, of course, had to break in and nothing lasts forever. Soon, I was entrusted to the tender care of the Christian Brothers where, I have to say, I did not entertain any romantic notions in relation to the teaching staff. As a matter of fact, the boot was on the other foot and there were certainly some who had an unhealthy interest in little boys. They were, indeed, a mixed bunch, but I have to say that I encountered only one

31

completely sadistic bastard. Of course, they did use physical punishment even more casually than the average *mafioso*; regularly, during each school day, those of us who had got too many sums or spellings wrong would have to troop up to the master's desk to receive a blow on each hand from a thick leather strap. This, did we but know it, was designed not simply to chastise us but also to hone our skills of reaction. If you didn't withdraw each hand as soon as it had received the assault, there was a real danger that it would be slapped again amidst the welter of little palms.

Daily life with 'de brudders' was fraught with danger. The chances of escaping without at least one dose of corporal punishment during class time were virtually nil and extracurricular activities were either spartan or character-forming, depending on your point of view. The only ones I remember were the ritual humiliation of Irish dancing lessons and learning the rudiments of Gaelic football in a field liberally dotted with fresh cowpats. For somebody with my lack of physical coordination both of these pursuits added to my sense that school was, essentially, a hostile environment.

In time – it seemed like aeons, but I suppose it amounted to about two years – I said goodbye to national school with considerable relief (all that indiscriminate whacking having made me pretty resentful), and headed off to the preparatory school at Belvedere. The Junior House, as it was called, had parquet flooring, a different teacher for each subject and a curious calm which made the Christian Brothers' place seem like a hedge school conducted on the no-frills policy since championed in another sphere by Ryanair. I mean, even the quality and frequency of the whacking was different. Boys were not biffed in the heat of the moment; instead they were sent to the headmaster, or Prefect of Studies in Jesuit parlance, with a note in Latin. '*Nomen puer*' identified the culprit and '*quam ob causam*' was frequently followed, in my case, by the words, 'day-dreaming'. The Prefect of Studies could then administer the lashes in cold blood.

As a system of having grown men deliberately hurt little boys, I reckoned Belvedere was a great improvement on national school. Indeed, I thought it was the last word in sophistication. There were no cowpats on the playing fields and most of the teachers, denied the opportunity to beat an education into us, employed more subtle methods.

In my time at Belvedere the senior school was ostensibly run by a series of headmasters, all of them decent men who meant well. It became apparent, however, as I got older that the real power was wielded by someone else: a rank-and-file Jesuit (if you can imagine such a thing) who, the story went, had been removed from Clongowes after he had broken a boy's jaw. There was even a suggestion that he had broken the jaws of several boys, but this may have been inspired by the French text he used in class, a little tale entitled '*Sept d'Un Coup*', or 'Seven with One Blow'.

He was a huge man, with ham-like fists and a head the size of a Hallowe'en pumpkin; he exuded a curiously seductive combination of charm, intelligence and sheer menace. A bully, a sadist, a brilliant teacher, a highly talented man, he was also an active paedophile. His influence was everywhere. In that cynically subversive way that can be so appealing to teenage boys, he would speak slightingly of other teachers and even impute pederastic tendencies to several blameless colleagues. Anyone who was made a prefect had to have his seal of approval.

Every year he produced a Strauss operetta, and I still find it astounding that nobody seemed to think that there was something fundamentally skin-creeping about having – to take just one example – a first-form boy in a long dress and blonde wig singing 'Pink Champagne' in a prepubescent treble.

This remarkable Jesuit insisted on measuring the members of the junior chorus for their costumes: individually, stark naked and in the privacy of his own room. Favoured pupils were taken on a summer trip to Vienna where accounts vary as to what kind of sexual assaults took place. I don't think there was a boy in the school who was unaware of what this charismatic monster was getting up to; I have no doubt that many of his fellow Jesuits knew, too. We used to refer to 'Tales from the Vienna Woods'. Yet this man was let continue for many years in direct – and I mean very direct – contact with boys whose parents felt that they were providing their sons with the best education they could afford. Eventually he was moved to parish duties, but only after a group of parents, including the late and much maligned Des Traynor, had refused to yield and forced matters to a head. These days, I would like to think, he would have received a custodial sentence.

Some years before this deeply disturbing man died he

officiated at the funeral Mass of the father of one of my old school friends. I had no idea who he was – this much frailer figure – as he emerged onto the altar in St Francis Xavier's in Gardiner Street. But when he spoke in that deceptively gentle voice, I felt the same sinking sensation as would assail me when he called me up to the front of French class for some form of humiliation. And I had never been one of his physical victims.

This man's legacy is varied. I know people who became nervous wrecks, some laughed it off, some refuse to acknowledge what happened to them, at least one has been in therapy for years. As for me, I have been left with an innate distrust of authority figures and a visceral loathing of the humiliation of human beings, in whatever form. In that sense he was, perhaps, a valuable part of my education.

A few years ago I received a letter from a group of classmates who were seeking funds for a new building project at Belvedere. They pointed out that this was an opportunity to give something back to the school that had 'given us so much'. I'm afraid I wrote a rather terse reply.

Belvedere, in my time, was a smug and self-satisfied school, very different from the vibrant establishment that is there now. In the 1970s it was coasting along on its reputation and some of the teaching was frankly abysmal. But there was one teacher at Belvedere who really inspired me and who has remained a lifelong friend. Gerry Haugh came as a callow H. Dip. Ed. student in my first term in the senior school and he is there still. He introduced me to Shakespeare and to real theatre, handed out criticism and encouragement and, above all, was a grown-up to whom we could talk about absolutely anything. If I had not had his example, I doubt I would have entertained any notions of returning to the classroom after graduation. And that, some-what to my own surprise, is what I did after Trinity College, Dublin.

The year 1981 was not an auspicious one in which to gradu-ate and go about the business of getting your career on the road. The country was in an appalling state and everybody seemed determined to leave as soon as humanly possible. I had spent four relatively easy and carefree years at TCD pursu-ing a degree in History, discovering the opposite sex in greater detail, drinking prodigious quantities of stout at the pavilion bar in College Park and spending considerably more time on what one might loosely call extracurricular activities than on my studies.

As far as academic matters were concerned it was, in my case at any rate, an example of youth being wasted on the young. Some of the finest brains in the land were on hand to teach me and my thirty-nine fellow students and yet I failed to be gripped by the story of the Guelphs and the Ghibellines and the emer-gence of medieval Europe. The only light relief in my Junior Freshman year was an unfortunate misprint in an impenetrable tome which referred – or was meant to refer – to King Cnut.

Eventually, I came to accept that I was going to end up knowing more and more about less and less. I developed a vast and wholly unexpected enthusiasm for the wool industry in medieval England – purely because my tutor, Dr Christine Meek, was a brilliant teacher – and I ended up producing a mini-thesis on how the cloth industry financed Edward III's military campaigns. I still have a sense of mild disbelief when I realise that I managed to pull this one off.

I was taught by the legendary Professor RB McDowell, a man of immense erudition and charm who dressed like a particularly down-at-heel tramp and whose office was – literally – ankle-deep in papers and books. On one occasion, when I had gone to collect an essay, he told me brightly: 'You take that side of the room, I'll take this and I'm sure we'll turn it up eventually.' It took less than an hour.

McDowell's great interest was in eighteenth-century Ireland and I worked with surprising enthusiasm for him. Other courses failed to grip me. I drove Professor Louis Cullen, the great expert on Irish economic history, to distraction; on one occasion, when reading a seminar paper on the price of potatoes in the nineteenth century, I was asked by him, rather sharply, to 'spare us the further details'.

When I was struggling to come up with a suitable essay subject on twelfth-century Ireland, I made the mistake of telling one of the leading experts in the area, Professor JF Lydon, that I found the whole subject rather boring. I can still hear the explosion that followed.

However, despite my patchy enthusiasm for history, I came

out after four years with a creditable 2.1 and decided that I would pursue a part-time MLitt. Of course, it was not a foregone conclusion that I would be accepted for postgraduate work, and I am eternally grateful to the School of Modern History that they decided to give me the benefit of the doubt. Professor KG Davies, then the Head of Department, told me, 'in the parlance of the English football league, you're a flashy player'. I am still awestruck at his powers of diplomacy.

The MLitt (which was on the development of surgery in late eighteenth-century Ireland, since you ask) eventually fell by the wayside. The original source material dried up after a few months of desultory research and so did my enthusiasm. In any case, I was enjoying the other part of my life. I had decided to try teaching.

Despite the economic black hole that blighted our career prospects in 1981, my tutor was quite upbeat. 'All of our History graduates get jobs,' she told me brightly. 'Eventually. That's the great thing about a degree in History. It teaches you how to think.'

I had yet to discover that this is, to some extent, true, but I was glad to hear that she thought that all of the class of 1981 – a wide-ranging assortment of characters if ever there was one – would find jobs. I was slightly dismayed, however, when she admitted that this process might well involve moving across the water.

I rather liked Dublin and I thought it would be good to stay put, at least for a while. My initial problem lay in the fact that my education at TCD, while teaching me to think, did not fit me for any particular occupation. I rather envied my friends in the Medical School: they had to work very hard, but at least they knew where they were going, even if it would inevitably involve short-term jobs in various parts of the English-speaking world. I almost envied my friends in the Law School, but I realised that legal science would have bored me rigid.

The only answer was for me to defer my decision as to where my career was to lie and the best way to do that was to sign on for the H.Dip.Ed. This course of relative inaction would allow me to hang around TCD for another year and, if I did a modicum of work, I would end up as a qualified secondary schoolteacher. Even then I knew that I did not relish the prospect of spending my entire working life at the chalk face, but it seemed like a good idea at the time.

Having been accepted for the H.Dip.Ed course my first task was to find a school that would be prepared to unleash me on its pupils and, oddly enough, my first thought was of Belvedere. Nothing would have been easier than to return to the familiar environs, despite the fact that I had not enjoyed my time there as a pupil. I am eternally grateful to the then headmaster who turned me down flat on the very sensible basis that I would be much better off going to a school with which I had no connections.

Amongst the establishments which responded to my plea for teaching practice hours was a boarding preparatory school in Bray, which was excessively anxious to sign me up, sight unseen. 'I can't do games,' I told the Head with perfect truthfulness. 'No problem, old boy,' he said. 'I'm sure you would be a great asset and, of course, you would be saving on rent because we can give you full board and lodging ...'

I nearly gave in. Much as I appreciated my home life, this offer of food and shelter held out some hope of independence. But the Head's eagerness suggested that he had difficulty finding people prepared, at the age of twenty-one and upwards, to share accommodation with a group of small boys. A ghastly vista opened up before me and I decided to decline the kind offer if I got another from elsewhere. Anywhere.

In the end, I got two offers on the same day and the choice was a tough one. Mount Temple Comprehensive came up trumps and so did St Columba's College, Rathfarnham. Mount Temple was close to home and to Trinity, but St Columba's was intriguing. I knew dozens of Old Columbans and even liked quite a lot of them. They tended to be clannish in a way that suggested that their schooldays had formed some sort of immutable bond between them. Having kept up with a handful of Old Belvederians despite the fact that we had been at school together rather than because of it, I was intrigued by a place where the pupils seemed to enjoy each other's company even after they had left.

St Columba's is a curious old place, perched in the foothills of the Dublin Mountains overlooking Marlay Park and, latterly, the M50 motorway. Founded in 1843 by William Sewell, an enlightened English clergyman who went on to establish Radley in Oxfordshire, it was designed to be a school that would educate the sons of landlords in their own country rather than in England, as was then the fashion. And so, St

Columba's was modelled on the Victorian English public school, with the boys divided into houses. Even today, St Columba's belongs to the Headmasters' Conference in Britain, the representative body of the so-called public schools.

In the early 1980s it was a small school, with just under three hundred pupils, boys and girls, the vast majority of them boarders. As I walked up the steep driveway in early September for the first staff meeting of term, I thought it seemed like a pleasant enough place to do my teaching practice. I had no idea that I would end up spending four years there. Or that it would change my life.

The first thing that a visitor will notice about St Columba's is that all of the pupils wear academic gowns. I was once delivered to the school by a scarily myopic taxi driver who peered through the windscreen at a group of second formers while I fumbled for the fare. 'My God,' he declared, 'you have some very young staff here!'

The second thing is the fact that the school is accommodated in a rambling series of buildings with well-tended flower gardens scattered between them. St Columba's doesn't look like an institution. The Gothic Revival chapel looks out over the school and – in the distance – a panorama of Dublin and the Bay. Stroll up the hill through the deerpark and you are in the foothills of the Dublin Mountains.

I learned rapidly. Unlike at Belvedere, the students were not expected to stand when a master entered the classroom. Their gowns were invariably filthy (the school doctor insisted that they be removed before entering the surgery) and embellished with slogans and pictures crafted in the medium of Tippex. The food was terrible. My colleagues were welcoming and supportive. Everybody was expected in chapel at 8.15am, and I mean everyone. Junior boys were called 'the ducks', junior girls 'the greenies', punishments included doing 'sides of blue' (essays on special paper which could only be obtained from one's housemaster), everything you wanted to know about the school was in something called 'the green book' and pupils were expected to stay within bounds known as 'iron railings' if they didn't have an *exeat*. The place had its own language, tradition and code of behaviour.

The pupils were friendly, lively and approachable; and so, for the most part, were the staff. What struck me in particular was what an easy relationship seemed to exist between the two. True, you were always called 'Sir', but the boys and girls of St Columba's would never dream of letting anyone take himself too seriously, teacher or pupil.

Young, single members of staff were expected to get as fully involved in the life of the school as possible (while older, married ones did not get off too lightly either). I ran the junior debating society, produced the junior play, took mini-busloads of sailors to Greystones on Saturdays, read bedtime stories to 'the ducks' in Tibradden House (or 'the duckery'), and even took camping trips. At lunch the staff ate together on the high table at the head of the dining room, but at supper we ate with the troops. As a result of all this, I got to know my pupils extremely well. I discovered why some of them were difficult or withdrawn. I learned about their families, their enthusiasms, their weaknesses. I came to care about them in a way which I had never thought possible, having always regarded teachers as a rather aloof bunch. With older ones I'd find myself discussing the meaning of life and other adolescent issues; with the younger ones I would occasionally have to deal with tears and homesickness. St Columba's was a community. I was part of that community with certain roles to play and I was appreciated. It was exhilarating, challenging, tiring, fulfilling, and I was introduced to the notion that I could, in however tiny a way, influence people's lives. I learned a vast deal more during my four years at St Columba's than I had during my ten at Belvedere.

But how, you may ask, did it change my life? Well, teaching O-level history to a mixed-ability group gave me my first experience of trying to explain something complex. In an odd and roundabout way my history lessons ('What's a dichotomy, Sir?; you're not at Trinity now!') paved the way for my consuming interest in helping people to understand and enjoy wine. St Columba's also gave me many lifelong friends, some of them members of staff, but most of them people who are big enough to ignore the fact that I once marked their prep and ticked them off for not having their top button done up.

But in terms of life-changing, by far the biggest element was the fact that I fell madly and silently in love with a blonde, blue-eyed girl in the sixth form called Johann McKeever, who helped out with the junior play. I certainly don't recommend young schoolmasters to entertain romantic feelings towards the girls in their school, but in this instance there was absolutely nothing I could do about it. I was smitten and, as it happens, fate was on my side. On her last night of term she and I ended up strolling down Dún Laoghaire pier by moonlight. We have been married to each other since 1984.

People sometimes say to me that it must have been quite strange marrying a pupil. The simple answer to that is that I didn't. I never encountered Johann in the classroom, and in the curiously egalitarian atmosphere of St Columba's in the early 1980s, we started off our relationship as friends, pure and simple.

On a school trip to Russia in 1983, very late at night in a Moscow bar, I told her – in an unguarded moment – that I thought she was wonderful, an opinion which I have never since revised. When we returned to school I was spared any real embarrassment by the fact that Johann was clearly going out with someone else. But our friendship grew and, at the end of term, blossomed into something else. The timing was impeccably respectable.

I was, at the time, a rather immature twenty-four-year-old while Johann was an eighteen-year-old wiser than her years would suggest. When we got married, at twenty-five and nineteen respectively, I think it is fair to say that we did so to keep our deeply conservative parents happy. Otherwise we would have cheerfully cohabited. However, it's remarkably good to have been married to her for just over twenty years.

Johann has been a full-time homemaker ever since our eldest daughter, Sarah, was born in 1989. Georgia followed in 1993, and Roberta in 1996. However, she has managed to snatch some time to develop her artistic talents, something that she plans to develop further when Roberta heads off to boarding school in five years' time. She has often said that she would quite like to be a relatively young grandparent – ours had all shuffled off this mortal coil before we reached our teens – but not, she adds, unexpectedly or prematurely!

I recently had a consultation with a particularly thorough homeopath. 'What is the best thing that ever happened to you?' was one of the questions she asked. No prizes, then, for guessing my answer.

Careering About

I have always been a bit wary of people with strong views and very clear ideas. So many of them don't appear to be very happy. The truth being rarely pure and never simple, in the words of Oscar Wilde, I have always tended to be a little vague. Vagueness can go too far, of course, but I like to think of it as the opposite of fundamentalism. And nobody has, so far, managed to put the fun into fundamentalism.

Perhaps vagueness is not quite the right word, but I have always been interested in too many things to get entirely obsessed with just one issue. And, no, I don't think I'm obsessed with food or wine. If I am ever in danger of becoming fixated on the *terroir* of a Bordeaux commune, or the finer points of asparagus growing (is salt really necessary as a top-dressing?), I get distracted by the throaty music of an old Aston-Martin, or a book on architecture, or a political conspiracy theory. Or just about anything, really.

People who are not vague or unfocussed in this kind of way enjoy certain benefits, of course. They are free to be single-minded in their pursuit of fame and fortune, or the breeding of budgerigars, or whatever. They set out, more often than not, with a very clear career plan and they get what they want. In this respect, of course, they have the great advantage of actually knowing what they want. Exactly what they want. I'm afraid I've always been rather hazy on this point.

And so, my career – for want of a better word – has never been actually mapped out. I have convinced myself that I was, indeed, making career plans, but so far I am forced to admit that the various jobs I have done were rarely what I set out, in the first place, to do.

I did, of course, deliberately become a teacher and spent four very happy and contented years in the classroom. Despite how comfortable I found myself in that job, I felt that the lure of teaching would pall eventually; I had a horror of teaching the same courses for donkeys' years and ending up obsessed with the microcosm that every school, however good, really is. My only problem was that I had no idea what to do next.

It was difficult to leave St Columba's. It had, in a sense, become my world and I was surrounded by colleagues who were variously interesting, eccentric, brilliant, great company, or, in some cases, a combination of all. I am thinking, in particular, of the late Charles Guinness, the classicist Richard Brett, the ceramics artist Peter Watts and his wife, Grainne, and my contemporary, Julian Girdham, who is now Sub-Warden at the College. The pupils, for the most part, were open, friendly and enlivening company. During my last academic year at the school I was married to Johann, who had only left a couple of years previously. I have to say that nobody – staff or pupil – seemed to bat an eyelid. At least in my presence. When we had announced our engagement in *The Irish Times*, I mentioned to the Warden, David Gibbs, that I had said nothing previously on the basis that we wanted the news to be a surprise. 'Well, you've certainly succeeded in that,' he replied. But he and his wife, Sally, were the first to offer us both their congratulations.

When I left St Columba's and went off into the wide world I applied for any number of jobs, but a combination of the times that were in it (we're talking about 1985 when the country was on the verge of bankruptcy) and my inability to persuade any employer that I was capable of multi-tasking meant that I found myself, in common with hundreds and thousands of my fellow citizens, signing on.

Meeting a friend of mine one day who was in public relations, I decided to try that particular sphere of activity. Why I should have done so is still a bit of a mystery to me, but I suspect that it was largely because the PR business was, like Mount Everest in the phrase of Edmund Hillary, 'there'. And I suppose I had an idea that anyone who could take school children on camping trips without any fatalities could make a fist of event management. I was also convinced, without a great deal of evidence beyond producing history essays at TCD, that I could write.

Considering that the public relations industry these days has a disproportionate number of semi-literate airheads working away happily in it (and failing, daily, to have any notion of how journalists really work), I suppose I should have been pretty depressed at my inability to get a job in the business. But perhaps it was different in those days. I was advised that I should first get some journalistic experience, and so I sat down and wrote a few features – including a rather hard-hitting one, of which I'm still proud, on the pharmaceutical industry – which I posted off to the features editor of the *Irish Independent*. Those were the days when 'hard copy' was the order of the day.

To my amazement, they were published and a cheque duly arrived. To my further amazement, the features editor 'phoned me up and asked if I had any more ideas. In no time I was spending most of my days – still as a freelance – in that grim building in Middle Abbey Street which was known to its inmates as Château Despair. Officially, it's Independent House.

The money was modest, but the experience was remarkable. I had not set out to be a journalist, but I was soon capable of sub-editing copy (in the days when that task was no mean feat, as it was done without any computer technology), cold-calling Very Important People for quotes, working on the news analysis team and becoming a nascent political pundit ('Whither Fine Gael?'). I had also become wine columnist at the *Sunday Tribune*.

Had I not been thrown in at the journalistic deep end and acquitted myself with reasonable ease, I would never have dreamt of trying to become an advertising copywriter. I read, one day, an interview with the late Peter Owens, one of the doyens of the industry, in which he said that if, on a scale of one to ten, you value job security at anywhere above two, advertising is not a sound career choice.

Well, it sounded about as secure as freelance journalism and the pay, I was told, was better. I wrote to thirty advertising agencies and got one reply, to the effect that they would keep my letter on file. I didn't hold my breath.

And then, one day, I got a call: not from the agency which had filed my letter but from one of the non-responders. They asked if I would come and see them about a once-off writing project that needed to be done double-quick.

The agency in question must have been desperate. They needed someone to research and write a pamphlet entitled 'PMS Can Leave a Woman Shattered', and deliver the copy within twenty-four hours. I was so delighted with the opportunity, and the vast cheque (by comparison to the admittedly paltry sum I was getting from Independent Newspapers), that I managed to turn the job around by ten o'clock the following morning.

The agency gave me occasional little jobs from time to time, and when I wasn't writing features for the *Indo* I was dreaming up straplines for Nissan cars, or punchy copy for life assurance companies. And then a new features editor was appointed at the *Indo*. He had an interesting approach to freelancers and would set the bar, so to speak, so high that we poor hacks would end up pushing at the bounds of what was possible to publish in a newspaper without getting sued.

In the meantime, I had become a parent. This was a very deliberate decision for Johann and me. Ruth Buchanan (also known as Mrs Shane Ross) had told us that there is a great deal to be said for having children when youth is still on your side. Babies are emotionally and physically very, very demanding, she said, and she was grateful that she and Shane had had their two children when they were in their twenties.

I was thirty when Sarah was born in 1989; Johann was twenty-four. It was not an easy birth and I still recall, with horror, the feeling of being unable to do anything practical to help. And also the sense of something akin to shock that descends upon you, even as a mere father, during the whole process. But within the experience there was a sense of complete wonder and true joy. When the midwife handed me the tightly wrapped bundle that was Sarah and I held her in my arms for the first time, I realised that the love I was experiencing was so acute that it was close to pain. I also knew, in the words of our friend and neighbour Alan McGurdy, that 'when you become a parent you surrender some of your peace of mind forever'.

Parenthood concentrated the mind. The crunch came when the features editor at the *Indo* asked me to produce 1,200 words on 'unconvicted criminals, with pictures of them'. I was less concerned with the fact that such a project would lose the paper several million quid in damages and more worried about the integrity of my kneecaps and other, more vital, body parts. I said no, and 'phoned up the advertising agency in a desperate attempt to persuade them to give me a job.

Having got to the bit where I was pointing out that I had a baby daughter to support, I was stopped short in my tracks by a wholly unexpected agreement to take me on, on a probationary basis. I spent the next two years writing newspaper and magazine ads, TV and radio commercials (most of them for baby food, fencing wire and highly poisonous agrichemicals), and patient information leaflets for all manner of medicines. I even ended up attending international medical meetings and writing a précis of the proceedings; I became quite expert in anti-hypertensive therapy, the role of H2-antagonists and bronchodilators. I have a vague idea that I once wrote a prescription for a colleague for a ringworm cream, but I may have been dreaming. One of the finished artists, Niall Clancy, pinned a sign on my office door which read,

'The Doctor is IN'. I know that I did decline to 'prescribe' the contraceptive pill for a colleague and pointed her in the direction of the Well Woman Clinic, saying that I thought the money would be well spent.

Little did I know that I would soon become what I suppose you might call a major player in contraception (perhaps, on reflection, that is an unfortunate phrase). After a couple of years manacled to my desk at the advertising agency, I decided that I had learned as much as I wanted (and perhaps rather more) about the ad business and that the time had come to move on and plough my own furrow. Despite my vagueness I had, at the age of thirty, decided that if I started my own marketing agency, I might be able to retire by the time I hit forty. 'Might' being the operative word.

The advertising agency people were very kind and they kept me well supplied with small jobs and projects which allowed me to set up on my own. Thanks to the fact that I was still writing about wine – for the *Sunday Business Post* at this stage – I was able to land the PR account for Irish Distillers' wine portfolio, and set about the task of trying to build Jacob's Creek into a household name. I promoted pharmaceuticals for Glaxo and various other drug companies. I even produced a two-hundred-page brochure for a window company, a task that was so catatonically boring that I almost lost the will to live.

But my sights were set on one brand I felt could be big in Ireland if it had the right marketing support on the ground. I focussed on getting the Durex account and, in the words of one client whom I subsequently lost, 'corrupting the young people of Ireland'. Well, someone had to do it.

I don't think my mother would have approved. The poor woman died, at the relatively early age of seventy, just a few weeks before I was, at last, asked to pitch for the business of our flexible friends. I was not optimistic, being up against two other agencies. Real agencies, with the kind of offices where you could invite your clients, with people who answer the 'phone and 'put you through'. Not one room with peeling wallpaper, a clapped-out PC, a fax machine and a hideously expensive, brick-sized mobile phone. This was, after all, 1991.

I'm not sure what swung it for me, but I have an idea that it may have been my insistence that there were dark forces in Ireland – the ranks of the extreme Catholic Right – who would stop at virtually nothing to slow the advance of contraception. I produced stickers I had peeled from lampposts and bus-stops which read, 'Condoms Cause AIDS'. This kind of campaign had to be tackled, I said, whatever about the every-day task of persuading people to embrace the idea of safe sex.

Well, perhaps that was it. I can't imagine the other PR agencies trawling through the poisonous rantings of those extreme conservatives who wanted to keep the country in the Dark Ages (otherwise known as the McQuaid Epoch). Or maybe it was the fact that I cracked a joke during the presentation. A rather limp one, if you will forgive the expression, but it got a laugh. I told them about the Irish condom company that had agonised about its packaging formats before deciding to present its wares in 4s, 8s and 12s. The 4s were for junior civil servants: Monday, Tuesday, Wednesday, Thursday, and then home to the Mammy in the country for the weekend. The 8s were for young, urban professionals: Monday, Tuesday, Wednesday, Thursday, Friday, Saturday and twice on Sunday. The 12s, on the other hand, were for married couples: January, February, March ... Oh well, it was worth it.

The best idea I presented to my new rubbery client was not mine at all. Ali Purdon (now Guy), whom I had first met when she was a pupil at St Columba's and who was now a formidable public relations consultant, suggested that Durex should commission the first ever research into the sexual behaviour of the Irish. It was a brilliant idea and a very simple one. The ensuing *Durex Report* came out in 1992 and attracted a vast amount of attention. By the time I was driving the Durex personnel from the press conference in Buswell's to lunch in The Commons, we had already hit the headlines in the evening papers. I had a very happy client on my hands.

When we launched the first ever radio commercials for condoms in Ireland, in 1993, the story made not just the BBC News but also the national network news in Canada, to say nothing of Sky News. The normalisation of condoms in Ireland – the process of tweaking the Irish psyche so that we regarded condoms as nothing more heinous than useful little pieces of rubber – was world news. The Catholic Right went – again, if you will forgive the expression – bonkers.

Durex, for a time, almost took over my life. I will admit that I was fired with missionary zeal. This was not just a commercial occupation – although I have to say it paid well – it was more than that. It was, for me, about more than promoting a good product in which I had great faith; our three children were conceived according to plan thanks to Durex. It was about assisting the country in the process of growing up and accepting the realities of sex and sexuality as we approached the millennium. We had campaigned hard to have the law on condoms changed. When I took on the Durex campaign in 1991 condoms could only be bought, legally, by people over the age of eighteen, from pharmacies and for '*bona fide* family planning purposes'. I have never been sure which family planning purposes are not *bona fide*, but they must surely include the old party trick of wearing them as a hat. A few years later condoms were being sold, to anyone who needed them, from every conceivable (well, you know what I mean) kind of retail outlet, including vending machines.

Condoms had now been exorcised; they were no longer sinister little foil-wrapped devices with an inherent demonic capacity to send anybody who touched the packet into a frenzy of what the conservative elements liked to call 'casual sex'. I often wondered what they meant by 'casual'; would you actually know that you were doing it? Condoms rapidly became as commonplace as toothpaste and dental floss.

Although Durex came close to occupying all my working days, I still found time to write on wine and had by now returned to my old berth at the *Sunday Tribune*. In 1994, the legendary Helen Lucy Burke hung up her boots as restaurant critic and I was invited to step into her place.

On one of my early outings in this capacity I invited the then editor, Peter Murtagh (now Head of the Foreign Desk at *The Irish Times*), to join me at Cooke's Café, and it was over that meal that we created a new columnist for the paper. I was telling Peter about my work in the rubber industry and how I kept a watchful eye on the extreme Catholic Right through the simple expedient of reading their house journal, a weekly newspaper called *The Irish Family*. I mentioned to him that I had had several pseudonymous letters published in it, including one which purported to come from a retired GP warning against the fatal side-effects of self-abuse in the young. (Oddly enough, the editor clearly twigged what was afoot when I wrote again, this time condemning the immorality of tampon use, quoting a genuine article from *The Furrow*, published in 1944.)

Peter suggested that it might be fun to create a *Sunday Tribune* columnist whose *oeuvre* would reflect the concerns of *The Irish Family* and its readership, but which would be written in such a way as the average reader would be unsure as to whether or not it was for real. And so I became the septuagenarian Aodghan Feeley NT, scourge of the liberals, sage of the Midlands, spin-doctor to Youth Defence and advisor to myriad action groups, including the wholly fictional Mothers Against Dubious Doctrine (MADD) and Families United in Combatting Kinky Sex (FIX).

In the course of writing Aodghan's 'Real Ireland' column I invented dozens of characters (although it has to be said that some of *The Irish Family*'s correspondents were, indeed, stranger than my fiction). There was his wife, Breda, who kept trying to kill him. Brother Cathal (named in honour of, but, I must stress, not after my then colleague, Cathal MacCoille), a retired and infuriatingly pedantic Christian Brother, Briege 'Bioethics' Brannigan who was Aodghan's '*amanuensis*', Labhras 'Imperial Leather' Uí Laoire, his great rival for the hearts and minds of the Irish Vigilance Association, and Father Jesus Pinochet y Tonic, his Opus Dei mentor. There was even a particularly supine Church of Ireland rector, Canon Cecil Smallbone, who suggested that Protestants should avoid speaking Irish in public in case it offended the majority.

Aodghan's trick was to weave himself, Zelig-like, into real events and the activities of real people. They were the leading lights of the conservative Catholic movement, but pretty much unknown outside those realms until Mr Feeley catapulted them all into a national newspaper. He was simultaneously in love with Nora Bennis, a Limerick housewife and conservative activist, and some of the young female leaders of the anti-abortion group, Youth Defence.

Aodghan, I'm sure, did wonders for the circulation of the *Sunday Tribune*. It became compulsory reading for all those conservative activists who lived in hope of seeing their names in the column which, at the same time, infuriated them. I am told that it became something of a badge of honour amongst the myriad groups and splinter groups which sought to defend Ireland against 'secular humanism' to be lampooned by Mr Feeley.

Aodghan and his outpourings were abolished when Peter Murtagh resigned as editor. Colleagues told me that one of the

few smiles that brightened Peter's face during his last few difficult days in the job was when he read Aodghan's column in
which the great man had picked up on a reference by one
Joseph McCarroll, a leading conservative, to the evils of oral
sex. 'It could be happening under our very noses,' opined
Aodghan.

Peter's caretaker successor explained that she didn't find
'Real Ireland' funny and she axed the Sage of the Midlands,
something that I can forgive only on the basis that the woman
in question seemed to have had a sense of humour bypass.
But I have since met hundreds of readers who would have
strongly disagreed. I didn't meet them at the time of writing the
column for the simple reason that Mr Feeley's true identity was
a carefully concealed secret. In the days before e-mail, his
copy was filed by fax – but only after I had carefully turned off
the sender ID function.

I suppose that Aodghan was, in a sense, there at the right
time. The mid-1990s saw a ferment of debate about abortion
and divorce. He would be, perhaps, a little past his sell-by date
at this stage. Even *The Irish Family* newspaper, when I last
glanced at it, is only a shadow of its former self and, as far as I
can gather, conservative extremists seem to have stopped
founding political parties every second week.

At the time, of course, there was considerable speculation
as to who was behind the Feeley Phenomenon, as the character himself was inclined to call it (he did, I have to say, develop
a kind of quasi-independent existence and I frequently found
myself referring to him in the third person). Joseph O'Connor,

then writing a weekly column in the *Tribune*, had become intrigued with Aodghan and started to claim that he regularly met him around town. As a result, many readers assumed that Mr Feeley was, in fact, Mr O'Connor.

In one column Aodghan commented, 'I can sympathise with Joe when it comes to people saying to him, "You're Aodghan Feeley, aren't you?" I often experience the same kind of thing with people assuming that I am "David Quinn" of the *Sunday Business Post*. The last time it happened to me was when I was enjoying a late-night Club Orange with Sean Dublin Bay Loftus in The Chocolate Bar in Dublin. With as much dignity as I could muster I pointed out that the true identity of David Quinn was a closed book to me, but that Brother Cathal, an avid "media watcher", believes that this particular column is one of Joe O'Connor's "japes", albeit, in my view, in very poor taste.'

Perhaps I should explain that I have the height of respect for David Quinn, although I am not always in agreement with him. He seasons his journalism with a healthy sense of humour and I like to think he took the joke in the spirit in which I intended it.

During the last few weeks of the 'Real Ireland' column I became aware that Joe O'Connor was hot on the trail of Mr Feeley's true identity, and I decided to bring him in on the secret. A friend of mine, adopting the persona of Briege 'Bio-ethics' Brannigan, 'phoned up and told him that Aodghan wanted to see him and a meeting was arranged in the bar of *Comhaltas Ceoltóirí Éireann* in Monkstown. Joe took the opportunity to present me with a copy of his *Irish Male at Home Abroad*, which had just come out and which was dedicated, I was delighted to see, 'to Aodghan Feeley, with admiration'. I was horrified to hear, however, that this was not the first occasion on which he had been invited to meet the great man. Perhaps the wilder elements on the Catholic Right, convinced that Aodghan was Joe, wanted to persuade him to desist. We will never know.

Just as I had never planned to be a promoter of condoms or a thorn in the side of Ireland's most socially conservative elements, my next move in the media was not premeditated. Early in 1996 I was contacted by a TV production company that had been commissioned by RTÉ to do a series on food and wine. They asked me if I would like to screen test for the position of resident wine pundit on the show and, needless to say, I jumped right in. It involved doing a piece to camera about a couple of bottles of wine, and I was fortunate in having had something of a dry run a couple of years beforehand.

Kevin Dawson, now a very senior RTÉ executive, was then a trainee director with the station and had to produce a sample programme. His chosen subject was food, and he asked me if I would front the programme, despite the fact that I had never stood in front of a camera in my life. Brave of him, I'd say.

I suppose the fact that Kevin's televisual début was purely for internal consumption in RTÉ was strangely reassuring. It would have been a different matter altogether if I had felt that my performance would have been offered, on air, to the great Irish public. In the event, however, I was able to muster a certain confidence, however ill-founded.

Talking to a camera lense in which you can see only a distorted image of your own mug is a pretty bizarre experience. Let's just say that it doesn't feel entirely natural and, of course, the whole idea is to come across as naturally as possible. Well, I enjoy a challenge and it's amazing what a little practice can do. Having said that, it can be a little unnerving to do a longshot, where the camera is in the far distance and you have to wander along a crowded street, staring intently into the distance and apparently talking to yourself. Little old ladies have occasionally advised me to seek professional help.

The production team behind 'Moveable Feast' seemed satisfied with me and we proceeded to make two series of the programme, which involved my discovery of parts of Ireland the existence of which I had previously accepted on the basis of faith alone. Each week the programme was set in and around a different town and John Daly, Clare McKeown and myself would present bright and breezy pieces about food and wine. Towards the end of the second series, as our stamina began to flag and cracks began to appear in the relationship between certain members of the team, we renamed the programme 'Miserable Beast'. However, I have to say that, overall, it was fun, exhausting and an exceptionally useful experience.

When the opportunity came to do a series of my own, 'The Big Stew', in 1999, I had come to accept the strange experience of talking to my own reflection as being more or less natural. There is something reassuring about pre-recorded programmes, in that you know that if you make a hames of your performance you can always do it again. Having to do it too often, of course, means that the crew – the unsung and unseen heroes of the production – get a bit browned off. The first piece I did for 'Moveable Feast' was shot on the quay at Westport and involved me extolling the qualities of four wines. In my keenness to add verisimilitude to the act, I swallowed a little as I tasted, on camera. Unfortunately, thanks to me fluffing my lines, planes going by overhead, people starting up tractor engines, or, indeed, a combination of all of these hitches, I was forced to give up on the twenty-third 'take' in a state of some intoxication. As the director said, 'When you started to slur your words it was bad enough, but when the belching began, we had to give up.' It was a useful lesson.

On one occasion I had to present a selection of sparkling wines from the open-air jacuzzi on the roof of the Clarence Hotel, accompanied by several bobbing rubber ducks. It was cold and wet in the jacuzzi, but it was even colder and wetter outside of it as sleet was beginning to fall and a stiff Arctic breeze was whipping up.

I did have the advantage of not being able to get wetter than I already was, but I have never seen a more bedraggled and uncomfortable crew as I faced the camera and prepared to do a six-minute piece, without hesitation, deviation, or repetition. I think I must have gone into a form of auto-pilot because I remember being aware, as I reached the four-minute mark, that I had not yet cocked it up. As I approached five minutes I could see the crew, with the exception of our steady-handed cameraman, beginning to resemble a group of spectators watching their chosen horse heading for the finishing line. When, to my own astonishment, I managed to finish the piece without a hitch – something which I'm not sure I've ever managed before or since – and held the closing smile for a few seconds, there was an outburst of cheering and an immediate exodus for well-deserved hot whiskeys. Sparkling wine? Not on your nelly!

By the time we had finished 'The Big Stew' I was about to pack up and head, with my family, for County Cork. I had said goodbye to Durex and my other PR clients some time before as my television work was quite demanding. I was writing more than ever, doing various editing and publishing jobs and consulting on wine for a number of clients. Not the road to fortune, admittedly, but it was the kind of work that I could do from pretty well anywhere, thanks to modern technology.

Moving to the country seemed like a good idea at the time, and so it proved. In some respects, at least. But the devil was in the detail and I made a complete hash of certain important aspects.

Apprentice
Gardener

Very few Dubliners are more than a couple of generations away from the soil of rural Ireland, and I am no
exception. But I have to say that moving to the country did not really feel like returning to one's roots, despite the
fact that I have a few drops of Cork blood coursing proudly
through my veins.

Of course, it was a return to roots in a different sense. It may
be significant that my great-grandfather's address was The
Gardens, Irishtown, Tara, and it was there that he grew fruit
commercially in the rich soil of the Royal County, sending his
produce to the market in Dublin by rail from the little station at
Beauparc. Another forebear was an apple grower in the Calva-
dos country of Normandy. Maybe it's in the blood.

During her student days one of my sisters, nine years older
than me, was inclined to look askance at the investment of
time and effort in such a self-indulgent pursuit as gardening
for pleasure. She would point out to me, as I pored over seed

catalogues – an unusual pursuit for a small boy – that there were more important things in the world, such as feeding sub-Saharan Africa and righting the numerous wrongs that blight the planet.

She was right, of course, but within a few years she was growing her own vegetables on the banks of the River Tay in Scotland – not because of a Pauline conversion, but because she had discovered that such an activity helped to make ends meet. And that was just the first manifestation of her green genes; she and my two other sisters are all active in the garden and, I'm sorry to say, are much more knowledgeable than me when it comes to flowering plants. While I might have to pause and struggle to remember what an *Alstromeria* looks like, they can reel off a list of cultivars.

Like many things that are in your blood, a yen for gardening can lie dormant, like seeds, for many years. And that is what happened to me. Before taking the plunge and heading south, I had served a kind of gardening apprenticeship.

The first stirrings of my horticultural renaissance manifested themselves when Johann and I were just married and were living in a little house near Rathfarnham, which had been built, like dozens of others in the area, for soldiers returning from the Boer War. In those surprisingly enlightened days it was considered a good idea to provide sufficient ground to grow as much of the family's food as possible. Not an idea that would get much of an airing in these days of soaring land prices and the scandalous shortage of affordable housing, of course, but our little house had a garden not much short of half-an-acre. Old-timers in the area recalled people keeping pigs.

At the bottom of our long, narrow garden there was a high mound and it rapidly became apparent that this was not just a rallying point for the local urchins, some of whom were exceptionally tough nuts, but a dumping ground for several tonnes of gloriously fertile top soil. The previous owners had, for some mysterious reason, taken a JCB and scraped the top six inches of the garden into this great heap, leaving just a large expanse of yellow clay subsoil on which fine crops of scutch and dandelions thrived, but little else.

There was, however, one small patch at the back of the house that had been spared – probably because it contained a couple of old apple trees which a former owner had, for some reason, decided to paint purple (along with the house, incidentally, which had since been thoroughly sandblasted). The original occupiers were legendary in the area. We had a garden of subsoil, a possible burial mound and day-glo apple trees. We have always tended to live in eccentric properties, and this was no exception.

The small patch was fertile enough, but there was a narrow strip, maybe three metres long, which was so rich that I still dream about it; this was dark, crumbling, fine soil, a veritable pin-up of a growing medium. I mentioned this to one of the neighbours one day and he explained that this was adjacent to the site of the old outside privy, long since demolished. It had been the practice, he said, to empty the contents of the latrine into a trench and then to cover it with a little soil. So the wonderful fertility was the result of decades of composting human waste.

Years and years of work by soil bacteria had turned what had once been pretty disgusting and dangerous stuff into gardening gold. These days I would leap upon such soil with whoops of joy, but I was too squeamish then even to contemplate growing any edible crops there. I'm still ashamed to admit that I ignored it and set about clearing a few square metres of lawn in which I grew a handful of crops, with the aid of artificial fertilisers and a few handfuls of bone meal. I confined myself to a few courgette plants, which rapidly produced such a glut that this potentially delicious vegetable was demoted on our list of desirable produce. And I produced a fine crop of shallots, probably the easiest edible item it is possible to grow, with the possible exceptions of bean sprouts and radishes. The spuds were a complete failure because, in my stupidly thrifty way, I used tubers which had sprouted in the vegetable rack.

This mild flirtation with growing things proved to be just a brief fling. We soon moved up in the world – literally – when we exchanged our cottage for a top-floor apartment in leafy Ballsbridge. Johann kept the horticultural flag flying in the form of potted-up herbs and scented-leaved geraniums, which grew quite happily on our high-altitude balcony (which was, in fact, the top of the fire escape). Freelance journalism and the whole process of scraping a living was not, I discovered, conducive to the gentle art of gardening.

My real apprenticeship started when I rented my allotment from Dún Laoghaire Corporation as recently as 1997. England is crammed with allotments because local authorities have for many a year been committed to providing the means to grow food to those who do not have the space at home. It goes back further than the Dig for Victory campaign during the Second World War, although the need to feed the nation during those dark days saw a huge increase in the amount of land made available for allotments.

I had never heard of any allotments in Ireland, although I had a vague recollection of seeing some vegetable plots along the railway line to the west of Dublin. I decided to phone Dún Laoghaire Corporation and discovered, much to my surprise, that they had plots to rent in Goatstown. I applied in writing, enclosing my cheque for £29, and the following January I was given a huge, completely weed-infested plot to rent in conacre – which means that I got to use it for eleven months of the year. Johann and I went to see it on a dark, wet February day and came within a hair's breadth of handing it back and taking up some easier form of recreation.

Taking on the allotment was, I suppose, the thin end of the wedge. We had always eaten well at home, but Johann and I found that our table was greatly enhanced by the delights the allotment provided. We also realised that the allotment took a lot of time and some of that time was spent in the utterly pointless exercise of driving there and back through ever more sluggish Dublin traffic. When I took on the plot, it took ten minutes to get there. When I relinquished it to Dún Laoghaire Corporation in 1999 it took twenty, and rising. Heaven knows what it would be by now.

Now, allotment-holders are an interesting breed. In my experience they are almost all male and in the autumn of their years. An interest in growing vegetables is desirable, but not essential. What united many of my neighbours at the Goatstown allotments was a desire to get out of the house; indeed, I suspect some were ordered out by their long-suffering wives. I, on the other hand, was trying to snatch an occasional few hours up there during what was invariably a busy, if reasonably flexible, schedule.

I would rush off after a business meeting in town, still wearing a pin-striped suit, and descend on the plot armed with wellies and a battery of gardening tools which lived permanently in the back of the car. I will freely admit that I must have been a strange sight. I once even collected one of my clients, the marketing director of Durex, from the airport only to remember that I had a few bags of well-rotted stable manure acting as a rather unusual air-freshener in the rear. She may have had a defective sense of smell, or, more likely, was too polite to comment.

My fellow allotmenteers dug vigorously and weeded thoroughly, but because they had all day – literally – to pursue such activities, many hours were whiled away as they leaned on spade handles and chatted. It was a tightknit community and, in effect, you were only as good as your allotment. Mine was a disgrace, and despite my best efforts it never really matched up to even the shabbiest of the neighbouring plots. I was constantly letting the side down. For Heaven's sake, some of my neighbours had their third-of-an-acre *entirely* weed-free, with the edges of the beds cut as sharp and precise as the creases in a Guardsman's trousers.

Life was simply too short and I had a great deal of other things to do, including the making of two entire television series. One elderly allotmenteer was so obsessed by digging that, in spring, I counted how many times he turned over the soil on his plot. I reckon he dug the allotment, from top to bottom, twelve times, but I may have missed something. When, at last, his spuds, onions and cabbages came up, he would look rather forlorn without the spade welded to his boot; he then had to make do with frantic hoeing and constant complaints about the weather and the horticultural short-comings of his neighbours.

Daunted as I was, I never entirely gave up. The produce was too good. Once, one entire family descended on their new and weed-filled plot and spent a whole weekend trying to clear it. From early in the morning until the light had faded almost completely from the south Dublin sky they toiled away, parents and assorted children. Then they packed up and never came back. They must have been watching too many garden make-over programmes.

As for me, I never managed to dig the whole plot; indeed, I managed to produce an abundance of fresh stuff to eat from a fraction of the total area. Digging of the kind you see in the gardening books, where the spade cuts into the soil like a hot knife through butter, was not possible because the allotment was covered with scutch grass, the roots of which produced a dense, almost impenetrable mat. Pushing the spade through this canopy was hard enough, but it was even more dispiriting to realise that every time I cut through a scutch root, I was multiplying the number of potential scutch plants. The only way forward was to dig with a spade and then to fork through the soil and remove every single fragment of root.

Did it work? Not really, but it was the best I could do. I missed thousands of root fragments, all of which joyfully sprouted and threatened to engulf the plot as soon as my back was turned. Some of my more vociferous neighbours told me that this was a fool's errand and that my only hope was to wait until the weeds were in full leaf and then spray them liberally with Round-Up, the glyphosate weedkiller developed by Monsanto, the champions of genetic engineering. Needless to say, my organic principles did not allow me to follow this advice. Well, not quite to the letter.

I managed to clear enough ground for my first crops, but I blush to admit that I did use weedkiller to prepare a further patch for stuff that would be planted in the autumn, and I have to report that it performed pretty well. I comforted my conscience with the thought that most of my neighbours were applying so many chemicals to their plots that my little bit of glyphosate would make no difference.

The neighbours tended to think that organic growing was strictly for the birds – and they didn't mean it ornithologically. They also seemed to have learned what they knew about growing vegetables from a kind of bush telegraph, and most had never opened a book on the subject in their lives. When I was found sowing broad beans on a bleak, late February day, they gathered around and told me, quite categorically, that I was wasting my time.

The books did not agree and nor did my immediate neighbour, John, a retired meteorologist who was one of the best and most helpful gardeners I've ever had the pleasure to meet. He was regarded by the others with almost the same level of suspicion as myself, but at least he had crops to show that he knew his onions – and a great deal more besides. John had dug a shallow well on his plot and it would fill with water at all but the driest times of year. He very generously let me use it, which was a great relief as I had been in the habit of filling huge plastic containers from the tap at home and lugging them up to the plot. Dún Laoghaire Corporation resolutely refused to install a standpipe for the allotments, so water became a very precious commodity during the summer. Digging was hard work, but watering was a soul-destroying business. On one occasion I had to do an emergency resuscitation job on my lettuce seedlings with a bottle of Ballygowan. Having a few garden taps when we moved to the country was sheer luxury, and even today when I turn on the hose in my polytunnel I wallow in the convenience of it.

Despite the scepticism of many of my neighbouring allotmenteers, and the lack of water, I found myself harvesting glorious broad beans in late May. For the most part the neighbours maintained a dignified silence; some expressed amazement; others clearly thought it a fluke. The spuds did famously, the onions swelled to a fine average size, parsnips (a tricky crop, I had been led to believe) started to show their broad shoulders, beetroot was a revelation, especially when roasted, and leeks, which went into the well-manured bed vacated by the early potatoes, defied the winter winds and frosts and provided fresh vegetable matter from December onwards. I was hooked. For the first time in my life there was no need to buy vegetables and the flavour was ten times better. Or more.

But the allotment was still a disgrace to the district. It was simply a matter of my available time versus the ability of scutch grass to grow exponentially. I persuaded myself that leaving patches of weeds – perhaps rather larger than absolutely necessary – would be a help to the ecosystem. The slugs certainly appreciated it; vast hordes of them lived happily in the long grass during the warmth of those summer days and would venture out at night to cut swathes through the potato haulms. Such was the extent of the plague that I had, for the only time in my gardening life, recourse to slug pellets. In the mornings I counted literally thousands of the brutes, all shrivelled in an orgy of repulsive slime.

The allotment had a much bigger compliment of slugs than anywhere else I've ever tried to garden, and it's easy to see why. Most of the allotmenteers used a veritable arsenal of poisons in their battle against pests and diseases. As a result, the only birdlife in the area was confined to the virtually indestructible magpies and pigeons, neither of which I've ever seen tackle a slug. And, of course, the obsession with neatness meant that there were no wild places to support a hedgehog population. At one point magpies became such a problem that one of the more manic plot-holders tried shooting them in the early morning, with the result that nobody would risk life or limb by turning up before midday. The thoughts of this particular gentleman brandishing a firearm struck terror into the rest of us, and he was eventually taken to task by the Gardaí for discharging a shotgun in a built-up area, but not before he had peppered an overhead power-line and left much of Goatstown without electricity for the better part of a day. The magpie population continued to thumb their beaks at us.

My second year working up at the allotment was the clincher. The freshness of the vegetables revolutionised our cooking habits and the abundance was breathtaking. We gave away boxes of produce to friends and neighbours. I grew the best peas I have ever tasted (they have given me a benchmark to strive for ever since), and I grew a bewildering array of other vegetables. The Florence fennel and celeriac failed to perform, but I had courgettes, squashes, lettuce, carrots, parsnips, broad beans, beetroot, leeks, scallions, shallots, onions, garlic, rhubarb, chard, sprouting broccoli, spring cabbage, Brussels sprouts, turnips, rocket, winter cress, radicchio and even cardoons, the close relative of the globe artichoke. When these bulky plants hit six feet and burst into flower they were the talk of the allotments, and opinion varied widely as to what they were. Some even whispered that they were a form of marijuana. I have to admit that I never got around to eating them as the allegedly edible stalks, which look a little like celery when blanched, were so full of fibres that you could have used them as ropes. I even planted asparagus, but it eventually got lost in one of the eco-friendly patches of long grass. The fact that such patches would occasionally be strimmed by one of the neighbours in my absence would not have helped this finicky vegetable to thrive; I'm sure the strimming was kindly meant.

While other allotmenteers were to be seen casting fistfuls of Growmore fertiliser onto the soil, I stuck with well-rotted stable manure, four bags of which I collected every Saturday morning from stables in – appropriately enough – Glenamuck Road in Carrickmines. Even in the two short years I spent cultivating the soil in Goatstown, I could see that this natural food was working wonders. Fertility and yield kept going up and it was more than worth the effort of digging it in – a process that makes one aware of hitherto uncharted muscles.

The Goatstown Apprenticeship turned me into a gardener in that I suddenly realised that anything – well, almost anything – was possible. It meant that I could read up on fruit-tree growing, not just as an academic exercise but as preparation for actually doing it. The fact that I never did so at the allotment is beside the point. Time was, as ever, a limiting factor, but the tendency of some of the local children to stage occasional pitched battles, using our fresh produce as missiles (onions can be swung by their stalks and then released to gain maximum ballistic effect) was another. And at least two little old ladies used to help themselves to whatever took their fancy, believing, no doubt, that the vegetables were growing wild.

Despite the constant scrutiny to which my horticultural efforts were constantly put by the old-timers, I think I was probably fortunate in having cut my teeth as a serious vegetable gardener somewhere other than right outside my back door. I was more than willing to make a complete fool of myself at the allotment, while I would probably have been rather more circumspect at home. And, in an odd way, the constant scrutiny made me more willing to take risks. In fact, it only encouraged me. Yah! Boo! and all that.

As an apprenticeship, the allotment experiment taught me lots. But it was also highly entertaining. Many of my fellow plot-holders loathed each other with an almost frightening intensity. The competition was fierce, and amongst the hardcore group the shame

of letting your cabbage get clubroot, or your potatoes succumb to blight was so great that I would not have been surprised to find one of them impaled on his fork having committed *harikiri*. I and a few others were regarded as barking mad – not for the first time in my life – and therefore not to be judged by the conventions of the majority.

In time, I began to yearn for a little privacy. I didn't mind the sceptical scrutiny so much as the company of the Allotment Bores, of whom we had several. These people would wander over and proceed to talk for hours on end. At first, out of politeness, I would interrupt what I was doing and listen with a semblance of attention. By the end I would carry on and emit muttered half-replies, but they just kept going.

The thoughts of having a private garden of reasonable size, one in which I could do anything I liked and not be interrupted, became very attractive. And so, when the time came to wind down the allotment I made myself very unpopular: having harvested the bulk of the crops for the summer, I left the maincrop potatoes to fend for themselves and the plot in general to grow wild and free as I set off with the family for our new quarters in Rushbrooke, County Cork.

When I returned in the autumn to harvest my lovely Caras, I had a great surprise. They had been stolen, which I suppose is flattering, given that the culprit must have been a fellow allotmenteer, a casual passer-by being very unlikely to know what lay beneath the weed-infested ground. Whoever it was had had to act quickly and furtively; in their hurry they had left about a sackful in the ground, which I lifted and bore home to

Munster in muted triumph.

Leaving the allotment for the last time that October evening – without much regret, I have to say – I saw the greatest bore of the whole lot emerging from the gloaming. He was highly excited because one of the country's leading gardening experts had just taken one of the plots. He had been watching her carefully, just as he had watched and ultimately despaired of me. 'Do you know what I'm goin' to tell ya?' he enquired, rhetorically, through a wreath of Sweet Afton smoke. 'These experts know nuthin'!'

Getting Out of
Town

W riting at my desk in Dublin, at the top of our tall
house in Monkstown, I could glance away from
the computer and out to sea, glimpsing Dún
Laoghaire pier in the distance and a goodly portion of Howth.
Not bad as views go. We had moved to Belgrave Square in
1988 when, amazing as it seems now, large old houses were
quite hard even to give away. The vast house was sadly
neglected and required a lot of money to be spent on it, but
we bought it for the kind of sum that would not quite buy a
Range Rover these days.

Here at Carrigeen Hill, our current abode, the view is quite
different but no less attractive: a vast panorama of East Cork
and West Waterford stretches away into the distance beyond
the little valley of the River Bride. If I stroll up the hill behind
the house – rather difficult to do if you're writing, but I sometimes take the laptop – I can see the blue haze of the Comeraghs and the Knockmealdowns, with the groove in which the

Blackwater flows in the foreground.

Life in the country is good. The air is pure, provided you don't settle in the shadow of a rendering factory, or an intensive piggery. The people are friendly and genuinely neighbourly. There's a lot more space than you tend to have in the suburbs: space for growing things, or just leaving wild as a habitat for the teeming diversity of life, or just through pure laziness – the effect is the same.

Having said all that, we made a bit of a botch of our move to the country and it has taken several years and a great deal of stress to put right. That's right: stress. Exactly what you move to a rural location to avoid.

Our mistake – mine more than Johann's, I think – was to fall in love with The Hermitage, a rambling Georgian house complete with a walled garden extending to almost two acres. And the paddock, of course. And the view of the River Lee. Falling in love with a place is the easy bit; knowing what you are letting yourself in for is a different matter entirely. Please don't let me discourage you if you are contemplating a move to the country. But don't do it lightly. And if you can, learn by our unfortunate mistakes.

First of all, why did we do it? Well, the simple answer to that is that we wanted a bigger garden. A much bigger garden. Our eldest daughter, Sarah, is still, in her own words, 'gobsmacked' that we went to such extremes to achieve that ambition. She was ten when we moved to County Cork and although she approved in principle at the time, she found the uprooting pretty traumatic. 'If you just wanted a bigger garden, surely you could have found one nearer to Dublin?' she still asks in amazement. 'Or even *in* Dublin?'

Well, I suppose we could have, but we liked the idea of the clean air and the fresh start and all the myriad other reasons which everybody who contemplates a move to the country can reel off like a prayer. We had a glorious house in Dublin, the vast Edwardian terraced home on Belgrave Square, the only problem was that the garden was in inverse proportion to the 5,000 square feet of accommodation in which we rattled around very comfortably.

The back garden was little more than a yard, much of it concreted over, and such soil as there was contained so little organic matter that it was not much more than the kind of grey dust with which I had grown up. There was enough room for herbs, roses, a glorious paeony that came with the premises and a gigantic horseradish, which demonstrated that this exceptionally resilient plant will grow just about anywhere. However, I hankered after fresh vegetables and perhaps even some raspberries. I indulged and encouraged such fantasies by buying dozens of gardening books, many of them old and well-thumbed, and I eventually decided to see if I could rent a garden plot somewhere. I even conjured up visions of an apple-cheeked old lady who would let me have her vast back garden in exchange for all the fresh produce that I would draw forth from the dark, crumbly loam ... In reality, however, I simply took on the allotment.

And the allotment had much to do with us ending up in the country. We wanted to live right beside our vegetable garden and be able to snatch a quarter-of-an-hour here and there to go hoeing or potting-up. We also felt that a greenhouse would be a bonus, and that an established orchard would be fun. So enthused were we that we decided to look for a house that had a walled garden, an enclosure that would provide a sympathetic microclimate for what we wanted to grow. Walled kitchen gardens have always held a certain fascination for me, with their lovely weathered brick and paths glimpsed through shadowy doorways, lean-to greenhouses and espalier fruit trees. I put it down to having read Ted Humphris's *Garden Glory* when I was a teenager, the autobiography of one of the last Big House gardeners who could remember the great days before the First World War. What a source of romantic notions about gardening.

At first, we thought of moving to Greystones. We wanted a decent house with a large garden. It seemed like a good place to start, but there was nothing suitable in a price range lower than the stratosphere. We looked at properties all the way down the coast, along the edge of Wicklow, Wexford, Waterford and eventually came across The Hermitage in Rushbrooke, County Cork – perhaps a little closer to civilisation than I would have liked, but it had a certain seductive magic. It was close to the pretty town of Cobh, half-an-hour from Cork City and, we noted with innocent enthusiasm, right beside the railway line, which would make trips to the glorious English

Market so convenient. The railway line was, of course, to be the Achilles heel.

Needless to say, we took professional advice: the house was unlikely to fall down, even if it needed a bit of work. This advice turned out to be hopelessly optimistic, but perhaps, in our enthusiasm, we were not listening as closely as we should have been. The property was, perhaps, a little expensive, we heard, but it promised to be a sound investment. And so, we were sold.

In reality, The Hermitage had a damp problem in the same was as the Niagara Falls are moist. The central-heating boiler gave up the ghost within days of being turned on and had to be replaced. The new boiler was very efficient, so much so that the ancient central-heating pipes, probably dating from the 1920s, could not cope with the unfamiliar pressure and sprang leaks with gay abandon. Putting this problem right threatened to cost a small fortune. The kitchen was in a gloomy wing, as far from the living areas as possible – doubt-less a relic of the times when the cook and indoor staff were kept out of sight and out of mind. Some of the electrical arrangements had been installed by an enthusiastic amateur and held out the distinct possibility of causing a fire. There was a lot of dry rot, judging by the smell, but it was hard to say where exactly. When we were expecting guests I would take the tongs and remove a smouldering log from the dog grate in the drawing room. I would then wave it around, like a thurible of incense, so as to disguise the fungal pong. The bedrooms had been created in the former attic of the house some time in the 1970s, but no insulation had been used during the transformation. As a result, it was like Siberia in the winter and on summer evenings it was like a sauna, even with all the windows open. But these were things with which we could have coped, given time.

Then, the *coup de grâce* fell. It seems that the dogs in the street had been aware that all of the surrounding land had been earmarked for County Cork's largest ever housing development. Cork County Council is amongst the most sensible local authorities in the country; it was doing its best to ensure that high-density development was concentrated along existing or mothballed railway lines. And what did we have at the bottom of the garden? In addition to the usual fairies, there was the Cobh–Cork line.

It turned out that The Hermitage would end up as a kind of island, or oasis, in the middle of a development of 750 houses, through which our long, rambling driveway (all three hundred metres of it) would snake its alien way. There would be new houses literally all around us. Not a rural idyll by any means.

As we waited for the hammer blow to fall we investigated the possibility of selling, only to find that nobody, not even a commercial developer, would be prepared to buy a property in such a location. We set about tackling the planning process, determined to fight the inevitable. It was not a cheery prospect and it got even more depressing when bulldozers moved in at the fringes of what would one day become a vast building site. But what could we do? We could, at least, do something in the garden.

When we moved in, the garden contained precisely 248 rhododendrons and, fond as we are of this Himalayan shrub, we felt they needed to be culled. We gave away over a hundred of them to friends, and to the previous owners, provided they were prepared to come and dig them up. Some we even sold – rhododendrons can be very valuable plants – and put the money towards garden equipment.

Nine tonnes of farmyard manure was imported from an organic farm in County Tipperary and barrowed up the long, narrow driveway. Much of this was used to feed the starved soil of the bed along the southfacing wall, now denuded of rhododendrons and ready to be returned to its original purpose of fruit and vegetable production. The previous owners had been rather chemical in their approach, and we watched as gradually the number of bees, lacewings and ladybirds increased under our almost entirely organic regime. A south-facing lean-to greenhouse provided me with my first experience of growing tomatoes and cucumbers. Indeed, I had started the seedlings in Dublin on the windowsill of our drawing room as a kind of joyful celebration of the fact that I would soon be able to grow under cover.

I dug up a large area of rough lawn and put in enough potatoes and onions to keep us going through the year; I reinvigorated the overgrown apple orchard with judicious pruning; I planted gooseberries, currants, raspberries (both summer and autumn varieties) and a quince tree. We ate well. This, incidentally, was the garden in which I planted the lavender cuttings from my parents' place.

Our garden walls had been built no later than 1820 and quite possibly several decades earlier. They were imposing, to say the least, and when I first managed to get an extension-ladder to the top in order to remove some of the brambles that inevitably put down grasping roots into the old mortar, I realised that this task, which at first appeared to offer a degree of worthy satisfaction, was both highly dangerous and essentially endless. But absolutely necessary.

The previous owners told me that they had poured paraffin

into the thatch of brambles, ivy and miscellaneous plants that covered every square inch of the top of the walls. I assumed that this application helped to suppress the plants but, no, it was necessary, they said, to then set fire to it. Now, I had two objections to this. One was that the heat would almost certainly crack the masonry and make even more footholds for flora, the second was that I had no desire to start a conflagration as I stood vertiginously on a ladder twenty feet off the ground. So, I am sorry to say, the flora went unchecked.

There was fauna, too. The rats of Great Island are legendary and there was a large colony in what we used to call The Wilderness – a patch of overgrown land that had originally contained the hen house and Heaven knows what else. Rats being rats, of course, they did not confine their perambulations to there. The first we knew of their further adventures was when the Conference pear tree, which had been trained against the garden wall, was denuded of its fruit in one night. The only evidence as to the culprits was a half-eaten pear that bore the unmistakeable marks of sharp rodent teeth. Closer examination of the crime scene revealed small holes in the wall through which the beasts travelled.

They travelled further. The old garden wall passed through the centre of the house and eventually the rats discovered the pleasures of our well-insulated attic, where they would perform what sounded like war dances above the bedrooms. They say that when you hear what you think are rats in the attic, they are in fact mice. This is perfectly true. Rats sound like a herd of stampeding elephants and they do – believe me

– cause sleepless nights. Sometimes they would fight and piercing rat screams shattered the still darkness. The cheerful men from Rentokil waged a losing battle.

The rats left the vegetables alone – unlike their cousins over by Ballyandreen, where friends of ours had their broad beans neatly podded and eaten in the course of a single night by their local rodents. But back at The Hermitage, something was devouring the peas as soon as they poked a tentative shoot above the ground. There was no sign of slugs – indeed the garden was curiously low on molluscs – and I suspected pigeons. When we first moved in, the house was surrounded by cereal fields and the local pigeons ate their fill, developed steroidally plump breasts and struggled to fly. You could see them struggling as they climbed, in grave danger of colliding with the garden wall. They reminded me of old war movies with the pilot of the stricken Wellington bomber yelling, 'We're losing power, chief!'

The obese pigeons, however, seemed to insist on a balanced diet and they gorged themselves on any member of the cabbage family they could find. They, like me, seem to believe that the best of the brassicas is sprouting broccoli and our annual crop had to be grown in a makeshift cage made of two-by-one and garden netting (which made harvesting quite a challenge, especially at dusk).

I assumed that the pigeons were in pursuit of an even more balanced diet when the delicate, sweet shoots of the peas started to vanish, and so I constructed a fortress of chicken wire which even a golden eagle would have found daunting;

but still the decimation continued. I then remembered that old-fashioned gardeners used to roll peas in red lead before sowing – a further example of how the use of deadly poisons in the garden is nothing new. They didn't do this just for the fun of it, or to make the peas easier to see (which it certainly does), but because mice, sensible creatures that they are, find that red lead disagrees with them. Could it be mice then?

I set a few traps and in the course of one night every single one of them slew a mouse. The next night it was a similar story of derring-do and carnage. By night three the moist climate had corroded the pin of each trap to the extent that a bus could have driven over it without producing the deadly snap. New traps every night would have meant that this crop of peas would turn out to be the most expensive in the history of horticulture.

I decided to put my faith in the notion that mice are enchanted by the peas when they are just producing their first root and first shoot. I have no doubt that they are at their sweetest at this point. I sowed a new row of peas in an old plastic gutter and kept it in the mouse-free greenhouse until the plants were three inches high. I then slid the row of peas, compost and all, into a furrow in the ground and my faith was vindicated. The mice, who quite clearly were still raising large families in the long grass nearby, ignored the new crop completely.

Soon the cereal fields had turned into a building site and acre upon acre of old scrub and hedgerows were bulldozed. The only good to come out of this was the fact that our garden, and the further acre or so of rough land attached to the house, became a sanctuary for birds and the dawn chorus could, on occasion, be deafening. Had the hedgerows survived, of course, the local bullfinches would have had lots of natural food at their disposal. When they moved into the garden, however, they decided that there was nothing so good as our plum blossom. We tried netting the trees and this great effort saved two Victoria plums, both of which tasted great not least because they were ours.

The walled garden with its very sheltered microclimate and the proximity of the broad River Lee, where the cross-river car ferry plies its trade, meant that we could enjoy some rare and tender plants that had come with the property. A vast mimosa tree, with its distinctive fronds of greyish, incredibly delicate fern-like leaves, was covered in a mass of fragrant yellow blossoms in the middle of winter. Big, prehistoric-looking *Dicksonias*, the tree ferns I had coveted in my youth, flourished and dozens of rare rhododendrons enchanted the serious gardeners amongst our friends. We tended to prefer the much more common but fabulously scented *R. luteum, R. fragrantissima* and *R.* 'Lady Alice Fitzwilliam' with her amazing fragrance of fresh nutmeg. I have always believed that a plant needs to be pretty spectacular if it doesn't have a scent. I am prepared to forgive delphiniums and lupins for having no fragrance because of their colour and form; I can overlook the lack of smell in the euphorbias and other stalwarts of the herbaceous border; but I insist that the plant without perfume has to work hard to justify its place. *R. henryii*, named after the

Irish botanist Augustine Henry, overcomes this lack by virtue of its stunning blue blossom, which shimmers in the distance.

When we arrived there was just one rose in the whole garden, straggling valiantly through a vast ceanothus bush. A garden without roses, plenty of roses, is not a garden at all in my view, so I planted over sixty highly scented versions in order to provide some sort of counterbalance to the hordes of rhododendrons. I propagated swathes of lavender, both the French *L. stoechas* and the traditional English version, *L. spica*. These, along with honeysuckle, provided the scents of summer. In early spring, sometimes even in January, the tiny star-shaped blossoms of *Clematis armandii,* which climbed in profusion on the south-facing wall, would fill the air with its strangely exotic scent.

I felt like a vandal destroying the winter heliotrope which threatened to engulf the vegetable beds. This plant, which looks like butterbur or coltsfoot and is just as invasive, produces a small pink head of tiny flowers in the depths of winter that give out a heady, honeyed fragrance. The flowers of viburnum look and smell surprisingly similar, although they are borne on the leafless branches of an upright shrub. Nevertheless, I ruthlessly eradicated the heliotrope, digging down as much as two feet in pursuit of its fleshy but infuriatingly brittle

roots. The notorious bindweed is even worse, but at The Hermitage I had to deal only with the less virulent hedgerow form and, thank Heaven, there was relatively little scutch to torment the gardener.

Digging out weeds or preparing the soil for the first of the potatoes to go in on St Patrick's Day, I would often come upon reminders of the garden's long history. The soil had been cultivated for over two centuries and there were plenty of ancient oyster shells, a legacy of the feeding of the soil with seaweed; at low tide it could be pitched into carts down at the river's edge. Hundreds of broken clay pipes – *dudeens* – were also turned up by the spade; I suppose when a gardener's pipe snapped he just dropped it where he was digging.

Gardening at The Hermitage taught me many things. One was that having the garden right outside your door, as distinct from on a distant allotment, does not necessarily mean that you will spend more time working on it. It would have been a different story had I been able to spend all day in the garden, whiling away the evening writing my latest best-selling novel; in fact, I was gardening while reviewing restaurants, writing about wine, pursuing broadcasting ideas, doing business consultancy work and visiting vineyards in both hemispheres.

The other lesson was that lawns, however attractive to look at, take a great deal of work and, to add insult to injury, contribute to global warming. A third was that a big formal garden, which is what The Hermitage had *par excellence*, really does require the attentions of a full-time gardener, a luxury we certainly could not afford. At first I used to call on the services of a local character who, despite having the opposite of green fingers could at least, I innocently thought, manage to dig. In fact, he somehow contrived to cover vast areas of weeds with a thin layer of soil, collect his pay and vanish, leaving only a cache of empty Carling Black Label cans as evidence that he had ever been there. It took me several weeks to twig, trusting creature that I am. I suppose I should have known better. Everyone in the neighbourhood had warned me about Jeremiah (I will draw a veil over his real name).

All gardens, of whatever size, demand love and attention. Unfortunately, at The Hermitage I found it impossible to cherish the garden in an unqualified way. As I mentioned earlier, we kept waiting for the blow to fall and it eventually became clear what way the wind was blowing. The County Council was not going to give the developers exactly what they wanted, but the housing estate was still going to be huge.

The only people who had even a remote interest in buying us out were, of course, the developers whose site we almost completely bisected. However, we were in no position to hold them to ransom and it would have been perfectly possible to build their development with poor old us stuck in the middle. Eventually, after a process which I think of as being similar to pulling teeth without an anaesthetic, we agreed to sell to them and set about finding somewhere else to pursue the country life.

When we realised that we were free of The Hermitage, a great weight was lifted from our shoulders. Great as the relief was, this was the time to pause for thought. Had we done the right thing by moving out of Dublin? If we had made a mistake, we decided, it was in rushing into buying The Hermitage without taking the right advice. (I should stress that we did take advice; unfortunately, it was very bad advice.) But moving? Despite the three years of trauma it still seemed, on reflection, to have been a sound decision for me and Johann and our three daughters. Serious traffic jams were a distant memory at this stage, we were growing much more of our own food and the great gastronomic resources of Cork, city and county, were on our doorstep. We began to realise how the media is tiresomely obsessed with the capital. And when friends who were coming to visit asked if there was anything they could bring us from Dublin, we had to resist the temptation to answer, 'Of course not, thank you.'

In time we found Carrigeen Hill, our present home and a much stronger candidate for living the rural idyll, if such a thing exists outside the realms of glossy magazines. It certainly seems a good place to put down roots, both horticultural and personal.

Excursions in the
Wine World

I once had a chastening experience in the bar of what used to be called a gentleman's club. Actually, it is no longer a gentleman's club because, due to an unusually enlightened membership, it was long ago thrown open to women, or ladies, as I should probably say. The more curmudgeonly members would claim that it is no longer a gentleman's club for the simple reason that there are very few actual gentlemen on the membership list. I was admitted over ten years ago, so they rest their case.

The club is blessed with wonderful staff, all of whom have an admirable sense of discretion. This is essential in an establishment where, for example, a High Court judge, flushed with good Port, might find his tongue loosened, or, much more likely, any number of members might loudly relate totally true but perfectly slanderous stories about what pillars of the community still survive.

One of the staff, an admirable barman, now retired, used to

line up the hooch for blind-tasting by members of the wine committee. (He also, incidentally, had a way of elevating any member who happened to be a Peer of the neighbouring Realm to celestial heights. For example, when waiting on an elderly marquess he would request from his assistant, 'A large Powers for the Lord'. But I digress.)

On one occasion, just after lunch, I bumped into the secretary of the wine committee who asked me to join a blind-tasting, the object of which was to find a new Gigondas to replace the one that had become too expensive (clubs, unlike restaurants, care about niceties such as this). The line-up of tasters was pretty knowledgeable: the managing director of a wine company, a doctor who had come within an ace of becoming a Master of Wine only weeks before, a chap whose veins are flushed regularly with the finest claret and, finally, me.

Such tastings tend to be conducted in virtual silence. Our excellent barman had four glasses lined up and our mission (should we decide to accept it) was to choose the best of the four wines. We took it in turns to taste, gurgle and spit, and then we fell to discussing the wines. There was virtual unanimity, which is always a good sign. The first was quite good, but a little coarse. The second was very good on the nose, but although the palate was quite elegant, we felt it finished a little short. The third was really not in the running at all; it was lean and one of us (possibly me) thought there was a suggestion of volatile acidity, as we wine bores call vinegar. The fourth was head and shoulders above the rest: balanced, sound fruit, nice backbone, tannins rounded, good length, quite stylish really.

We had been so intent on the wine that we had failed to notice that our barman had been champing at the bit throughout the proceedings. 'Gentlemen,' he eventually spluttered, 'I've been trying to tell you: these are four glasses of the same wine.'

There was a short silence and a certain amount of coughing before we simply got on with the job. The excellent staff are so discreet that this story never emerged into the vulgar glare of publicity or, worse, *The Phoenix*. However, it only takes one irresponsible member to pull the rug from under all that, and the job has fallen to me.

You would imagine that I, once bitten, would be twice shy. Not a bit of it. I seem to court ritual humiliation the way moths drop everything the moment they catch a glimpse of a bright light. No sooner had I decided that the one Gigondas was, in fact, four quite distinct wines than I found myself answering the 'phone to a charming researcher from the BBC. Would I be prepared, she enquired sweetly, to taste Champagne – blind, of course – in Lisdoonvarna on a live link to the 'Watchdog' programme, presented by the dreaded Ann Robinson? Nothing, I declared, would give me greater pleasure, and the miserable fee of a hundred quid would do fine. As you will have gathered by now, I should not be let out on my own.

In this instance the job looked deceptively simple. A certain Champagne house was selling its goods at a pretty high price in the UK and very cheaply back home in France. Ms Robinson smelt a rat and investigated. The Champagne company told her, however, that the stuff they sell back home was a very young and therefore relatively inexpensive blend (presumably on the basis that the French would lick battery acid off a sore leg provided that the label is suitably posh), while the British demanded, and got, an older and therefore dearer blend.

The programme-makers wanted to know, not unnaturally, if anybody could taste the difference. Or, more specifically, if *I* could taste the difference. Why me, you may well ask. It turned out that 'Watchdog' was doing a feature on the Lisdoonvarna Bachelor Festival and they thought it would be fun to do the blind-tasting with an Irish wine writer in a pub, surrounded by people swilling pints of Uncle Arthur. Logic has never been the strong suit of primetime television.

The BBC is nothing if not thorough. We rehearsed the piece for the first time at eleven o'clock in the morning, at which point the running order dictated that we would have a comfortable three minutes in which to do the job. Six o'clock, six rehearsals later and about to go live, this generous slot had been trimmed to one minute, thirty seconds. Estimates of the audience figures varied, depending on whom I was asking, from six million to fourteen million. Nervous? Oh, just a touch. And there was no sneak preview of the wines.

With five minutes to air, I sweetly asked the floor manager if it would be possible to have a quick taste, and she thrust a couple of glasses in front of me. They looked distressingly similar, but wait! Was one of them just a smidgin darker, in which case it was probably older? I glanced at the bottles. One seemed to have a French tax stamp on the foil. The other, presumably British, didn't. Oh dear God! Was I cheating?

It was then that my overworked Guardian Angel intervened. One glass smelled much better than the other. This must be the older, UK blend! And with that we were on air and I was trying manfully to avoid spilling the precious fluids, not easy when you realise, too late, that you have lost control of your hands. And yes, I was right! Actually, it was a doddle. Or it would have been without a full outside broadcast crew, a veritable octopus of cables, forty ballroom dancers (all of them accommodating a great deal of free BBC drink) and Ann Robinson, back in Television Centre, rattling through proceedings with that grim determination for which she is justly famous. In the end we did the piece in just over fifty seconds, but it felt like five hours. I took the next day off, lying in a darkened room.

It was probably the relief at having got through this unscathed that softened me up for the next request, which came from RTÉ. Daire O'Brien, standing in for Pat Kenny on his morning radio show, wondered if I would taste three wines, blind, on air, and have a stab at identifying them. It sounded like fun, but, of course, I had not reckoned with Daire's mischievous sense of humour. At least, that is what his friends call it.

I should have guessed that something was amiss when it was explained to me, just before we went on air, that I would have to spend a few minutes in the men's loo while Daire introduced the piece. The reason for this curious arrangement is that the RTÉ lavatories are the only place in the Radio Centre where you are unable to hear Radio 1.

In the studio I was presented with three glasses of red wine. The first was chock full of blackcurrants, not unlike *crème de cassis*, with a lick of vanilla and plenty of tannin. I always think you should go with your first instinct when blind-tasting. And I did. Cabernet Sauvignon. New World. Probably South America. Chile, if I had to name a country.

So far, so good. Correct in every detail. Then came something very different. Grenache? European, anyway. But what, exactly? Blind panic. No idea. Cheapish. Maybe Grenache? French? I had a blind stab and said Côtes du Rhône. Wrong. It was, in fact, a rather ropey Châteauneuf-du-Pape, and I suspect the fact that a light example of this wine is very similar to Côtes du Rhône was lost on most of the audience who were, I thought, probably squirming with delight at this stage. Pride before a fall and all that.

The third wine stumped me completely. It was, I said, like nothing I had ever tasted before. It wasn't bad, though, and I would be intrigued to know what it was. The answer made me very grateful that I had not voiced any wild surmise. It was, in fact, a blend of the first two wines, but I was too shocked to get cross about this sleight of hand.

The audience, however, was appalled. Dozens of callers protested that this was a terribly unfair thing to do to a poor wine writer. Kind as these sentiments undoubtedly were, I had only myself to blame. I don't do blind-tasting anymore. Not in public, anyway.

I never set out to be a wine writer, of course, but it is a truth universally acknowledged that freelance journalists are prepared to write about anything, ignorance notwithstanding. A young journalist on the threshold of his career is not so much concerned with what he can write about; it is more a question of what he can get away with writing about. That was certainly the case with me.

I was blessed with virtually teetotal parents. Had they been the sort of people who were forever opening bottles of this and that – or even indulging in a nightly Sherry – I might have grown up regarding the fruit of the vine as being just another grocery item. When I was a nipper our groceries were delivered by Findlater's in their distinctive dark-red vans with gold lettering on the side. I was forever sticking my head into the back to see what other customers were getting – indeed, I will now confess, for the first time, that I once swiped a small bottle of Schweppes Indian Tonic Water from Findlater's pantechnicon, sometime in the winter of 1967, I think, just to see what it was like. (I have been left with a distaste for quinine ever since and an occasional urge to slip an unexplained half-crown into Alex Findlater's hand.)

Anyway, it was through observing the orders of other, more worldly customers that I grew familiar with the sight of dusty old bottles, each of them with a flash of white paint on the side (to identify where the sediment or 'crust' lay), wrapped in straw protectors. I was in my early teens before I knew what these beguiling old bottles actually were: Vintage Port, probably classics like the 1945 and 1947, though I'm sure they still had some of the legendary 1927 in stock after forty years. Those were the days.

I think I was fourteen when I came across a copy of the simply-titled *Port,* by Rupert Croft-Cooke (Putnam, 1957), and was entranced by both the illustrations and the wonderfully evocative account of this most Anglophone of wines. Sadly, the world which Croft-Cooke describes has changed beyond recognition, although some of the essentials remain. When I first visited the Douro, I felt I had been there before – what greater tribute can you pay to a writer?

Huyshe Bower, who, despite the name, is from Dorset, is a partner in the three-hundred-year-old Port firm of Taylor, Fladgate & Yeatman. He went to work in Oporto over forty years ago, and he told me that he took Croft-Cooke's book with him on the tortuous train journey up to Vargellas in the Douro. We agreed that it may not tell you much about the current state-of-play, but my goodness, it makes you thirsty for a glass of something old and good. And all this without resorting to a single reference to the likes of cassis, toasted hazelnuts, or acacia.

Anyway, my love affair with Port began at an indecently early age; I persuaded my abstemious family that a bottle of Port would add considerably to the general *bonhommie* of Christmas 1973. And so it proved. My father and I peered in the window of Thompson D'Olier, on the Green, and contemplated Taylor's Late Bottled Vintage 1967, but in the end it was a bottle of Cockburn's Special Reserve, bought in Mitchell's, which we bore home.

The family tradition on Christmas night was for my father to read the passage where the Pickwickians descend upon

Dingley Dell for the Festive Season, and on this occasion it was enlivened by Port. I'll never forget that first taste of Port and the appropriateness of the occasion: people gathered around the fire on a winter night.

Later, I encountered full-blown Vintage Port for the first time and was initiated into the mysteries of decanting. Around about the time I was doing my Leaving Cert. and during my first few years at TCD, Dow's 1960 was remarkably cheap and I can still remember discovering the extra dimensions of fruit and concentration that came with real Vintage Port, even in this lightish and long since faded year.

In the meantime, I have been lucky enough to drink a glass or two of some of the great Ports of the century: Cockburn's '08, Cockburn's '27, Graham's '48, Croft's and Taylor's '55, Taylor's '63, Dow's '70 and, infanticidally, all of the top wines in the superb '77 vintage. They all have something indefinable at the heart of their appeal: the wholesome sweetness, the warmth of both the spirit and the baked fruit, the elusive scent of violets that is the hallmark of Taylor's. But there's more. Perhaps it's because Vintage Port is the most sociable of wines, best shared around the fire on a cold and windy night.

So, perhaps Port was the spur to my interest in wine. If so, it was helped by spending several Christmasses, during my student days, working with Mitchell's of Kildare Street. Initially, I was put on gift-wrapping fatigues, but as soon as my complete inability in this area was noted I was politely, but firmly, transferred to delivery duties.

Those were the days when a fine old family business like

Mitchell's could afford to offer a very personal service. Once a week the van would deliver a bottle of £2.99 University Cream Sherry to an elderly lady in Blackrock, whereupon I would be tipped a princely 25p. I delivered Krug Champagne to Sean Kinsella's ostentatious Mirabeau Restaurant where the mohair-coat brigade went to consume conspicuously; Montrachet (or mon-trashy, in the argot of the wareroom) to the Dún Laoghaire yacht clubs; and a weekly dozen of malt Scotch to a crusty old colonel in Wicklow. I once delivered a bottle of Château Margaux 1966 to Bord Iascaigh Mhara, which the receptionist said she would chill straight away. Well, the customer is always right, I suppose. I even delivered a gift-wrapped bottle to Charlie Haughey in Kinsealy. Even at the time I wondered if it were Château Lynch-Bages 1970, if you see what I mean.

In those days the late Bobby Mitchell was the patriarch of the family firm – Mr Robert, as we called him – and he ran the

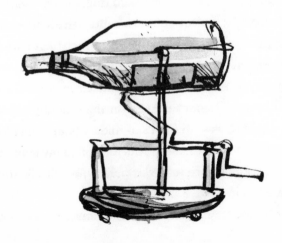

business with a kindly rod of iron. I'm quite sure it made very little, if any, money in those days, given that the lady in Blackrock with her weekly bottle of bargain Sherry was not alone and that the most loyal and demanding of customers were often those who spent the least. I remember Bobby becoming virtually speechless when I requested a raise from £1.25 to £1.50 an hour. 'Do you want to ruin us?' he demanded.

Bobby's wife, Mrs Robert, would send in trays of sandwiches and a big pot of chicken broth when we were working late in the wareroom. On one occasion she mistook a large saucepan of water, which had been left to soak with a generous dash of washing-up liquid, for the wholesome broth. One of our colleagues, who was rather generously described by the foreman as being 'a brick short of the load', had consumed three mugs of the liquid and pronounced it very good by the time the rest of us had been surprised by the thick layer of soapy foam on top.

In the late 1970s Mitchell's was still doing some bottling. Huge casks of Noval Port would be broached, the bottling line would crank up, corks would be flogged into place and the whole atmosphere became intoxicating – literally – with vaporised wine at 22% alcohol.

I learned how to decant Vintage Port during my Mitchell's sojourn. In those days – and I'm sure they would still do it – Mitchell's would decant old Port, which is full of sediment (or 'sentiment', as our foreman called it) into a fresh bottle if the customer wanted to serve it the same day. The bottle was slid gently out of its bin and into an ancient wooden decanting cradle, the cork was withdrawn (often in several pieces) with the bottle constantly at an angle of forty-five degrees, and the wine then poured through a funnel lined with muslin into the clean bottle. I was mildly disappointed that no candle was used, but it was pointed out to me that Port bottles are so opaque that you can't see a guttering light through them.

It was a curious apprenticeship for a young history student whose background was robustly abstemious with subtle nuances of Calvinism. My parents had neither the interest nor the wherewithal to lay down the likes of Lafite, let alone Lieb-fraumilch. My mother would enjoy an occasional glass of Mateus Rose or Spanish Sauternes on high days and holidays, and it invariably reduced her to a fit of the giggles. My father's long career as a total abstainer was marked by only a handful of attempts to consume the hard stuff and this, I must stress, was on doctor's orders.

He once told me that he quite liked the taste of altar wine, so I rushed off and returned with a bottle of twenty-year-old tawny Port, which is the kind of altar wine that only the Pope and the Archbishop of Canterbury would use on a regular basis. It was no good. 'It tastes brackish,' he declared, and I have to admit that I'm still stumped for a definition of this quaintly Victorian word. Muscat de Beaumes de Venise was no good either, despite its sweetness and grapey wholesome-ness. Eventually, I prescribed a glass of apple juice spiked fairly liberally with vodka. This did the trick. The poor man lapped it up like mother's milk, became uncharacteristically garrulous, came within a hair's breadth of singing 'Sliabh na mBan' and retired to bed early vowing never again to touch alcohol in any form. We never discussed the matter afterwards. It was clearly not from my parents that I derived my fascination with wine.

Years ago, when I had been producing features for the *Irish Independent* for a few months, I got a call from Deirdre McQuillan who was then features editor at the *Sunday Tribune*. She had decided that the paper needed a wine column – a pretty revolutionary move, this being 1986 – and told me that Peter Dunne of Mitchell's had suggested that I might be the man for the job, on the basis that I was a freelance writer with a considerable enthusiasm for the stuff. Convinced that enthusiasm is a reasonable substitute for knowledge, I grasped the opportunity and suddenly found myself charged with the unlikely task of writing a piece on Greek wines: difficult enough now, but well-nigh impossible in 1986.

I embarked on my wine-writing career equipped with nothing more than a liking for the stuff, a copy of André Simon's majestic tome, *The Wines of the World,* and a brass neck. Even now it makes me blush prettily to recall that I had been laying down the law on fermented grape juice for several months before I realised what oak tasted like.

The revelation was somewhat unusual. I was sharing a vegetarian dinner with Lingard Goulding, then headmaster of Headfort School in County Meath, when he disappeared to the cellar and returned with a dusty bottle. He drew the cork and carefully poured some red liquid into a beautiful old crystal decanter. He then filled my Luminarc tumbler (preparatory

school headmasters don't stand on ceremony). Passing me the bottle, he remarked, 'You don't see much of that these days.' He was right. It was Château Lafite 1952, one of the greatest wines of Bordeaux and in a pretty good vintage. And even though the school-issue tumbler, used no doubt for administering orange juice to the children in Lingard's care, was not the best vessel for swirling and sniffing, the wine's aroma wafted upwards and I was entranced. Amidst all the complex smells and tastes that a wine like this was throwing at my olfactory system, I was puzzled and enchanted by a rich whiff of something resembling a mixture of poster paints and vanilla essence. I had encountered oak – very expensive French oak – for the first time.

Good Plain Food?

Food is now much more than just fuel for the body. Food is fashion. Food can be dangerous; it can be the focus for guilt. Food, according to some, is the new sex. Food has never been more confused, more controversial, more commercialised. How on Earth have we got to this point?

Food fascists are amongst the most irritating features of modern life, and Heaven knows there's lots of competition. The phrase may be new to you, but I'm sure the key characteristics are very familiar. If they had their way we would be eating a mountain of dietary fibre, minimal saturated fat, no sugar to speak of and our daily ration of so-called functional foods. They may sound upbeat when they talk about such things, but when you examine their edicts there is a distinct lack of joy.

The more extreme elements amongst the food fascists are obviously very browned off at the notion that people are actually allowed to eat what they want. If they had their way we would have food police; I can't help thinking that in another era they might well have been keen proponents of eugenics.

Eugenics, essentially the idea of selectively breeding out all human imperfections, was especially dear to the heart of Adolf Hitler. Hitler – when not masterminding genocide and marching, uninvited, into whatever country took his fancy – was a strict vegetarian and lived according to a rigorous dietary regime. Fanatics tend to be fanatical about everything, I suppose.

The food fascists like to say that Britain has never been healthier than it was during the Second World War, and for once they have a valid point. A society in which white bread was virtually unknown, fats and sugar were available only in minute quantities and red meat was a treat was arguably running on better, purer fuel than is the case today. However, when you factor in the stress, grief and carnage of the war years, plus the propensity for cooking everything to a mush or a crisp, it's a wonder they survived at all.

Now that many of the old taboos – mainly to do with sex – have gone, the food fascists, descendants of the puritan zealots and Jansenists who made life so jolly over the centuries, have to focus on our new guilt: food and how to use it.

The Second World War was indeed a watershed as regards food. While our neighbours across the water were forced to eat a theoretically healthy diet, things were quite different in Ireland. Meat was freely available and, generally speaking, we ate quite luxuriously by comparison to most of Europe, but butter and tea were rationed, oranges and bananas were unheard of and white flour was but a memory. Indeed, my grandmother is said to have sieved a year's supply of wholemeal flour in order to make a 'proper' cake for my mother's wedding in 1945. British servicemen on leave came to Dublin to feast on steaks at The Shelbourne and The Dolphin.

War has much to do with the advent of industrial agriculture. The British swiped the secret of synthetic nitrogen production from the vanquished Germans at the end of the First World War, while the development of a whole range of artificial fertilisers and organophosphate pesticides was made possible by the fact that the Allies had to find a use for stockpiled explosives and other weapons of mass destruction after the Second World War.

Politicians, even in the 1940s, loved a soundbyte. Having won the war, they spoke of the need to win the peace, and part of that process involved feeding the people of Europe. This was the age of the boffin; in those innocent days, blokes in white lab coats had a strangely God-like aura. The most obvious way in which science could be seen to be working for a better world was in the production of hugely increased amounts of ever more affordable food. Nature was seen as something to be conquered, to be subjected to the will of governments and scientists; the fact that organic pioneers like Lady Eve Balfour had written of living 'in harmony, not only with our own species, but with with all others' fifty years before notwithstanding. Mind you, such peace-mongering, at a time of military victory, was not likely to win friends and influence people. Even today, to be fair, I'm not sure I'm all that keen on living in harmony with *all* species. Rats and slugs, for example: I'm sure they perform some useful functions in the great symbiotic network of life, but I will do my damndest to keep them in check whenever they venture near my plants.

Not only did the brave new world provide new and deadly effective agents to combat pests and diseases in agriculture and horticulture but the whole nature of the soil, the medium in which vegetables and fruit are grown and which sustains the grass and other feedstuffs on which meat has been traditionally reared, was to be radically re-evaluated.

Synthetic plant nutrients were now available, easily assimilated, coveniently applied in their pure form and, above all, cheap. In the past the soil had been fed with organic matter, in the form of manure or compost, but why bother when there was a new, improved, cleaner way? Only a few cranks, or prophets, saw the soil as a complex, living thing. Now the farmer was being encouraged to view the soil as just a medium which provided a convenient anchorage for roots; all nutrition could be provided in a handy, easily measurable and concentrated form produced not in the gut of animals or in heaps of decaying vegetable matter but in chemical factories. The soil, in any sense in which it had existed for centuries in farming, was doomed. And farming was well on the road to industrialisation.

Although our faith in science has been severely rattled in recent years – witness the horrible spectre of BSE – it is taking a long time for the average consumer to question the basis of modern agriculture. The first chink in the armour of the brave new agriworld came with the publication, in 1962, of Rachel Carson's *The Silent Spring,* which drew attention to the disastrous consequences of DDT – the most infamous of the organophosphates – and its terrifying persistence both in the environment at large and in the food chain. Nine years later DDT was banned in the USA, not a country noted for its sensitivity on environmental issues, and it took even longer, and less stringent governmental action, to see its eclipse in Europe.

Other organophosphate pesticides, including the one implicated in Gulf War Syndrome, are, of course, still in widespread use and the authorities tell us that they are perfectly safe, if used appropriately.

The industrialisation of food started with changes in the soil, but it was not long before food processing made its contribution, too. Contribution is, perhaps, not quite the right word. In some forms of food processing natural elements tend to be subtracted and 'value' is added.

It is not long ago that people who were convinced of the health benefits of 'wholefood' were regarded, at best, as harmless cranks. For much of the twentieth century the vast majority of the population strove after 'refinement', both in food and in behaviour. Leafing through popular magazines from the 1940s and 1950s, I am always struck by the advertisements which, on the one hand, offer courses to help you improve your grasp of the English language, and on the other, suggest you calm your digestive system with scientifically concocted invalid foods.

Well within living memory there were households in Ireland which feasted on brown soda bread when alone, but when expecting company, especially the priest, would splash out on white bread from the shop. As recently as the 1960s it would have been considered much more sophisticated to reconstitute some diced, dehydrated vegetables, produce mashed potato from a packet, and finish off with Bird's Angel Delight than to produce a meal from fresh, raw materials. In a land like ours, which seemed eternally doomed to poverty, such behaviour was seen as progress.

In the wider world the industrialisation of food formed one of the greatest movements for change in the last century. What this meant was that the distance – literally and figuratively – between producer and plate became ever bigger. Go into a supermarket in Ireland today and the chances are you will find tomatoes from Saudi Arabia, lettuce from the Central Valley of California and asparagus from Peru – even in June. What this means is that freshness is sacrificed, huge quantities of fossil fuels are consumed (a kiwi fruit from New Zealand uses more than its own weight in fuel to get here), chemicals are often used as preservatives, and seasonality is a thing of the past. Most of us no longer know when a particular food is in season. Instead of looking forward to that wonderful burst of flavour we used to enjoy for a few weeks when the asparagus was available from local growers, we now eat the stuff all year round and the taste has been reduced to a dull, attenuated average. Yes, it tastes of asparagus, up to a point, but it doesn't sing.

Strawberries are no longer a treat when you can buy them

in December, but this is not entirely down to food miles. It is also because we – or, rather, the supermarkets acting on our behalf – demand perfect, shiny fruit with long shelf-life. As a result, the horticulture industry has produced a series of strawberry varieties with all the charm of an elderly turnip. But they look lovely.

I will be the first to put my hand up and admit that I quite like to brighten up the dark winter days with a few red peppers from a massive polytunnel in the south of Spain, and that my savage appetite for aubergines is such that I will occasionally buy one that has come all the way from Israel or Holland, but I will defend such behaviour on the basis that (a) the only stuff I have in the garden in January is root vegetables and the odd Brussels sprout, this being the penalty we pay for living in this part of the world, and (b) I have nothing against world trade as such.

However, if you want to experience the sheer exuberant joy of the first of the crop, well ... it has to be just that: the first of the crop. The difference between the first of the early potatoes and the 'new' potatoes which I madly bought in a Dublin supermarket one dark December day is like the contrast between the morning dew and photochemical smog on a bad day in Los Angeles. No, actually, it's greater than that.

The wallpaper vegetables and fruit – by which I mean the ones that are always there in our daily lives – usually taste of very little. Even one of my own onions stored through the winter and sliced open in late spring is just an onion, although it tends to be a little denser in texture and more pungent in flavour than the conventional ones you buy in a shop. Apples, of which we consume a prodigious quantity in this country, are generally pretty unexciting, even if you avoid the awful and grossly ill-named 'Delicious' varieties. But try an Irish-grown Worcester Pearmain in October and your teeth will crunch through crisp flesh to release the sharply sweet essence of the fruit, and you will taste an apple so good that you will have considerable sympathy for poor old Eve while understanding why God is supposed to have issued such a stern prohibition on picking. The reason, again, is simple: the season. Let's face it, an apple, no matter how good, that has been kept in an atmospherically controlled, chilled warehouse under a blanket of inert gas just isn't the same thing. It's useful to have it, of course, and it may be crisp and juicy, but it's not the same. It is unreasonable to expect it to be any different.

Most of the food industry is essentially concerned with what they call 'adding value', but what would be more accurately described as adding to the cost that the consumer is willing to pay. Sometimes, it can be worth it. If you don't have time to cook for yourself you can, with care, get pleasant and nutritious dishes that just have to be reheated. I do it myself from time to time, and Marks & Spencer makes a lot of money out of this kind of convenience food.

But for some food companies, manufacturing involves buying raw materials as cheaply as possible, processing them, making the finished product look more substantial than it really is, and charging as much as possible for it. There is a whole branch of the industry whose sole function is to produce chemicals and equipment which make the food product appear better than it is. We all know about artificial flavours and flavour 'enhancers', but there are also chemicals and processes which make food hold water and air so as to make it look bigger and better. There are chemicals to change texture, add a gloss or a sheen and even to slow the process of oxidation. Antioxidants are a vastly important weapon in the arsenal of the food processors because fat, as we all know, can taste quite good. Salt and fat give many processed foods their immediate appeal, but fat will oxidise and taste rancid after a relatively short time. Step forward the antioxidants and the fat in the product will taste fresh for much, much longer.

Salt and fat have taste appeal, but the food processors know that adding sugar to the equation gives you a product which is, in terms of the mass market, a real winner. To be fair to the industry, it has not conditioned us to react in this way, although it has been encouraging our natural inclination in this direction for decades.

And it is a natural inclination. Anyone with a functioning set of tastebuds knows that pork crackling which has been sprinkled with salt is one of the most moreish things on the planet. We know that a meringue is quite tasty on its own, but when you add whipped cream – and all the fat that it contains – you have something quite celestial. The reason that we should think so probably goes back to our earliest days as a species. Early humans had it tough. The taste of wild honey was a very rare treat; meat and fat did not come their way every day. Indeed, our ancestors probably realised that sugar and fat not only tasted good but also tended to extend the waistline. Many aeons before Weightwatchers and Slimcea, people believed that putting on a few pounds was a happy and a wholesome thing to do because they had noticed something in their battle for survival. When food supplies grew scarce, it was the skinny people who perished first.

These days the situation has reversed, and it is not just a matter of fashion or perception. Our sedentary twenty-first-century lifestyle, combined with the ready availability of fat and sugar at every meal (and between meals), means that obesity is a serious problem. Being overweight does increase your chances of developing heart disease, high blood pressure and even diabetes. On balance, it is better to be skinny – not through avoiding fat and sugar altogether, of course, but through eating a balanced diet (which can contain the occasional morsel of pork crackling) and plenty of exercise.

Most of us in the western world are fatter than we should be and most of us want a quick fix, hence the diet industry, which in many ways is just as pernicious as the worst elements in the food processing one. In the maelstrom of advice on how to lose weight certain important facts are lost, or perhaps suppressed. First of all, if you lose weight rapidly, you will put it back on again just as quickly. Secondly, it is possible to be fit while being technically overweight – and fitness is an essential weapon in warding off cardiovascular disease. Thirdly, you can virtually forget about calories if you eat a balanced diet that completely excludes refined carbohydrates. The down-side is that refined carbohydrates include white flour (and therefore pasta), sugar (even the brown variety) and honey. The late Dr Atkins made a fortune through promoting a rather extreme version of this diet.

The link between refined foods and disease was first demonstrated in a meaningful way by a doctor of Irish birth, Denis Burkitt, who trained at TCD and at the late, lamented Adelaide Hospital. Working in Africa, he noticed that his patients never presented with diverticulitis and only very rarely with appendicitis. He established a link between a diet high in fibre – from unrefined foods – and a paucity of certain conditions common in western societies where fibre forms a very small part of the typical daily food intake.

Shortly after graduating, I shared a house with an old schoolfriend who had gone through the Medical School at TCD, and who is now a distinguished physician in Detroit. He discovered the works of Denis Burkitt and became quite obsessed with the need for dietary fibre, even unto consuming vast quantities of raw wheat bran for breakfast (a substance which, I can reveal, is almost impossible to remove from crockery once it has dried on). I gave him a copy of Dean Swift's essay, 'Of Human Ordure', as a wedding present after a dinner with myself and Johann (the Dean being quite obsessed with what children call 'poo'). As he was leaving, he cast an eye over our collection of Kilner jars filled to the brim with chick-peas, lentils and dried beans. 'My God!' he said. 'Just imagine the combined bowel-shifting power of all that!'

Swift had an instinctive notion that refined foods were bad news. The most common refined carbohydrates are, as I mentioned, white flour and sugar. And when I say common, I mean it. Just consider your average daily diet, especially all the sugar that you don't actually spoon on, the sugar that is hidden. When you eat foods that contain these substances you will get a fairly instant boost of energy, but the rapid peaking of insulin secretion that results from this encourages your body to store fat, ie, your physiology will start to convert the fat in your meal – the butter, meat fat, olive oil, whatever – into adipose tissue, or, as it is better known, body fat.

Eat whole foods – wholemeal bread, fruit, vegetables, modest amounts of meat, fish and what have you – while avoiding sugar and you will enjoy the 'slow burn' of unrefined nutrition, the sort of fuel on which we are designed to run. I will admit that I am perhaps not the most dedicated exponent of such a scheme, and that you would be well advised to go very easy on potatoes and bananas, which both contain carbohydrates that are as refined as any you will find in nature. Give such a diet plenty of time, however – ideally a few years – and you will be surprised at the effect.

The surprising thing about this advice – shocking, perhaps, to many – is that it points the finger at refined foods and not at that great *bête noire*: fat. The obsession with fat is one of the great modern con jobs and it dates back to the early 1960s when researchers established a putative link between dietary cholesterol and arterosclerosis, or hardening of the arteries. A lot of people who have heart attacks have perfectly normal cholesterol, by the way, but this is usually glossed over.

In the years since this discovery, the western world has become obsessed with saturated fats and we have come to believe that they are very, very bad and that polyunsaturated fats, such as sunflower oil, and monosaturates, such as olive oil, are very, very good. This is not, in fact, the case. Saturated fats in moderation, especially in the context of a diet rich in fresh fruit and vegetables, are fine. Polyunsaturates and monosaturates are, indeed, beneficial but, on the other hand, they are liquid fats. In order to turn these oils into a form which can be spread on bread, they must be processed. So much so, indeed, that many margarines and spreads based on healthy oils end up containing distinctly unhealthy transfats.

The huge con job – the scale of which really does beggar belief – lies in the food industry's successful efforts in persuading the vast majority of our population that dairy and olive spreads actually taste good. What they have done, in effect, is to imply that only people who do not care about their health eat butter and that butter is, in effect, a killer. It is this wickedly misleading 'health' message that has caused vast numbers of Irish people to turn their backs on a great Irish product which, when used in moderation and in the context of a good diet, will do you no harm at all. The truly galling aspect of this shameful exercise is the connivance of the Irish dairy industry; who are the people, after all, who make so many of these so-called spreads? And the medical profession, by and large, has bugger-all interest in real nutrition, preferring to swallow, uncritically, the now rather old-fashioned dictum that minimal fat is, in itself, a panacea.

So-called good oils, and the spreads based upon them, are presented to us as exemplifying the bounty and benificence of nature but, in fact, many of them are highly unnatural. At the commodity level – where volume is the biggest issue, not flavour – olive oil and sunflower oil are so over-extracted as to be indistinguishable the one from the other. Indeed, high-quality extra virgin olive oil is often added to so-called pure olive oil in small amounts so as to ensure it tastes of anything at all.

Basic oils are extracted using pressure, heat, solvents, phosphates, alkalis and deodorising agents. Every last drop of oil is sucked out of the seed or the olive and the quality is, frankly, crap. Cold-pressed oils are produced simply by squeezing the unheated raw material and no chemicals are used. The oil yield is very small, of course, and so the price is high, but you actually get to taste the olives or the sunflower seeds.

Looking for the magic words 'extra virgin olive oil' is a good start if you want an oil that has not been abused by industrial processes, but the range of character and quality is as wide as the range of prices you will be expected to pay. Cheap versions are often quite bland (and therefore fine for cooking), and will usually be a blend of many different extra virgin olive oils from many different sources. The 'Italian' extra virgin olive oils that you find on the supermarket shelves are almost invariably, in fact, the produce of Spain, Portugal and even North Africa, blended and packaged in Italy, but at least they are cheap. The best oils, the ones you drizzle on bread or use to dress salad or vegetables, will be deep in taste, complex, delicate and not at all greasy. They will also cost as much as a very good bottle of wine; €30 for 75cl of exquisite oil is actually not a lot to pay for something so delicious and which can be used so sparingly.

Drizzling very good olive oil onto bread demands serious baking, the sort of stuff that is palpably the staff of life, the kind of bread that is made by hand from the best raw materials. We are not talking about industrial bread, the sliced pans and other manifestations of the science of the modern bakery and its triumph in making air and water stand up. The sort of bread that the average family eats these days – whether it is white, or 'brown', or even 'wholemeal' – is actually the product of a highly automated and industrial process that bypasses all of the skills involved in traditional, slow, craft baking. Vast, high-speed mixing machines, and a whole range of so-called flour improvers, means that the fluffy, insubstantial gunk that we know as bread is produced as cheaply and as quickly as possible.

We may seem to eat quite a lot of bread in Ireland but, in fact, we are second lowest in the EU scale of consumption, with only the United Kingdom coming in below us. All of our Continental European neighbours have managed to retain the respect that is due to craft bakers and they are prepared to pay for real bread. In almost every village in France you will see a sign promising '*pain cuit au feu de bois*'; in Ireland, we regard the rather bland offerings of Cuisine de France (a company owned by IAWS, the big Irish agri-company) as sophisticated.

Of course there has been a reaction to the onward march of the sliced pan. There are enough people to support the work of such proper bakers as La Maison des Gourmets in Dublin and Declan Ryan in Cork, but, unfortunately, a whole swathe of the population think that tarted-up bread is actually the real thing. Sundried tomatoes and olives and Heaven knows how many other additions are often designed to trick your palate into thinking that the actual bread is worth eating. Often it is not. One bread product (I'm sure that is how it is described in the marketing material) bearing the moniker of a well-known Irish chef smells strongly of margarine. Check the ingredients and, sure enough, it contains hydrogenated vegetable fat, which is the technical phrase for marge.

In-store bakeries are very often just a mini version of the vast industrial ones, but they are there to provide the homely smell of freshly baked bread to which we all seem to have a Pavlovian reaction. It makes us feel more comfortable and therefore happier to buy more. The bread itself is made using flour 'improvers' and the result is pretty underwhelming. The so-called French versions shatter into a kind of dust when they go stale; I think this tells us something. In fact, when you consider the state of bread in Ireland, it is perhaps not so surprising that most of it is smothered in 'dairy spread' before it ends up in the average stomach, churning about with lots of other industrial grub.

When I was a child we had two kinds of bread: Boland's batch loaf, from which it was always a pleasure to peel those slightly doughy flakes on the sides; and traditional Irish brown soda bread, which owes its leavening not to yeast but to the action of the acid in buttermilk on sodium bicarbonate. In our house, my mother tended to use milk that had been allowed to go sour. These days milk doesn't go sour, it goes off in a thoroughly nasty way; another example of change in the production of basic foodstuffs.

Wholemeal bread, like all whole foods, is good for you. At least in theory. The problem is that cereal production in modern agriculture involves high inputs of what the agri-chemical industry likes to call 'crop protection agents', or nasty chemicals, as the rest of us would say. Cereals also tend to be treated chemically so as to keep them from deteriorating in storage. It is hardly surprising then that wholegrain flour tends to contain a much higher degree of chemical residues than white flour, which is made from the grain stripped, literally, bare. So, while there are countless boffins to reassure us that the residue levels are so small as to pose no danger to human health, I think I would prefer to use organic wholemeal flour, thanks all the same. This is, of course, another example of how the industrialisation of food and farming gives us more than we want. In this case it is not the hidden fat, sugar or additives, it is residues of chemicals used to protect crops against attack from insect and microbial infections.

It would be a mistake, of course, to think that there was a golden age when all food was natural and wholesome.

Nineteenth-century legislation to outlaw food adulteration was a response to a real problem. Food products, in general, are arguably a lot safer than they were in mid-Victorian times. The romantic view of our agricultural past sees our forefathers producing a mixture of crops, both animal and vegetable, in the pursuit of virtual self-sufficiency, with the surplus sold at market to provide life's little luxuries. For many Irish farmers this was, indeed, the norm until well into the last century. Others, like my grandfather and great-grandfather, grew for the market – in their case raising fruit for the growing metropolis of Dublin, but they also had a house cow, kept poultry and had a kitchen garden to feed family and employees.

My great-grandfather, Michael MacKeown, trained at Kew Gardens and established a fruit farm in County Meath where he grew the usual staples, but he also managed to build a heated greenhouse in which he produced grapes, in the days when the vine fruits of South Africa and Continental Europe were dear enough to justify the large expenditure on fuelling a coke furnace to offset the gloom of the Irish climate. One of my mother's earliest childhood memories was of the cool, spotless, tiled home-dairy where the milk was separated and butter was churned exclusively for the use of the household. Another was of soaring on her swing into the plum blossom of the orchards in spring.

Of course, even in this rural idyll gardeners, especially the professional gardeners, used poisons in their battle with nature. We tend to imagine that there was once an innocent age when every food crop was produced without the aid of a chemical armoury, but this is not entirely true. Arsenic was used as a pesticide from at least the middle of the eighteenth century and every walled kitchen garden attached to a Big House had a locked cupboard in the bothy where deadly substances were stored.

Biological controls, now very much back in fashion, were eclipsed by the development of modern pesticides in the early 1930s, although the first recorded example is when mynah birds were imported into Mauritius in 1762 in a successful attempt to keep down the devastating locust infestations. Geigy, the Swiss chemical company, isolated the world's first wonder pesticide, dichlorodiphenyltricloroethane, later to be known as DDT, in the late 1920s. Its superstar status was confirmed when it came close to eradicating malaria in Europe just as the Continent was plunged into the Second World War.

Science may indeed have delivered cheap food for some years in the 1950s and 1960s, but it doesn't take an economist to look at the agricultural policy of the EU over four decades, however well-intentioned, and decide that the real cost of food is actually higher than ever. In fact, most of us now realise that Europe's Common Agricultural Policy (CAP) is a time-bomb and that urgent action is required. It may seem an oversimplification to say that Europe's farmers have been encouraged to spend their working days producing commodities nobody wants, but it is hard to put any other interpretation on what the EU has been doing for decades. Cheap food, which seemed so important in those bleak post-war days, has turned out to be very expensive indeed.

Irish farmers, whose real job is to produce food that people need and want to buy, received a total of €1.6 billion in direct payments from the EU in 2002. This represents 70% of agricultural income. The EU shells out €2 every day for every dairy cow in Ireland which, as Fintan O'Toole has pointed out in *The Irish Times*, is considerably in excess of the daily income of half of the population of the planet. This is not just obscene, it makes no sense whatsoever.

CAP reform is long overdue and the future of Irish farming is going to be very different from what we have seen since we joined the EEC. Some argue that the only viable future will be based on bigger and bigger farms with ever greater economies of scale and enhanced competitiveness which, when translated, means more and even cheaper food. Do we never learn?

The future for our farmers – the only game worth the candle – lies in the production of exceptionally high-quality food for the only sector which more and more consumers throughout Europe support: natural, sustainable and, ideally, organic food. Vast monocultures suit huge farms; organic agriculture suits the generally small farms of Ireland. It is blindingly obvious, especially when combined with our image abroad as a green, clean country. For God's sake, it's our national colour. But try telling that to the IFA, an organisation so devoid of visionaries that it vies with Youth Defence for the title of Ireland's Most Conservative Organisation. And perhaps with less excuse.

Europe's farmers make more money out of knowing how to play the system than from honing their agricultural skills. There is a scandalous divorce between good husbandry and farm incomes, and it is a credit to the many people who still take pride in what they do on the land that we can still buy superb Irish grass-fed beef, if we know where to find a traditional craft butcher with an eye for exceptional meat. The concentration of the Irish meat industry in the hands of a few very rich and successful businessmen has done nothing for farmers, consumers, or for those few remaining retailers who are concerned about quality rather than price. Successive governments have played right into their hands and, at the time of writing, there is no indication that this cosy relationship is going to change.

The average consumer distrusts both farmers and government agencies and not without good reason. They are not particularly impressed with 'traceability' schemes for meat, probably because the implication is that products will only be traced if something goes horribly wrong. We have come a long way from the days when we knew the butcher and the farmer who put meat on our plates. I am reminded of the story told by Myrtle Allen of Ballymaloe of how she commented to a neighbour that she was very impressed with the butter that his sister was sending her. 'Oh yes,' he said, 'that field always gave good butter.'

There are reasons for optimism, of course. A lot of people want to know more about their food, scientific claims are treated with healthy scepticism and the Irish organic sector is growing at a rate of knots. How long it will take real, natural and ideally local food to go mainstream is anyone's guess, but a lot more of us aspire to that situation than did a decade ago.

The Way We
Eat Now

S heila Dillon, who presents 'The Food Programme' on BBC Radio 4, once came to lunch, a couple of years ago. She was doing a piece on the Irish Food Revolution (we tend to think of such phrases as having capital initial letters) and was starting her quest in County Cork. A few weeks before her visit the *Daily Telegraph*'s food writer, Tamsin Day-Lewis (Daniel's big sister), had written a paean of entirely justified praise for Cork's English Market under the rather neat headline, 'The Tuck of the Irish'. It was becoming clear that the message to our brethren in Britain was that Ireland had been undergoing a tumultuous change in its attitude to food and how it is produced and presented. Well-intentioned as these stories were, they did seem to imply that if it was not impossible to throw a brick at random in Ireland without hitting an artisan producer, the day was not far off.

After Sheila and I had lunched frugally but well off lentil soup made with organic chicken stock, hunks of excellent brown soda bread (both of which Johann had left ready for us) and a makeshift salad from the garden, we proceeded to record an interview. The process was not helped by the fact that our dog had secretly devoured the sponge microphone cover as a snack, but we spoke softly to compensate.

The interview never saw the light of broadcast day, through no fault of the BBC; they were trying to do an upbeat piece on Irish food and there was me saying that, yes, there were scattered outbreaks of excellence, but the balance was still pretty unexciting. I would love Ireland really to be The Food Island, to use Bord Bia's admirably aspirational phrase, but I did feel – and still do – that we have quite a way to go. So does England, Wales and Scotland, of course. Put it like this: you need a really good guidebook to eat consistently well when making a tour of these islands. In Italy, you just follow your nose, sometimes literally.

So has there been an Irish food revolution? Well, perhaps there has, but we are exceptionally eager to congratulate ourselves on anything that we do even vaguely well. Hence, where a few but growing number of far-sighted people decide to produce wholesome, natural, handmade food in Ireland and when a modest proportion of our chefs cook supremely well, we tend to exaggerate the picture.

The pioneers of real food in modern Ireland,

starting with Myrtle Allen in the early 1960s, have had to struggle against all the odds, and many of them still do. We live in a country where small, high-quality producers have it rather tough. They are prey to the Draconian application of EU food safety laws (which don't seem to operate in quite the same way in places like France and Italy), where government policy always seems to favour large-scale, factory-based production, and where we are still conditioned to expect all food to be cheap. Despite being still an essentially rural country, your chances of buying food that has been produced within a few miles of your home are slim and taking food seriously continues, unfortunately, to be regarded as an élitist, middle-class affectation. Even today in Ireland, an enthusiasm for fine food is seen as something rather alien and above our collective station; no wonder so many of the pioneers of real food here have been foreigners.

As is the case in so many other areas of our national character, our approach to food comes heavily laden with historical baggage. We have a guilt about eating well because we are the descendants of the people who survived the Famine, the ones who not only avoided starving to death, and somehow didn't succumb to cholera, but who managed to stay in the land of their birth. We are here because our forebears had enough to eat – maybe only just enough in order to cling onto life and produce children. In this context it is no surprise that our attitude to food is rather short on joy and celebration.

And so it dredges up uncomfortable collective memories if we decide to spurn inferior food. It seems faintly indecent to demand the best that we can afford because the stock of which we are born survived by eating what they could. And when we failed to clear the plates of childhood meals we were told – if we were Roman Catholic – that the starving children in Africa would give anything to be offered such nourishment. Not having achieved an adult level of logic – or what passes for it in the grown-up world – we would fervently offer our congealed meat and three veg (especially the veg) for immediate transfer to Africa on the basis that we were not starving. That way lay a clip around the ear.

Add to this kind of experience the obsession with calorie-counting and the alleged evil of fat and it is no wonder that we bring to food a curious combination of rather twisted emotions. It is alright to eat to live, but living to eat is sinful.

In most Irish families you don't have to delve very far back into the ancestry to find dire poverty. It is very much to our credit as a people that we have always prized education as an engine of advancement and that whole generations of Irish parents strove against appalling odds in order to give their children a leg-up the social ladder. But woe betide the upwardly mobile who got 'notions'; the consumption of wine and fancy foreign food would elicit a sharp condemnation: 'Sure, t'was far from that you were reared!'

Times are indeed changing, but slowly. These days the national staple is no longer potatoes, it is pasta. Wine is consumed not just at Christmas but weekly in middle-class homes throughout the land. The Jacob's Creeks and Piat d'Ors have come to be accepted as part of normal behaviour. It may not be much of a revolution, but it's a start. We eat and drink very differently at the dawn of the twenty-first century than we did when I was growing up the 1960s and 1970s – largely thanks to television and travel.

While we bring home from holidays abroad a braver palate and a willingness to eat foods of which our parents may never have even heard, we don't import what I think is the most infectious aspect of food culture in Europe: the passion, the excitement and the demand for quality. The French, the Italians, the Spanish will happily debate food for hours on end – ideally over a table laden with various dishes – and they will go the extra kilometre and the extra few euro to get the best they can afford. Watch them in the markets, even in the super-markets, as they prod, sniff, squeeze, consider.

Our Continental cousins take so much time and effort to select the raw materials for cooking not just because this sense of discernment is bred in the bone but, I believe, because they have retained the sense of sharing and communion that used to be part of breaking bread together. Many Irish families sit down together around the dining table on only a handful of occasions throughout the year. Most people, according to the statisticians, eat in front of the television, so that the consump-tion of food is a communal activity only in the sense that the family eats more or less the same food while watching the same programme. As multiple televisions become the norm in Irish homes, even this sense of communion may well be lost as the younger element watch 'Buffy the Vampire Slayer' while parents settle down in front of 'Sky News'.

Most houses these days still come with a dining room, but it is usually deployed for some purpose other than eating. If a family eats together it is probably in the kitchen, something which I have never been keen to do. I believe there is a greater sense of occasion and significance if the meal is carried through into another area and seen and consumed in isolation from where it was prepared. Not always, of course. We eat in front of 'The Simpsons' from time to time and have been known to refuel in the kitchen, but we like to have several, proper family meals in the week. Apart from anything else, it's an opportunity for conversation.

As a restaurant critic, I always try to approach each meal with enthusiasm and high expectations. However, despite great strides over the last decade in particular, the norm remains pretty uninspiring. The function of the average, bog-standard Irish restaurant seems to be to convert mass-produced ingredients into tarted-up pictures-on-a-plate, and to charge an arm and a leg for the privilege. They are mind-numbingly predictable. When a waiter asks me, yet again, the extraordinary question, 'Do you want to see the menu?', I want to reply, 'No, I'll just guess'. In fact, I have been doing a few trial runs by leaving the menu closed and choosing by ESP. I turn to my companion and say, 'I'll have whatever they have managed to do to goat's cheese to start, followed by whatever they have done to the lamb.' It rarely fails.

The predictability of Irish restaurants has changed, of course, and it now hinges on doing silly things with the raw materials. There are two reasons for this. The first is that the raw materials are often pretty dull and bland, the second is because chefs feel that they have to justify their existence and produce something that the punter is unlikely to do at home. Cheffing about is a very common practice and is sometimes, tragically, extended to excellent raw materials, whereupon it becomes a crime.

Too many Irish chefs and Irish customers appear to have a horror of simplicity. There is nothing – simply nothing – as good as spanking fresh fish dusted with flour and cooked in a little butter until it is just done, served with a wedge of lemon. A piece of beef that is well-reared and properly matured by a craft butcher (as distinct from mass-produced and vac-packed in a vast factory) needs only to be lightly anointed with olive oil, salt and pepper and placed on a very hot grill. A salad of fresh, organic lettuce needs just a drizzle of olive oil and a squeeze of lemon juice.

Bread needs to be made slowly using the best flour and a lot of skill; it does not require sundried tomatoes, curry powder, fried onions or chunks of cheap olives. (If Shakespeare asked today, 'Where is fancy bred?' he would be directed to the

nearest restaurant.) Mashed potato needs to be made from a variety of potato suitable for boiling or steaming, into which a lot of hot milk and melted butter is whisked. If the spuds are good it doesn't really need to be flavoured with mustard, or sage, or bits of bacon.

This feverish desire of chefs to appear clever seems to desert them as soon as the vexed question of vegetables arises. Most will have recourse to what they can buy pre-prepped: chunks of potato, lumps of calabrese broccoli, batons of woody carrot. This is vegetables as wallpaper, as muzak, as a token gesture. In many European countries there is a tradition of serving vegetables as a separate course, where they have to sing for their supper and keep up with the meat or the fish. Of course, in such places vegetables tend to be grown with pride, with an emphasis on flavour, texture and, above all, freshness. They are not produced as a commodity.

We have dozens – perhaps hundreds – of small-scale, organic growers, producing stuff like cavolo nero (the Tuscan cabbage), myriad squashes, asparagus peas, proper sprouting broccoli (not those big heads of calabrese which are supposed to be so good for us), tiny courgettes, okra, all sorts and colours of tomato, artichokes, green onions, baby leeks, dozens of salads, lots of different kinds of oriental brassicas. And what does the typical restaurant do? It serves the kinds of vegetables which would not be out of place in a 1950s' factory canteen.

This sort of attitude reveals that restaurants in Ireland almost invariably serve vegetables – and other foods, too – not because they are any good, or because they are in season, or because they really compliment whatever else is on the plate, but simply because they are there, day in, day out, and are sold cheaply. There are restaurants in West Cork – a dwindling number, thank Heaven, but present nevertheless – where the chef buys his vegetables out of the back of a van that has travelled all the way from the Dublin market. Meanwhile, within a few miles there are organic producers who are ignored because they have to charge more to make a living and cannot guarantee a year-round supply of red peppers and courgettes.

Great chefs care deeply about their raw materials, vegetables included. It is, perhaps, invidious to name some personal favourites, and I'm sure I will leave out many who are doing wonderful things. But amongst the visionary chefs of Ireland I would have to mention Derry Clarke of L'Ecrivain, Guillaume Lebrun of Guilbaud's, Ross Nugent of Chapter One, all in Dublin; Paul Flynn at The Tannery in Dungarvan; Rory O'Connell at Ballymaloe House; Denis Cotter at Café Paradiso in Cork. These guys are superstars, but there are dozens of good, modest restaurants which do a superb job and rarely get much recognition for it: places like The Farmgate in Midleton, Grapefruit Moon in Ballycotton, 101 Talbot in Dublin, The Crawford Gallery Café in Cork, The Wine Vault in Waterford, Country Choice in Nenagh and La Dolce Vita in Wexford. The good news is that they are a growing band, but you can travel long distances between them.

I once found myself in a small town in Umbria with a couple of fellow wine writers – one English, the other American – getting peckish. Although it was well into siesta time, we decided to find a restaurant the American had visited some years before and which he said was eccentric but very good. We came across it eventually in a side street off the sleepy *piazza* and entered the cool, empty, dim interior. The elderly owner looked surprised and a little embarrassed. She told us that she had nothing to give us and that fresh supplies would not be delivered until later in the evening. Would we like to come back then? We said that some bread and cheese with a bottle of wine would do fine and she pottered off to see what she could find.

The crusty rustic bread arrived in no time, along with a round of a local semi-soft cow's cheese and two bottles – a nice touch – of something red and palatable. As we ate we were gradually surrounded by a wafting, delicious smell and shortly afterwards our hostess emerged with duck breasts which had been grilled over wild fennel, and a vast bowl of crisp salad. She told us that we looked hungry and she had managed to produce these few morsels. The bill came to a little over ten quid a head, and we tried to assuage our guilt at having interrupted her afternoon's rest by pressing a large tip on her. She refused and said that it had been a pleasure to pre-pare such a simple snack for such appreciative foreigners (the implication being, I suppose, that English-speakers rarely show much appreciation).

It reminded me of Elizabeth David's story of stopping at a wayside *auberge* somewhere in deepest France and being told that there was nothing – *rien* – to eat, but that she and her companion would be welcome to some bread, some *char-cuterie* and some of the local wine. They gratefully accepted, gorged themselves on *saucisson* and were somewhat emabarrassed to find a *daube* of beef plonked on the table at the point where they felt that they had eaten their fill. Followed by a *coeur de crème*, salad and cheese. I like the Continentals' idea of 'nothing'.

Eating abroad is fraught with potential embarrassment. Maeve Binchy tells a wonderful story about leaving her hotel in Taiwan in order to avoid the hideous imitations of western food served there. This was thirty years ago when tourists rarely ventured beyond the air-conditioned comfort of their accommodation. She found a place which appeared to have a menu in the window and went in to find that it was, indeed, full of people – all men, as it happens – eating and drinking. Not knowing how to read the menu she looked around and saw someone eating what appeared to be stir-fried prawns accompanied by a beer. She pointed and indicated that she would like the same, whereupon, frozen with horror, she saw the waiter snatch up the poor man's bowl and beer glass only to plonk them down in front of her. She ate quickly and left, with many thanks and abject apologies, and had her offer of a generous bundle of US dollars politely but firmly refused. She is still, she says, not sure if it really was a restaurant.

In rural parts of Europe and even, to some extent, in the cities, many restaurants are family businesses; the premises have long been paid for and everybody, young and old, has a role to play in what they see as a kind of community service. This is the key reason why it is relatively cheap to eat in countries which put a high value on food. Such restaurants have an organic link with their environment; in Ireland, for the most part, restaurants lack this sense of personality and place. Most are glorified sandwich bars and many of the rest are élitist and somewhat alien.

In many Irish restaurants we seem to suffer from a kind of Emperor's New Clothes Syndrome. The kitchen is pretending that the food is special and the customers are concerned to appear sophisticated. Look around you in a restaurant on the Continent and consider that communal sense of purpose and mutual respect that infuses every action that you witness. In places like that, both punters and staff know what they are about.

It may seem perverse to describe the average Irish restaurant – with all its silly cheffing about – as conservative, but considering that eating out is a relatively new experience for most of us, the typical menu is remarkably traditional. How many of us ever consider eating a starter, main course (meat or fish with three veg) and a dessert as the main meal of the day at home? And yet virtually every menu in the country is based on the idea that we do. Tapas bars and noodle houses, where you order a range of dishes which are served as they are ready, are much more in tune with the way we eat today and they are becoming more common. Wagamama's communal tables and decree that you get your dishes as they are ready are revolutionary, but it does a roaring trade.

The conservatism of Irish restaurants is most clearly expressed in their approach to wine. A few brave pioneers (an unfortunate phrase, in the context, I suppose) charge a standard mark-up on a bottle of wine, which makes trading-up an attractive option. Rather than having your bottle of house wine, you can have something quite serious while still paying €10 or so as a margin to the restaurant. However, in virtually every establishment in the land you will pay a percentage mark-up, which means that while you are being ripped off for a bottle of house plonk, you are being mugged and left for dead if you decide to have a bottle of half-decent Burgundy.

There are some monumental, legendary wine lists in Ireland. Places like Kelly's of Rosslare, The Lord Bagenal Inn in Leighlinbridge, Kenmare's Park Hotel and Delphi Lodge in Connemara maintain vast, eclectic lists. Even before you open the wine list you know that you will be able to drink something interesting and well-made from any major wine region in the world and that, should the humour take you, you can choose from a huge range of great classics. These restaurants are driven by a passion for wine and, to some extent, by missionary zeal. Not only are the lists big and eclectic, they often offer outstanding value for money, especially for older vintages.

This kind of wine list is a labour of love and nobody is really in it for the money. Offering mature wines is the sort of thing of which accountants strongly disapprove. This is why most restaurants don't even bother to offer serious wines that are ready to drink – with the occasional exception of some posh Bordeaux label with an extortionate mark-up – and source everything from a couple of the big wine distributors. Hence you open the list and see all the usual suspects from every wine-producing country you can shake a stick at – and none of them particularly good.

In places like New York, London and Sydney, many of the better restaurants have long ago abandoned the idea of organising wine lists on the basis of country: they prefer to offer a short list, carefully chosen, with interest and quality as the object, and comprising a range of styles rather than a clumsy geography lesson. This kind of restaurant will have a wine waiter who knows every single wine intimately and can tell you anything you want to know about any of them. He, or she, will expect you to ask for advice rather than plumping for the Irish favourites, *viz.* Sancerre, Fleurie, or 'a bottle of the house red'.

Such restaurants can provide you with a full bottle of wine, of course, but they are used to most of their customers ordering by the glass. By the generous glass, of course, not the mingy little thimbles we tend to get here. If you want to get a flavour of this kind of wine list (and some excellent, simply prepared organic food), try the Ely Wine Bar in Dublin, the success of which has yet to spawn any serious imitations. I find this curiously reassuring in that it suggests that the average restaurateur is aware of his or her limitations.

The limitations seem to be legion. The shunning of simplicity extends far beyond the sheer cheffiness of menus. Try ordering a green salad. Pretty straightforward, you might think: some lettuce, perhaps even a couple of kinds, a few leaves of rocket, maybe even a bit of basil. Is this what you get? Rarely. On most occasions the colour definition is by-passed and you will end up with cherry tomatoes, beansprouts, every conceivable colour of pepper, slices of cucumber (moderately green, I

know), chunks of red onion, layers of tough, leathery radicchio, shreds of red cabbage, lollorosso ... nothing limits the list
but the resourcefulness of the kitchen.

Even leaving aside the fact that nobody in their right mind
could regard this concoction as being green, it is also a total
nightmare of tastes and textures. The Irish mixed salad is whatever comes to hand, and, unfortunately, an awful lot comes to
hand. The most complicated salad I like to create involves
some lettuce, some rocket, a few snips of fresh herbs (especially chives and chervil, but when did you last see the latter in
a restaurant, let alone the supermarket?), perhaps a few mari-
gold petals and the odd nasturtium flower or leaf for a touch of
pepperiness. Yes, yes, I know I am admitting that the desire to
cut all the greenness with colour is a national characteristic
which, at heart, I share, but I insist that this is real salad, a salad
that has been thought out.

The average restaurant serves lettuce-dependent salad (with
all the other, inappropriate ingredients) right through the
winter. When did you last see a seasonal offering of beetroot
and orange salad, or winter cress, which provides the crunch
and refreshment for which we look to salad as a
palate-cleanser? Or a little bowl of lamb's lettuce and winter
purslane with a simple dressing? Or little strips of blanched
celeriac tossed with a touch of *remoulade*?

When I consider ideas like this I sometimes wonder if I
should be let out on my own. Perhaps I eat too well at home.
Indeed, I have given up eating chicken, except in restaurants
where I know the raw materials are sourced with considerable

effort and pride. Your typical chicken fillet, I'm afraid, tastes of sawdust to me, because I eat the real thing back at the ranch. But the blandness seems to be spreading. However well a piece of beef may be cooked – crusty outside and moist and rare within – it usually tastes of very little. Again, this is a case of poor raw materials, of meat that has not been aged for flavour and which, more likely than not, was produced in a farming system that rewards yield rather than quality.

Any system that works on that basis ultimately fails both producer and consumer, while it undoubtedly lines the pockets of those who come between them. And it is not confined to agriculture. Far too many restaurants look to yield (bums on seats, portion control, 'competitive' margins) rather than to quality and the giving of pleasure. Far too many of those who are involved in the complex process of feeding us, whether at home or when we eat out, have had a passion bypass. Why? Because too few of us care: never mind the quality, look at the quantity; and when we eat out, give us fashion, not passion.

Deep Delved
Earth

As I've already mentioned, Lingard Goulding was the first of several friends whose generosity fuelled my enthusiasm for wine when I was starting out. He did not, of course, snap up parcels of mature claret at auction – not on a teacher's salary. However, his father, the late and gloriously eccentric Sir Basil Goulding, had left him a few cases of very good stuff and he had the sense to enjoy them as they were meant to be enjoyed, without undue reverence.

Others who find themselves the inheritors of wine prefer to off-load it, often with unrealistic expectations. There is a curious notion that the mere action of time will snatch a wine from mediocrity and translate it into the realms of the sublime. Nothing, of course, could be further from the truth. Virtually all of the wine produced in the world is for immediate consumption and no amount of slumber in the deep delved earth will change that.

The triumph of hope over reality is what has driven several dozen cellar-owners to ask me to cast an eye over their dusty bottles. Perhaps, deep in their hearts, they know that twenty dozen Beaujolais Nouveau 1973 are unlikely to be drinkable, let alone saleable. But what about the Henkell Trocken 1927, and the half-bottle of 'the Widow' (as the cognoscenti call Veuve Clicquot) which appears to date from 1938?

One of the oddest collections I ever unearthed was in the nether regions of a very grand country house. It comprised seven bottles of the rather crude-sounding Fockink Orange Curaçao ('Not another Fockink Orange Curaçao!'), seventeen dozen bottles of what turned out, upon tasting, to be grocer's Sherry dating from the 1920s, and three dozen unlabelled, oozing bottles of clear spirit, each nestling in a decomposing straw cocoon. On closer inspection the bottles were embossed with what appeared to me to be the Imperial Russian crest and an abbreviated Latin inscription. My imagination, as estate agents like to say, ran wild.

This, I decided, might well be serious stuff. Obviously it was vodka specially distilled for the Tsar and given to the great-great-grandfather of my friend, who had just inherited the stately pile. It seems that great-great-grandfather was on first-name terms with all the crowned heads of Europe. I eventually found an expert on Victorian spirits – which makes him sound like a Theosophist, I suppose – and asked for advice. He became very excited and asked detailed questions about the quality of the glass and the smell – the very pronounced smell – which the bottles exhaled. If it were the genuine article, he said, we had something worth several hundred pounds a bottle. The Japanese, he added, were very keen on this sort of hooch.

A week or so later I was standing in a bar in Milan, marvelling at the odd concoctions that Italians insist on drinking. I was admiring the label of one, which appeared to contain extract of globe artichokes, when my eye fell upon a bottle of Grappa, the coarse grape spirit that is best used externally as an embrocation. The crest was identical in every respect. I asked if I could have a sniff and the dream of excited Japanese collectors trampling each other to death evaporated with the familiar pong.

On one occasion I was summoned by a rather dreamy old character in County Cavan who had decided to off-load several dozen Cockburn's 1963 – which is arguably the best thing to do with this somewhat patchy Vintage Port – and I drove miles and miles to collect the stuff. The cellar was beautiful – early eighteenth-century brick vaults, all recently restored because the owner had tackled a major outbreak of dry rot in an uncharacteristically clear-headed manner. The area was vast and echoingly empty. There, in a corner, lay the Vintage Port, beside it a few dozen Mommessin Vin de Table Franaçis 1977, three venerable bottles of white Dubonnet, a demijohn of Navy rum and, bizarrely, a half-bottle of Wincarnis which, as older readers will remember, was Empire Wine fortified with beef extract. I was reminded of those signs you sometimes see on bags of hospital refuse: 'Biohazard'.

But stay! What was this? A dozen bottles of Château Lanessan, a very sound claret, of the equally sound 1970 vintage. I murmured approval and the owner said I was welcome to them for a modest sum considering that I had sold his Port rather well. We shook on it and lovingly slipped the bottles into the back of my car.

As I was about to head for home, the vendor said, 'I do hope you enjoy the Lanessan. Decent wine, you know, and it's bound to keep well now.' I raised a puzzled eyebrow. 'The wooden case was devoured by the dry rot,' he said, 'so I rescued the bottles and soaked them in thingummy for a few days.'

'Thingummy?' I asked, with a note of alarm creeping into my voice.

'Oh, you know,' he said. 'A good strong solution of the stuff they pump into the wall to kill the wha'-d'ya-call-it ...'

Sometimes, of course, wine keeps well when you least expect it. I once cast an eye over some bottles for an elderly lady who was down on her luck. I prayed that the spectacularly unkempt cellar would throw up a few gems, perhaps an eighteenth-century bottle of Château d'Yquem, the greatest and longest-lived dessert wine in the world. That would be enough to buy quite a decent annuity.

Unfortunately, all the first few bins contained 'off' vintages of some of the famous names of Bordeaux, things like Château

Haut-Brion 1974 and Château Latour 1969. Such wines are hard to sell because even when spanking new they were no great shakes. But what was this over in the corner? Oh dear, a mountain – fourteen dozen to be precise – of Château Lascombes, a very sound Margaux, but from the execrable 1972 vintage. My heart sank.

And then she said, 'That stuff is drinking very nicely. I had a bottle last Sunday and I finished it all on my own.' We plucked another from the pile and went up to lunch and I discovered that she was right. It had the beguiling nose of old claret and a decent wallop of fruit. If only I could persuade someone to take a chance on it ...

The solution, of course, was to buy a few dozen at a figure considerably in excess of the pathetic market value and suggest to a benevolent and well-heeled, claret-loving friend of mine that he should take the rest. Fortunately, this man likes to drink wine rather than vintages or labels and considers that he did rather well. The sum realised fell well short of the putative Yquem, but it certainly helped a delightful old lady.

A considerably less delightful old lady threatened me with an ancient muzzle-loader as I was inspecting a binful of Taylor's 1927, one of the last century's greatest Vintage Ports. It struck me that the firearm was unlikely to be loaded, but I wasn't keen to find out the hard way. I had been invited to have a look at the wine by her stepson, with whom she was feuding at the time. He heard her footsteps and scarpered, leaving me to pretend that I was measuring up for a new dampcourse. The wine, which belonged to the stepson, was eventually spirited out of the house through the pantry window, over a flat roof and into a wheelbarrow for transfer to the gate lodge to which the rightful owner had been banished.

In one crumbling country house I came across a collection of bin labels, each written in a firm but flowery Victorian hand, in soft lead pencil, on unglazed ceramic tiles. They spoke of another age, and the one which the owner gave me did so with particular eloquence: '1892 Krug', it stated simply, '72 dozen'. Consider for a moment that vintage Krug, one of the greatest Champagnes, now costs over €100 a bottle. Consider, too, the effort involved in getting through 864 bottles.

Another find prompted thoughts on how life had changed over the last century. I came across a splendidly eccentric collection of three or four dozen bottles of what appeared to be old Sherry. On closer inspection I found that each bottle had a typewritten label which read: 'Bin 19. Amontillado. (Doubtful).' What unfortunate secretary had been given the job of tapping out each of those labels? What was the butler thinking as he gummed them on? Most importantly, to what did the 'Doubtful' refer? The drinkability of the wine? Or whether or not it was an Amontillado? Could there be a suggestion that it might even be a rare Palo Cortado?

I had to explain to the executors who wanted to sell this stuff that the label was not really helping the marketing process. Heaven knows, it's hard to sell any kind of Sherry these days, let alone one that boldly claims to be doubtful. I retrieved a bottle and opened it some days later with a wine merchant friend. The wine was magnificent – intense, long, nutty, of remarkably high quality. We decided on the spot to buy it for personal consumption. But is it an Amontillado, or a Palo Cortado, we wondered? 'Who cares?' we chorused.

Occasionally I have stumbled across very rare and valuable wines. There was the legendary Château Latour 1929. When I told the owner the sort of price such wine would achieve at auction, she blanched visibly, sat down and asked was it worth it. I explained how I had never tasted it, but that it promised to be magnificent, with its power, elegance, complexity, and concluded that it all depends on how much money you have to throw around. 'Bloody hell,' she said, 'I don't need the money. I'll keep the damn stuff and enjoy it.' And I'm happy to report that she did. With a little assistance from me.

Wine Whine

I am getting a little sceptical about all these claims about how democratic, how accessible, how much a part of popular culture wine has become. The implication is that wine snobbery has been banished, that the pretentious gobshite is no more and that the fruit of the vine is as natural a part of our diet today as boiled bacon and cabbage once was.

Well, hooray for that, but there has never been a time in the history of civilisation when wine snobbery has been more prevalent. In the so-called bad old days, wine consumption was confined to the sort of people who 'had' a wine merchant in much the same way as they had a tailor and a stockbroker. The mere middle classes made do with tea and an occasional glass of sweet Sherry. The working classes had the odd bottle of stout, or a Port and lemon.

In those days, the sort of people who bought wine would stick religiously to the classics: dry Sherry, Champagne, Bordeaux, Burgundy, Hock and Vintage Port. They would buy what their merchant recommended because ... well, because that's what their fathers and grandfathers did before them. The nearest thing to wine snobbery in those days would be an approving comment upon the age of the claret, the rarity of the Port ('Don't see much of the '08 these days, old chap'), or the choice of Champagne ('Splendid, a bottle of the boy', as Bollinger was affectionately called by the intimates of King Edward VI).

In these enlightened days when, in the immortal words of Auberon Waugh, 'even the merest dentist knows about the first growths', how down-to-earth is our consumption of wine?

Well, first of all, conspicuous consumption has now been applied to wine. Many of our most successful entrepreneurs have become label-drinkers and Château Petrus, the great Pomerol, is a must. These label-drinkers stick the famous Petrus 'logo' – as they would have it – in your face rather in the same way as a certain kind of consumer uses a S-series Mercedes as a kind of personal flag.

I once saw a well-known business figure lunching in the late, lamented White's on the Green. I could see that the wine in his decanter was Château Haut-Brion because, being a bit of a trainspotter, I know the unusual hue of that property's capsule. However, as he chatted to his companion he quietly turned the bottle around so that the label faced the rest of the dining room.

I know of at least two socialites who refuse to drink any Champagne other than Roederer Cristal, usually of the latest available vintage. Anybody who knows anything about Champagne will realise that Cristal needs at least ten years, preferably twenty, before it opens up. But, of course, it's just the label that counts and Cristal's presentation is very distinctive.

Modern wine snobbery is not confined, of course, to those who decide to match their wine to their income (one of the richest people I know drinks nothing but earthy Portuguese reds). Several different forms are known amongst what you might call the Pringle sweater-wearing/Volvo-driving classes.

There's the terribly tedious conservatism ('I discovered these wines a few years ago, now I don't drink anything else'), which usually revolves around a touching devotion to Wolf Blass President's Selection and/or Faustino Gran Reserva Rioja. They believe that they taste almost as good as a gin and tonic or a Budweiser, but, bloody hell, there are times when you're expected to drink wine!

Then there's the 'we buy it all direct from the *château*' type who loads up the car with claret and wrecks the rear suspension on the journey back from France. This sort will always lecture you on how much he or she has saved, will invariably serve the wines far too young and has never heard of decanting.

By far the most irritating type of modern wine snob, however, is the person who has decided that under €14 a bottle, or whatever, 'European wines just can't compete with the New World'. Needless to say, this kind of snob would be horrified if you produced a bottle of Jacob's Creek, although if you served it blind he would be in raptures. This creature actually finds European wines too complicated, has a taste for pretty obvious fruit flavours and plenty of oak and just can't be arsed, if you will excuse the expression, to take wine seriously enough to get fun out of it.

I once came across an example of modern wine snobbery as I ate a solitary meal in a rather upmarket restaurant somewhere down the country. The speaker was encased in Lacoste, the great branded tit, while his two female companions had blonde hair and black eyebrows. He was explaining how he had gone 'horse riding' in the Hunter Valley; what other kind of riding did he think his audience had in mind? Anyway, he told how he had found this 'wonderful little winery' and that the very wine which he had just ordered came from there. It was a boring, confected little number with fearful back-palate acidity.

Just as wine snobbery has evolved and mutated, so too has wine criticism. In the good old days when wine writing was a gentlemanly occupation requiring little more than a large private income and a few functioning neurones, the consumer was never exposed to winespeak beyond the basic and perfunctory 'full-bodied', or 'wholesome'. Then along came those wine writers, born since roughly 1940, most of whom do not have a large private income. There was a sudden realisation that consumers want more information and more entertainment. Thus was born what we might call fruit 'n' nutspeak.

But where did it all come from? Well, the likes of Emile Peynaud of Bordeaux and other oenologists began to list all the compounds that go to make up wine. They devised trigger words to describe smells and tastes and the University of California went so far as to produce a graphic representation of them, which has now been whittled down to a wheel-shaped diagram.

Some wine consumers – the ones who tend to say, 'I don't know much about wine, but I know what I like' – fall around in hysterics at the mention of blackcurrants in the same sentence as Cabernet. But the same chemical that gives blackcurrants their intrinsic ... er ... blackcurrantiness *is* present in Cabernet. So, it's not pretentious nonsense. New-mown hay may seem an unlikely whiff to get off certain white wines, but coumarin occurs both in your lawn and in some wines. I could go on, and on ...

Such smells are, if you like, facts. But taste and smell is a very subjective business and there is great scope for imagination. I know exactly what Martin Moran MW means when he uses the brilliant phrase 'singed fruitcake'. I'm perhaps less sure what Michael Broadbent, possibly the most experienced taster in the world, means by 'oyster shells', although I know that 'iodine' is a respectable tasting note. I have occasionally used the phrase 'TCP'; old-fashioned South African Pinotage tended to reek of hospital corridors. Honestly.

Mature Riesling does smell of petrol (or diesel, nobody seems able to decide). 'Farmyard' is another word that would not pass the marketing people unless translated into something anodyne but, again, it's spot-on. It is our euphemistic version of what the French tend to call *merde* when describing rustic red Burgundy. The fact that it is usually meant as some-thing of a compliment is not so surprising when you consider the smell of some mature cheeses.

Perhaps as an organic gardener I tend to come into contact with certain smells to which most people are strangers. Unless you've made plum or damson jam you won't know the kind of smell and taste I often associate with Merlot and some Syrah. An apple straight off the tree is the nearest thing I've ever tasted to a good, young Riesling kabinett. Grass clippings a few days old can smell remarkably like Argentinian Malbec, with the result that I sometimes use the tasting note 'compost'. And I know all about the distinctive smell of farmyards.

While wine writing these days is based on a pretty broad vocabulary, there does seem to be a tendency for both the commentators and wine consumers to look over their shoul-ders before making a judgement. This suggests to me that there is lot of Emperor's New Clothes Syndrome in the air.

Now this has nothing to do with the full-time iconoclast school of wine comment, which is, in fact, to be found at the opposite extreme. This tendency is characterised by wild, sweeping statements of a breathtakingly ignorant kind, for example, 'Australian wines are all crap', or 'Life is too short to drink anything other than the true French classics'.

The latter kind of attitude is easy to pick out, and perhaps a little less easy to avoid – especially at a certain kind of dinner party where a particular breed of diner, invariably male, enjoys nothing better than lecturing a captive wine writer. But at least you know what you are dealing with; in the case of

Emperor's New Clothes Syndrome, there is just silence.

I mean, for example, how many people think that Penfolds Grange is an amazing wine, right enough, but far too dense and ripe and concentrated to be really great? But who says this out loud? Who thinks the prices commanded by some modern cult wines are so outrageous as to beggar belief and – this is the vital bit – the wine is just not good enough, complex enough, even to begin to justify them?

Most of these so-called cult wines are over-extracted and over-alcoholic, flattering to the palate but, essentially, clumsy and obvious. There seems to be something of a correlation between high marks from Robert Parker, the most influential American wine guru, and high alcohol content, hence the scramble to hit 14.5%. Whole swathes of the world's wines are now too alcoholic for their own good, but do we hear serious objections? Not nearly enough of them.

Here in Ireland, despite the fact that some of our wine writers don't know their Arsac from their Elbe, much of our wine media does what it is supposed to do: offer criticism, both positive and negative. I think our neighbours across the water, on the other hand, are getting tired of the gushing enthusiasm of many wine writers for bland, commercial plonk.

Why the gush? I think it all started with Oz Clarke and Jilly

Goolden trying to demonstrate the truism that wine is for everyone. Perhaps in such a class-divided society as Britain they felt they had to protest just a little too much. Seeing Jilly going into ecstasy over some stg£2.99 Hungarian Sauvignon always makes me wonder if she would simply go up in flames if you gave her an example of what Didier Dagueneau does with this grape in the Loire. However, credit where credit is due. We – the British and us – are now wine drinkers. The fact that most of us drink boring, mass-produced, big brand wines is a start. But more and more people are being seduced by the real thing.

Wine, in huge areas of the world, has gone the way of all modern farming: intensive monocultures with high-energy inputs, involving the destruction of the countryside and its ecosystems. Talk to people in some of Australia's biggest wine companies about 'sustainable viticulture' and you will find they become uncharacteristically reticent. The big players in the Australian wine industry, by and large, are pretty contemptuous of organic production – which suggests to me that they are not taking the future seriously. Eventually, of course, it could be their biggest mistake.

It's not just the big Australian producers by any means. As every week goes by more and more of the world's wine brands are owned by fewer and fewer companies. They are responsible for vast areas under vine in many different regions of the world, including Europe. But as wine globalisation carries on apace, a lot of the wines that compete for our attention are becoming boringly homogenised in taste and style.

How many New World Chardonnays have individual character? Not enough of them, and those that do usually make exquisite white Burgundy look like a snip.

Big brand wines are designed to deliver consistency. Unfortunately, in many cases, they also deliver sheer boredom. When I say things like this – which is simply the unvarnished truth – I'm often accused of being anti-New World. Nothing could be farther from the truth. The New World is bursting at the seams with passionate, exciting wine-makers and not all of them are at the cottage-industry end of the business. You only have to think of the marvellous organic and biodynamic Fetzer Bonterra operation in California to realise that real wine, sustainable wine, does not have to be made in tiny quantities.

California is an interesting wine microcosm, from the ghastly jug-wine production of the Central Valley to the super-hyped hyperbolic wines of Napa – and everything in between.

There's a widespread belief in the wine business that Randall Grahm of California's Boon Doon winery is barking mad. He has experimented with batches of wine from his Le Cigare Volant vineyards by adding crushed rocks to the fermentation because he is passionately interested in enhancing what he calls the 'minerality' of wine. This did not prevent him, however, from making a rather startling claim when asked about the inspiration behind the project. 'Drugs,' he replied, without batting an eyelid.

The very name, Le Cigare Volant, is another example of Grahm's rather offbeat sense of humour. It means 'flying-saucer' in French (which suggests that aliens choose differently shaped craft depending on their terrestrial destination). Grahm discovered that the *vignerons* of Châteauneuf-du-Pape passed an edict in the 1950s expressly forbidding alien spacecraft from landing in the vineyards. Well, I suppose you can't be too careful.

Grahm was one of the first Rhône Rangers in the New World; when everyone else was getting hot flushes about Cabernet and Chardonnay, he was busily planting Grenache, Syrah and Mourvedre. Le Cigare Volant is, in music terms, a Chateauneuf tribute wine. Personally, I think he is one of the sanest wine-makers in the New World. Perhaps this is because he spends a great deal of time thinking – and not just about wine. He confesses to envying European wine-makers, not a comment that trips lightly from the lips of wine producers in the New World.

'If you are in Burgundy,' he says, 'distinctiveness and distinction arise from *terroir*. In the New World, the dilemma is how to legitimise your efforts without relying upon the usual suspects: concentration, big fruit, new wood, the *Wine Spectator* and Parker.' He goes on just as trenchantly: 'As the noise in the bazaar increases, one must shout louder and louder to be heard. Does the worthiest, most carefully crafted product in the bazaar outsell the products that are of shoddy construction but have all sorts of attractive, shiny features? I think not.'

Of course there are lots of shoddy wines with shiny features produced here in the Old World. It is thanks to the New World that our shoddy wines have changed; but they have changed only in their presentation. There is massive global over-supply of wine and some of the biggest players in the world market seem to have no sense of direction; they follow rather than lead. Does the consumer really need yet another range of bland New World varietals with pretty labels and a convenient price point? Why should the consumer buy X's Chardonnay if it tastes the same and costs the same as Y's? The New World big brands are the new Liebfraumilch: simple, unintimidating, easy to understand and ultimately as boring as looking at other people's holiday snaps.

Where's the innovation? Where's the palpable connection between wine and place? Where are the products that wean people off inoffensive ordinariness and on to a bit of interest, excitement and a higher price point?

You can, of course, look to Europe and to relatively small producers. Anecdotally there is lots of evidence that people who have adopted wine drinking as normal behaviour through buying and enjoying the big New World brands, eventually come to enjoy the greater diversity offered by the European classic regions. Having been bored, intimidated and sometimes disappointed by Old World wine during their ini-tiation phase, they begin to revel in the difference.

Old World wines have changed, of course. There is still an ocean of dross out there, but you are much less likely to stum-ble across a really lousy Côtes du Rhône these days than you would have ten years ago. And vast numbers of Irish consum-ers have twigged that trading-up generally delivers better qual-ity and enhanced pleasure.

According to Randall Grahm, wine producers can either make distinctive wine or they can 'create the illusion of distinctiveness by distilling and coalescing the needs and wants of the *zeitgeist* and amping up the volume.' Amping up the volume seems to be a choice that more and more producers of relatively expensive wines are making. At the bottom end, the challenge is to turn grapes which are often far from good into something drinkable. And technology is there to help.

I had my first face-to-face encounter with what one might call extreme wine-making many years ago when I made a trip to one of Australia's hottest and most isolated wine regions. It was typical of vast areas in that country in which irrigation has made the desert bloom. The local town was the kind of place that reminds me of low-budget horror movies, where the happy young couple in the camper van pitch up only to find that everybody, from the sheriff downwards, are all keen on human sacrifice by moonlight. I can't quite put my finger on why this should be, but there it is. I do know that the Mafia have long been active in this area and that most of their victims are found in the irrigation channels that criss-cross the landscape. As far as the eye could see were the vines that produce Australia's bulk wines and fruit farms measured in thousands of acres. You and I may not have seen a tinned peach since early childhood, but they are still canning them here.

A short drive out of town brought me to a winery where they use every trick in the book – all of them legal – to coax something drinkable out of the abundant but frankly rather vapid local grapes. A tour of the production process was a lesson in how to make cheap wine.

The first problem was that the grapes, generously watered and baked under the blistering sun, had a great deal of sugar in them, but the essential acidity which makes wine drinkable was almost entirely absent. Very tasty for nibbling or bringing on a hospital visit, but damn all use for wine. The solution? Simple. You bung a few sacks of tartaric acid into the fermentation tank and Bob's your uncle. The resulting wine may have a rather persistent acidity, reminiscent of the acid drops I used to munch in junior school, but it certainly perks up an otherwise flabby wine. It is made, oddly enough, by processing unripe grapes and is therefore usually produced in Europe.

Over at the red wine vats there was a slightly different problem. The acidity needed adjusting, but because the grapes were ultra-ripe the tannins had become so round and soft as to be barely noticeable. Tannin is the substance that makes stewed tea taste astringent and it is abundant in sloes. It is quite unpleasant in itself, but it is an essential element in the taste of most red wines. The tannin deficit was rapidly resolved by the addition of a few shovelfuls of tannic acid, a brown, highly soluble powder derived, apparently, from chestnut leaves.

It now remained to make the wines, both the white and the red, match up to the expectations of the customer's palate. Because they were to sell at a retail price point where, apparently, people expect a taste of oak, that is precisely what needed adding.

Traditionally, all oaky wines absorbed that distinctive

vanilla character from ageing in new oak casks, a highly expensive business. These days, new oak is kept strictly for the posh stuff. However, ingenuity – it's not quite technology – has the answer. Oak chips are placed in plastic mesh containers, known as 'tea bags' in the business, and dunked in the wine until they impart their magic scent and savour. Just as the manufacturers of expensive oak casks will supply them with the required amount of 'toast' (the degree of charring on the inside), the tea-bag people char varying proportions of the oak chips.

All of these techniques, if used with care and skill, produce wines which are attractive and affordable. However, most of us prefer to retain rather romantic notions of wine and whenever we see the magic words '*mis en bouteilles dan nos caves*', we imagine a bloke in a striped T-shirt opening a creaking cellar door. He indicates the serried ranks of barrels in the underground cathedral of wine and says, gutturally of course, '*Voilà, nos caves!*'

European wine producers generally operate within stricter regulations than those governing their New World counterparts. For example, adding sugar to grape juice is generally outlawed, but in poor vintages, in certain regions, it is permitted in order to boost the alcoholic strength to a normal level.

I was amused, though not terribly surprised, to see sacks of sugar stacked high in a small winery in ... er ... a famous French wine region a few years ago. It was quite a reasonable vintage, but the inspector from the *Appellation Contrôlée* had announced to all and sundry that he was taking his holidays during the harvest. The French and ourselves have much in common.

Old World wine producers often have to deal with the effects of a rainy growing season and downpours at harvest time. Dilute grape juice does not make good wine but, once again, technology can help. A process called reverse osmosis involves excess water content being pushed across a very fine membrane filter, while gently heating the grape juice, or 'must', under a vacuum allows water to be evaporated off at a temperature similar to that produced by fermentation. These techniques really do seem to work, even if we prefer to think of *vignerons* being entirely at the mercy of the elements.

Curiously enough, the dearer the wine, the more likely it is to have been produced by natural or traditional methods. Mind you, at the legendary Château Petrus, Christian Moueix has been known to fly a helicopter low over the vines to protect them from frost damage, a luxury well beyond the means of the average wine producer.

Modern wine technology, although it is used throughout the globe, is a product of the New World where the industry has never been in thrall to tradition for the simple reason that there wasn't one. However, one technological innovation was introduced in Spain in the late 1960s in response to the demands of the marketing people. It had been noted that while 'sophisticated' people drank pale, dry Sherry, most punters preferred brown, sweet Sherry.

Thus was born pale cream Sherry, a drink that tasted sweet but looked dry, and therefore upmarket. Croft started to pass their tawny-coloured cream Sherry through charcoal, which stripped out the colour. With the advent of this rather naff drink – produced for image rather than anything more tangible – came one of the first nails in the coffin of Sherry as a serious drink.

Sherry is one of the world's greatest wines, but the problem is that very few people – even the most ardent of wine buffs – have ever tasted the real thing. Sherry sales reached their peak in the 1950s when a bottle of Harvey's Bristol Cream cost roughly the same as a bottle of Château Lafite and rather more than the up-and-coming Château Petrus. Even modest Sherry was quite serious stuff in the old days, the sort of wine that Barbara Pym's curates and spinster heroines sipped when they let their hair down.

Most big brand Sherry these days is a very pale and sickly shadow of its former self, and the only reason it continues to sell is because virtual-teetotallers and others who have been snatched from the jaws of total abstinence like to nurse a small glass at Christmas. And, of course, for some bizarre reason of ritual, a certain kind of wedding reception never kicks off with anything other than a glass of cheap and nasty Sherry served in a gnat's bathtub.

Real Sherry, however, is one of the great joys of the wine world and the best producers are very poorly rewarded for their sublime produce. This is good news for us, selfish as it may seem to rejoice in the fact.

Even the best producers tend to perpetuate the central myth of Sherry. They will tell you, correctly, that it starts off as one of two styles of wine. They will imply that this process is completely spontaneous and will convey an impression that the *bodega* manager comes in of a morning, examines a butt at random and mutters, in accents of stage surprise, 'Bless my soul, it's turning out to be a *fino*.'

Actually, *fino* is *fino* because a thin film of highly specific yeast begins to grow on the surface of the wine. If the wine has an alcoholic strength of less than 16%, you get this yeast film, or *flor*. So producers fortify the young wine to 15% (by adding grape spirit) if they want a *fino*, and rather more if they want the other form of Sherry, *oloroso*. The *flor* keeps the wine from contact with the air and also imparts a certain flavour of its own – a kind of savoury yeastiness. A naked *oloroso*, by contrast, takes much of its flavour from direct contact with the air.

Fino Sherry is either sold young and fresh (Tio Pepe is probably the most famous brand), or is allowed to age in cask, turning amber and nutty-tasting and transforming itself into an amontillado. Good amontillado is nutty, concentrated, complex and dry. However, *fino* that is allowed to age on the off-licence shelf is one of the most revolting wines known to man and much more common than one would like to think.

Manzanilla is a *fino* that has been made in the seaside town of Sanlucar, close to Jerez. Very similar to Jerez *fino*, manzanilla has a distinctive salty tang which, they say, has something to do with its coastal origin. Who knows? The main thing is that it's very tasty. Fresh, chilled *fino* or manzanilla are the world's most civilised aperitifs and surprisingly good with food, too, especially grilled fish.

Oloroso, like *fino* and manzanilla, starts life bone dry. It can be sweetened by adding the intensely sweet wine made from Pedro Ximenez grapes, or, more commonly these days, with any number of cheaper and inferior substitutes. This turns it into an *oloroso* cream Sherry. If, as I say, this wine is then passed through activated charcoal, it loses its tawny colour and becomes, God help us, a 'pale cream Sherry', like the very untraditional Croft Original.

Proper, old-fashioned, sweet *oloroso* is very hard to find these days, but nothing else, not even old tawny Port, goes quite so well with walnuts. In those days, casks of sweet *oloroso* were shipped to the East Indies and back again in order to acquire a slightly 'baked' character: a case of singed fruitcake if ever there was one.

Dry *oloroso* does come as a bit of a shock to the normal palate. We are simply not used to being assaulted by so much taste, and we always associate the nutty, dried-fruits character of aged fortified wines with sweetness. Real Sherry such as this is well worth the search, and if I were to single out one category of wine that offers stupendous value, this would be it.

I only discovered real Sherry when I had become a wine writer and it was a revelation after the sickly stuff that tended to be served at receptions when I was at Trinity. Perhaps the most valuable book I was to discover during those far-off student days was *Cooking in a Bedsit* by Katherine Whitehorn, a well-thumbed Penguin paperback that carried battle scars in the form of splashes of bolognese sauce, cigarette scorches and the impressions of beer glasses. It also contained the most useful advice ever given on the thorny issue of what wine goes with what: 'White with carpet, red with lino,' it advised.

Does the world worry about matching food and wine these days? I'm not so sure. But if a wine really works with a particular dish – combines in some indefinable way with it – the whole experience is elevated to something rather more than a meal. However, having spent a great deal of time and money in my effort to discover as many such experiences as possible, I have to say that marriages made in Heaven are rare enough.

Top of my list is gently chilled Sauternes with ripe, tangy, salty Roquefort. Here the two flavours merge into something quite distinct; a creamy, seductive taste emerges on the palate and there is a hint of coconut there. Sweet wine in general does the same with ripe blue cheese. Good ripe Gewurztraminer from Alsace merges in similar fashion with the best aged Gouda, while a steely Sancerre makes fresh goat's cheese leap in the mouth.

Such impeccable matches are, as I say, not very thick on the ground, but this is no excuse for randomly partnering wines with whatever appears on the table. I have no idea what people drink with the favourite

British dish, chicken tikka masala, but I am sure that our favourite – pasta in many guises – is usually downed with a few glasses of inexpensive New World red.

The Italians, of course, would never dream of such a thing, and not just because Jacob's Creek is hard to get in Bologna or Rome. Nor is it on account of their perfectly understandable gastronomic chauvinism. It is because, throughout Europe, certain dishes have evolved alongside certain wines. The relatively high acidity of many Italian reds, and the tannins that frequently accompany it, work well with pasta. In the Veneto, home of the buttery, cheesey risotto, the tart backbone of Valpolicella and Soave could have been expressly designed to cut the richness, and in all probability they were.

The red wines of Bordeaux, of course, are very different. Leaving aside the fact that so many of the lesser examples are simply dull and overstretched, the firm Merlot fruit of a decent, inexpensive Claret, allied to the acidity and tannin that balances it, will enhance a mouthful of pink lamb or rare beef without dominating. A great Claret, if you are so lucky as to be taking a corkscrew to such a thing, will appreciate such simple food. An exquisite rib of beef partnered by a fine Claret with a few years' bottle age is one of the best things on Earth. But keep the horseradish at arm's length.

Some of the most food-friendly wines are, unlike the reds of Bordeaux, so out of fashion as to be barely visible. Manzanilla Sherry, dry and almost austere, is pure joy with salted almonds, grilled chorizo, or thin slices of melting jamón de Serrano. German Riesling – especially from the superb 2001 vintage – provides a sharp and slightly sweet counterpoint to goose, or to *rillettes* of pork. Banyuls, the sweet red wine from southern France, could have been designed to enhance dark chocolate.

Of course, if you really do want to drink Barossa Shiraz with your grilled sole, do so with an easy mind. I can't say that it would do anything for me, but I think it's essential always to be prepared to experiment. There are no rules in wine. It's an agricultural product made by farmers and once you've bought a bottle, you can do whatever the hell you want to with it. Just keep an open mind, and do try to get hold of some good Sherry.

The Concise
Veg Plot

Just as fashion helps to create conservative consumers of wine, it also determines the boundaries for what we eat. But within each of us, I believe, there is a passion for good food. It just needs to be released. Too many of us have never tasted real freshness – the modern world conspires to keep it from us – but when we do, our lives change. In every other sphere we are urged to take control, take responsibility. But what about food?

There is something very special about eating something that you have grown yourself. It's not just the fact that it has been tended with loving care, contains no nasty residues and is as fresh as it is possible to be. It's because it is yours. It would not have happened if you had not initiated the whole process.

When I was small, my first experience of growing things was confined to sprouting carrot tops in a saucer of water, which was fun but not really concerned with edibility, and sprouting mustard and cress on damp tissue. The speed of germination and the fact that you have an edible crop in a week was a bonus; the fact that children really just don't like the taste was incidental.

Most of us eventually develop a taste for stuff that most kids regard as rabbit food. Some grown-ups are known to sprout their own beans, for Heaven's sake, and even this process – which requires no soil, just a jar and a mesh lid – can be part of reclaiming your food. The fact that bean sprouts are highly nutritious, fairly tasty and add a glorious crunch to a stir-fry means that they are a good crop with which to start your journey towards ... er ... I was going to say self-sufficiency, but let's not get carried away. Towards producing some of your own food and taking control of what happens to it. Sounds good.

Getting beyond bean sprouts does not require a vast commitment. After all, most of us are fairly limited by space. You can, of course, go to immense trouble to create a very pretty *potager*, as the French call an edible garden, but I never look at one without wondering how so many lettuces, all ready to be picked at the same time, can be consumed. They are a joy to behold, of course, but I reckon that much of the produce of a *potager* ends up in the freezer, or on the compost heap.

Much as I enjoy looking at a well-tended *potager*, something in me rebels against this example of style over substance.

I also feel that an ordinary, bog-standard vegetable garden looks wonderful, but perhaps I'm mildly prejudiced. I derive great amusement from the diagrams in old-fashioned gardening books where the kitchen garden is carefully screened by a high privet hedge as if it were vaguely indecent. If you've got one, however small, flaunt it.

Mixing edible plants with decorative ones is perfectly feasible and sometimes quite effective in terms of visual impact, especially if you are prepared to let some of your vegetables go to seed. Why have expensive alliums when a few leek seedheads give much the same effect. Let your beetroot bolt (and believe me, it will if you don't keep it watered) and you will have fragrant flower spikes that will enhance any herbaceous border.

If I were confined to a small garden – the very small kind of garden that goes with the average suburban house these days – I would ensure that most of what I grew had a culinary purpose. And those that didn't would need to earn their keep by pouring out delicious scents: roses, lavender, honeysuckle and what have you. A garden is for the senses, all of the senses.

Reading magazines like *Country Living* can sometimes engender a rather over-romantic vision of growing your own. You end up with visions of a quaint, wooden wheelbarrow packed to the gunnels with wholesome produce, of your garden as a picture of earth's bounty, of bright tomatoes and tumescent courgettes, of a perfect herb garden that your friends will envy ... And the odd thing is that when you have harvested your first crops you will feel such a sense of satisfaction, bordering on smugness indeed, that it really doesn't matter that your achievement is not quite as photogenic as the pictures in those glossy magazines. Just as other people's babies often seem to lack the stupendous beauty, cleverness and utter adorability of your own, so it is with the productive garden.

Let's consider, for a moment, the objections to creating an edible garden. And then demolish them as quickly as possible.

Running a fully functioning and comprehensive kitchen garden is very nearly a full-time job, there's a long journey between seed packet and kitchen table: slugs may well eat most of what you plant, those wholesome wooden wheelbarrows are expensive and probably fall apart pretty rapidly. And, of course, the produce from your garden will actually cost a great deal more than the organic fruit and vegetables you buy at the market.

Let me explain. You may be a manual worker, a civil servant, a surgeon, all on different rates of remuneration. If you factor your time into the cost of producing your own vegetables they will become very, very expensive. Even if you are on the minimum legal wage. I visited one of the last working private kitchen gardens in England in the mid-1980s where the owner of the estate calculated that the cost of producing a cabbage came to just over stg£14. Down the road in Sainsbury's they were selling cabbages for 39p.

But who cares? If you're worried about such issues I doubt you will have ever given much thought to gardening. If you really enjoy being out in the fresh air, getting earth under your fingernails and doing something mildly active, you can forget about what your time costs. I have been amazed at how much satisfaction I got from putting up a rabbit-proof fence, not a task that you would initially rush out to do in a ferment of enthusiasm.

One thing binds all gardeners together, young and old, novices and experienced hands alike: if we didn't get a big kick out of it, we would give up and try something else. The slugs, the frosts, the plagues of aphids all, in a curious way, make the whole process a bit more exciting. They add suspense, just like you find in a good book.

In a small garden, allowing for the fact that children will need space for play, you can still supply a lot of your vegetable diet. Even if you have very limited time, the same applies if you are prepared to limit your ambitions to producing mainly salad crops and herbs. I reckon that it is with these crops – very useful, pleasurable and expensive to buy at the supermarket – that everyone who wants to start reclaiming their food should start.

You can, of course, buy a few herb plants and stick them in the ground, sow some seeds and hope for the best. Whatever the gardening writers tell you, this does actually work up to a point. For Heaven's sake, it's a start! However, it's always wise to regard your garden as a living organism that needs care and loving attention. It also needs feeding. By all means try growing things with benign neglect. But if you want to get your garden into abundant production, you will have to do some digging.

Digging is where your growing career starts. If you have an established garden, or one that has run wild, you will need to clear the soil and aerate it. But in the gardens attached to relatively newly built houses you may well have your work cut out for you. If you're lucky, the builders will have thrown a thin layer of top soil on the compressed territory of your garden. Very close to the surface you will have heavy, sticky soil which will not sustain very much plantlife, and the chances are that it is riddled with bits of brick and mortar, to say nothing of the stones that were there in the first place. This needs to be transformed into fertile soil and in some cases you may even need to buy a load or two of topsoil.

Most of us, however, will simply need to give the existing soil a bit of a treat. Dig it to a spade's depth and incorporate as much organic material as you can lay hands on. It would be lovely to think that you can produce enough from your domestic compost bin, but even the most dedicated home composter with a small garden will manage only a pretty modest output. You will need to acquire manure, nicely rotted-down manure, from somewhere. The best comes from stables, but farmyard manure – or FYM in polite circles – will also serve. Mature manure, to coin a phrase, should be full of worms and they will go on digging your soil while you are off-duty.

How much manure to the square metre? There is no simple answer to that question other than to say you should apply as much as your budget, your time and your back muscles will allow. The more the merrier. This applies even if your garden is established but neglected. Very few of us can acquire gardens where the soil has been nurtured over many years. If you have one, go down on bended knee and thank God for the wisdom of the previous owners. But don't be depressed if, even after digging in vast quantities of manure, your soil does not resemble the dark, crumbly substance that every dream garden is supposed to have. The bottom line is that plenty of organic material will eventually yield a rich growing medium, and even in the very short term it will allow you to grow stuff. And don't forget that even a little organic material is a great deal better than none.

The ideal time to set about feeding and aerating your garden soil is the autumn. Take your time. No need to rush, but try to have the manure dug in by mid-winter. Then leave the soil alone and the frosts will help to break it down and produce a decent texture. By spring you will be ready to start growing.

Why not start with a few herbs? You will need sage, rosemary, thyme and mint to start your perennial herb garden. Put these plants in the soil and, with a bit of care, you will have them for good – although it's a good idea to root cuttings from them every two or three years. One of the most rewarding perennial vegetables is the globe artichoke which, although it grows to a substantial size during the summer, will reward you in two ways: it produces an abundance of edible flowerheads and they are highly decorative, the sort of thing that gardening writers like to call 'architectural plants'.

Plant your artichokes three feet apart in the sunniest place you can spare and you can leave the rest to nature. When the big, fat flowerbuds have swollen in June or early July, but before they bloom, snip them off and boil or steam them until they are tender. Serve them with a ramekin of melted butter or a good vinaigrette into which you dip each 'scale' as you strip the 'globe'. The greater part of each scale is tough and fibrous; the bit you eat is the tender part at the base. When you have pretty well denuded your globe, scoop out the bristly 'choke' to reveal the fleshy base, which is the real delicacy: what the French call *fond d'artichaut*. Lap it up with more butter or dressing.

A lot of people are a bit daunted at the prospect of dismantling a globe artichoke, but it's more than worth having a go. First time, do it in private. The late Jane Grigson, one of the great food writers of her generation, did so but didn't realise that the bristly centre was inedible. She choked on the choke but developed a lifelong love of artichokes.

The gardening books will tell you that your herbs and globe artichokes need a sunny spot and well-drained soil. If you can provide this, well and good, but do remember that mint will grow anywhere. In fact, the trouble with mint is putting a stop to its insatiable desire to spread. One solution is to dig it up every autumn and reduce the roots to manageable proportions, but the lazier and equally effective way is to take a bottomless plastic bucket, plunge it into the soil and plant your mint within its confines.

Sage likes fertile soil so give it plenty of organic matter and try to keep it out of deep shade. Thyme, my favourite culinary herb, can be an awkward little plant and it often looks rather bare and straggly when you want luxuriant growth to provide lush bunches for the kitchen. Don't buy just one, splash out on three or four of them and apply the following tip. All the organic matter that you have dug into your soil will have made it somewhat acid; if you have acid soil in the first place, it will have increased the acidity further. Thyme likes alkaline conditions, so sprinkle a few handfuls of calcified seaweed when planting and give another dose or two during the summer. I could never grow decent thyme until I discovered this little trick.

Of all the herbs, rosemary is perhaps the most resilient and, in good conditions, can make a substantial shrub, five feet tall. If you can give it a sunny spot, all the better, but it will yield fragrant shoots pretty well anywhere. It also roots from cuttings with the greatest of ease, so if you have a friend with a bush, ask for a few sprigs, taken from where they join a main stem, dip the base of each in rooting powder and plant them firmly about two inches deep in late summer; in a couple of months you will have new plants ready to place where you want.

Growing your own salad may seem a very small step towards taking control of your food supply, but there are two reasons why it can make a very big difference to your life. First, commercial salad crops are amongst the most intensively produced and they incur some of the highest chemical inputs, some of which end up not just on your plate but in your body. Secondly, green, leafy vegetables are very high in folic acid which, as everybody should know by now, is essential for women who are likely to conceive. Folic acid, in sufficient quantity, hugely reduces the incidence of neural tube defects in children.

But what if – like me – you are not likely to get pregnant? Folic acid and vitamins B6 and B12 help to break down homo-cysteines, which are implicated in cardiovascular disease. There is a school of thought that believes that tackling homo-cysteines is much more important than banging on about cholesterol. Indeed, I believe that the coalition of doctors, pharmaceutical producers and the so-called functional food industry continues to focus on cholesterol and saturated fats because of who – and there are no prizes for guessing – funds the vast majority of research into heart disease. Homocysteines can be tackled by using materials which cannot be copy-righted: folic acid and B vitamin supplements on the one hand, and green, leafy vegetables on the other (although the GM industry, we should remember, is keen to patent plants).

So, your salad plot is important. Not only will its produce help you keep down your homocysteine levels, but the exercise involved in tending it will do you good, too. Here's what you can grow, with a minimum of space and time.

Lettuce comes in lots of different shapes, colours, textures and flavours. Most of us think of it growing in regimented rows, each head lying firmly and plumply against the well-hoed earth. In fact, whenever I see such a sight in a private garden I wonder why the owner wants to create a glut of let-tuces. No matter how keen we are on salad, there is a limit to how much the human frame can take. Much, much better to sow lettuces in very short rows every two weeks or so and get a succession of fresh salad material, rather than having to watch them bolt and produce flower spikes while you struggle to eat the little green triffids. The miniature cos lettuce Little Gem is my particular favourite, and I find it best to sow three or four seeds every six inches, thinning to one plant when the seedlings are about an inch high. Used like this, a single packet of seeds will keep you going for a couple of seasons at least.

In a very small garden, there is an even simpler way to provide a constant supply of lettuce from spring until late autumn. The family of lettuce which is known variously as salad bowl, looseleaf and cut-and-come-again (or CCA to the cognoscenti) can be sown thinly, not in rows but actually broadcast evenly over, say, a square metre. As soon as the first leaves are of edible size, all you have to do is pick them individually and let the rest continue growing. A square metre of CCA will keep you in salad for about two months, perhaps even three. Two such squares will cover your salad requirements for as long as

it is possible to grow lettuce outdoors in Ireland, with a first sowing in early to mid-March and a second one in June. The vigour and luxuriance of your CCA lettuce will very much depend on how much organic matter you have managed to get into the soil; lettuce is a greedy feeder and it likes moisture. If you have done your best but still feel that there should be more nutrition in the soil, there is no shame in occasionally liquid-feeding with an organic seaweed extract (but do remember to rinse the leaves before eating).

Slugs adore lettuce above all other plants, so be prepared. Make sure that your lettuce plot is well away from long grass, old walls, piles of garden rubbish and anything else in which slugs like to laze away their days before their midnight orgies. Go out at night with a torch and pick up as many of the little buggers as you can find – using rubber gloves or chopsticks. If you have a particularly severe slug problem – and believe me such an experience is far from uncommon – consider using the biological control that is marketed under the brandname Nemaslug. This involves watering on a solution of microscopic nematodes which kill the slugs; sounds messy and complicated, but it's very easy, especially in a small garden, and it involves no chemicals. Encouraging frogs and hedgehogs in the garden will help to keep the slug population in check. Indeed, the only pristine hosta I have ever had in my garden was close to a hedgehog nest. I believe geese and ducks are good slug predators, too, but I have yet to sign them up for the job.

Slugs are also keen on rocket seedlings, but this is a fairly resilient and very fast-growing plant; in very sluggy areas it may offer some hope amidst all the despair that the molluscs engender in even the stoutest-hearted of gardeners. There was a time when rocket was grown in Ireland only in the herb garden, but the peoples of France, Spain and Italy have been tucking into the stuff for centuries as salad; indeed, our ancestors seem to have done so too. These days it is one of the signs and symptoms of a trendy restaurant – rocket leaves, often all the way from Israel or Holland, with a balsamic dressing and shavings of parmesan.

I find the best way to grow rocket, especially if you like the leaves small, young and tender, is to follow the advice for CCA lettuce and broadcast-sow a square metre or so. Rocket grows rapidly – I have often wondered if that is how it got its name – and even a sowing made in mid-March should produce useable leaves by mid-May. By then, of course, with more sunshine and greater warmth, the rate of growth increases dramatically and I am inclined to sow smaller patches every two to three weeks. A final sowing of rocket made in late August should keep you in leaves right through the winter. Left in the open they can get a little tough as they struggle through the cold conditions. However, if you lightly cover the crop with horticultural fleece from the end of October, the tenderness remains.

American cress, or winter cress, is one of the hardiest salad crops. It looks and tastes rather like its close relation, water cress, but it has a more peppery flavour and when it is at its most pungent – in the depths of winter – it needs to be mixed with something a little blander. One of my favourite winter salads is a combination of oranges, scallions and winter cress with a light, mustardy dressing. For winter use, it should be sown in August or early September so that it puts on some growth before the days shorten, but it will also grow happily if sown in spring. Broadcast the seed thinly, just as for rocket and CCA. Again, some horticultural fleece will prevent the leaves getting unpleasantly tough in wintertime.

I always sow some miner's lettuce (or lamb's lettuce, as it is more commonly known) at the same time as I put in winter cress. In a combination of two parts to one of cress it makes an excellent salad when the days are short and spring seems very far away. The French call it *mache* and like to eat it all year round, enjoying the fleshy crunch of the little green stems which open into small, oval leaves of dark green. The plant is usually eaten whole as life is simply too short to separate each stalk and leaf, given that the whole thing is usually picked when not more than two inches round. Just trim off the roots (you would be surprised how many restaurants forget this elementary preparation) and any discoloured or damaged leaves, soak in salted water to get rid of any wildlife, rinse thoroughly and dry off in a salad spinner. This cleansing is important as the little plants hug the ground for dear life and can be unpleasantly gritty.

There is no point in growing radishes just because they are quick and easy. Let's face it: most of us have never exactly been seduced by a radish. But they can be delicious. It's just a question of having them young and fresh, straight out of the soil, and knowing how to eat them. We can take freshness as read if they are growing outside your back door. Here's how to eat them. Wash them, top and tail them and pile them up in a dish, just before dinner or a lazy lunch. Place a little container of sea salt flakes beside them and dip and eat. You won't need pepper; radishes are the pepperiest of vegetables, but the heat is counterbalanced by their cool crunchiness. Alternatively, dip them in soft, salted butter and munch away.

Growing radishes could not be simpler. You can sow them – very thinly, in rows six inches apart – from early March until September. When conditions are at their optimum – with long daylight and reasonable temperatures – they will be ready to pull in only three weeks, which makes them one of the quickest edible crops. The cylindrical variety, known as French Breakfast, is one of the best but the globe form, Sparkler, is good, too. The key thing to remember is this: pull them when they are just big enough to be worth the trouble of eating. Elderly radishes are woody and quite horrible.

Spring onions, or scallions as they are called here in Ireland and in North America, are an essential part of the traditional Irish Sunday salad. So, too, are limp butterhead lettuce and vinegary salad cream, but let's forget about those for the moment. If you are an onion fan – and there are many who are not – there is something really sensual in the green, fresh, youthful pungency of a scallion. The commonest garden variety is called White Lisbon and forms around bulbs with slender green leaves. To plump up properly in a naturally cultivated garden – where they are spared the force-feeding of NPK fertiliser – they need to be sown thinly in very fertile soil and grown as quickly as the weather permits. When they are good, they are very, very good, and when they are bad, they are rather weedy and over-strong in flavour. I prefer to grow the modern Japanese hybrids (Sutton's Seeds do several versions), which don't bulb at the base but resemble pencil-thin leeks when fully grown. The flavour is pleasantly mild, too, which means you can eat more of them at one sitting which, considering the health benefits of fresh onions, is a further blessing. Sow them thinly in short rows, a foot apart, from March to September.

What else can be grown with minimal effort? It may be worth trying a short row of jerusalem artichokes – the tuberous ones that resemble globe artichokes only in taste. It's worth choosing the variety carefully because the old-fashioned strains are exceptionally knobbly and by the time you have peeled them there may be nothing left worth eating. There are several relatively smooth varieties on the market, such as Fuseau, and you buy them, rather like spuds, in the form of tubers which need to be planted about four inches deep and two feet apart. The richer the soil, the better the crop and if you plant them in February, giving them extra growing time, they should bulk up nicely. Before the autumn harvesting they will produce very tall stems which look rather like sunflower plants (to which they are related). If they like where you have put them, they will hit eight or nine feet and will become a prey to high winds; a few stakes are a good idea.

You can leave the crop of tubers in the ground over the winter and dig them as you need them, but do remember that slugs find them tasty and you may lose a proportion of your harvest to the little beasts. It's also a good idea to dig them carefully, ensuring that no little tubers are left behind because they will start growing again and before you know it you will have an artichoke forest.

We usually peel the artichokes, slice them fairly thickly and throw them into a pan with a generous dollop of olive oil, a few cloves of garlic and a sprig or two of rosemary – nothing else. Then we put the pan on a low heat and cover it, shaking it vigorously every minute or so until the artichokes are tender. They also make exceptionally good soup if blended together with onions and chicken stock.

Leeks are one of the joys of the winter vegetable garden and because they grow slender and tall they give a good yield for the space they occupy. Leeks are prolific, hardy, surprisingly beautiful and infinitely useful. When they are little thicker than pencils they can be wrapped in Parma ham, blanketed in béchamel sauce, topped with Parmesan and baked. They can also be simply steamed and served cold with a vinaigrette, a dish which the French know as 'poor man's asparagus'. It's certainly just as good as asparagus, anyway.

Sow your leeks thinly in March; because you will be transplanting them later you can put the rows as little as six inches apart. By June you will have hundreds of baby leek plants which now need to be transferred to their permanent home – but, to be honest, you can delay this until as late as early August. Now, take a dibber – a blunt instrument with which you can make a suitably shaped hole (the handle of a rake is fine) – and push it into the soil to a depth of about six inches. Repeat this every eight inches and leave eighteen inches between the rows. Water your leek seedlings several hours before you lift them with a fork and then gently tease them apart to produce individual plants. Pinch off any straggling roots and drop a leek plant into each hole. Don't fill it in, however; the leek will need the space. Simply fill each hole with water and the leeks will settle into place, the water washing just enough soil down to their bases to provide a snug anchorage. After that, you just watch them grow. They will be ready from late October if you like them small, and will continue to grow through the winter until you dig the last of them the following March. If you like your leeks along the lines of Kate Moss, try the long, slender King Richard; if you prefer something more like Robbie Coltrane, try the ample Musselburgh. Slugs don't seem to like leeks – a further bonus. I plant mine after the last of the new potatoes have been lifted. They like the well-turned soil and the generous manuring that good spuds demand.

The broad bean is a vegetable of great antiquity and our only native European pulse. They are also a doddle to grow. They used be regarded with suspicion by the Early Church because if you look at the blunt end of a broad bean carefully – and they obviously had little else to do – it is vaguely reminiscent of the female genitalia. Doubtless others thought this a pro rather than a con. The pleasures of the broad bean have been vouchsafed to the few who have eaten them young and spanking fresh. Big beans with tough grey skins are as horrible to eat as they look. They can, of course, be skinned and then turned into various quite pleasant dishes, such as falafel and byessar, and this is what we do when the crop is so prolific as to defeat even our ability to eat them young. But when they are small and tender they are superb: perhaps steamed and dressed with a little first-rate olive oil and some chopped summer savory, or tossed in butter with some garlic and lardons of bacon.

You can sow broad beans in late autumn for an early crop in the spring, but be sure to choose a winter-hardy variety, such as Claudia Aquadulce. In spring the even more delicious Windsor varieties can be sown from as early as mid-February; my favourite of these is The Sutton. Soak the beans overnight in water and sow them eight inches apart in a double row, with a foot between them. Zigzag the beans so that the two rows don't crowd each other. A second double row needs to be about three feet away, although two feet will do if you're short of space. If they are reasonably sheltered, the plants will support themselves; if they sag or get knocked about by the wind, use some short bamboo stakes and string.

The white and black flowers have a wonderful scent and bees have orgies in them. Pick the first of the crop when the pods are five inches long and keep picking in order to encourage further fruiting. If black aphids invade – and they simply adore broad beans – just pinch out the fleshy growing tip of each plant as this is the part they are after.

Onions require quite a bit of space in order to produce enough to keep you going for an appreciable amount of time; their near relation, the shallot, however, can be very productive in a small space. Shallots resemble small onions but tend to be more slender and tapered; they have a mild onion flavour and I would find it hard to do without them in the kitchen.

The joy of growing shallots is the sheer ease. You buy your shallot bulbs in the garden centre in the autumn, press each one into the soil so that about half of it is buried, spacing them about six inches apart with a foot between rows, and they will be ready to pick the following July. At this stage each bulb will have divided to produce several new shallots. It's almost like magic. Shallots are arguably the easiest thing to grow next to bean sprouts and, to be honest, they are rather more useful.

There are other easy vegetables, of course, but this would be my core selection, the ones which deliver huge pleasure for a tiny output of energy and maintenance. Grow the vegetables I have mentioned in this chapter and you will, I am quite sure, be bitten by the vegetable gardening bug. Within a year or two you will be eyeing the lawn and considering how much more you could grow if you could persuade the family to let you dig it up. Either that, or moving house in order to get more space. While considering either of these options, try reading the next chapter.

The Complete
Veg Plot

Lavishly illustrated gardening books give us a very misleading idea of what the soil really looks like – certainly in comparison to any garden I have cultivated. You know the sort of thing: there's a series of six colour photographs showing how to plant leeks, for example, and the soil is completely bereft of stones, dog's bones and weed fragments. There it is, all uniformly brown and perfect, looking as if it was sterilised and sifted before being carefully placed in situ. I expect they buy the stuff in bags.

It can get a little disheartening, then, when the fruits of your back-breaking labours yield a patch of earth that looks ... well ... rather tatty. But don't worry, it will sustain plantlife just as well as the manicured version. Consider, for a moment, how luxuriant were the weeds which you have just – at least partially – removed.

If you want to create a kitchen garden – a real fruit and vegetable plot, not just a few patches of salad and whatnot –

your first step will be the hardest. You have to clear the soil. Now, you can grow lots of your own produce in a very small garden, but if you are looking at houses with a view to becoming a keen kitchen gardener you're going to need something in the region of eighty to a hundred feet long. And if it's south-facing, so much the better.

Don't be seduced by the idea of the 'no-dig' method, which many organic growers like to use. This form of permaculture, where a permanent mulch of compost covers the soil and seeds are sown by simply scraping back the top layer, starts with thorough digging in order to remove all perennial weeds. 'No-dig', then, is a bit of a misnomer. It should really be called, 'More digging than you ever thought physically possible, followed by a lot of other work.'

So, no matter how you intend to cultivate your plot you will need to start by clearing it. This is never easy and you will experience pain in muscles you never knew you had. But, believe it or not, there are few things more satisfying.

There are two common starting points: you will have either a garden that has run wild, or a lawn that you are prepared to sacrifice for the greater good. In the case of the untamed wilderness, start by strimming or mowing it down to ground level and then cover it with something that completely excludes light. Newspapers covered with black plastic film is a very effective combination, but you may have some old carpets that will serve just as well. The idea here is that you are depriving the weeds of the light they need for food production. Autumn or winter is the best time to attack and if you leave your mulch in place for a year, you will be amazed to see how much destruction has been wrought. However, you will need to tackle the deep-rooted perennial weeds, like dock, thistle, dandelion, brambles and nettles, with a garden fork.

Black plastic, newspapers, cardboard, old carpets: all of these are effective mulches which both suppress weeds and hold in moisture. Straw and well-rotted manure are less effective at keeping down weeds, but once the ground is clear and the crops are in, they will be a big help. They also feed the soil.

If you are amongst the dwindling band of chemical gardeners, you may prefer to use a glyphosate weedkiller when your weeds are in full spate. Two applications, a few weeks apart, will kill most plants right down to the roots, but do bear in mind that this is not a natural method and that these so-called translocated weedkillers are descended from Agent Orange. However, there are plots that are so densely overgrown that the temptation to resort to such chemicals may prove very hard to resist. I have used glyphosate in the past when I was dealing with very, very stubborn scutch or couch grass, but I still feel uneasy about it.

Converting a lawn is, in many respects, a lot easier. The idea here is to remove the layer of turf to reveal clean soil below and this can be done – albeit slowly and rather tediously – by slicing off the grass, to a depth of two inches or so, with a spade. Remove it in squares and stack them carefully, with the grass side down. Then cover the pile with black plastic and leave it alone for a year. It will have rotted down to yield lovely, rich soil which can be barrowed back to the plot and applied as a top dressing. Be careful, however, to remove any perennial weed roots as you do so; if there are none, look more closely. If you really can't find any, get down on your knees and thank Providence. Or have an eye test.

However you clear the soil your next step will be to dig. For most purposes you need only dig to a spade's depth. Turn over the soil and leave it rough for the frosts to work on. If you do your digging in autumn you will need only fork over the soil in spring. As I have mentioned elsewhere, digging performs two functions: it breaks up and aerates the soil and it also provides an opportunity for incorporating lots of bulky, organic material like manure or compost.

If – like me at Carrigeen Hill – you are creating your kitchen garden from a rough field, you can take some shortcuts. My plot has emerged from old pasture and I had no hesitation in using any mechanical aid that I could reasonably get hold of. I started by asking a neighbour of mine who is an agricultural contractor to plough it during the winter. It was, we agreed, a bit like taking a sledgehammer to crack a hazelnut; he can plough forty acres in a day and my vegetable plot is a scant one-third of an acre. The blades of the big plough cut into the surface like a scalpel and turned the turf right over to reveal lovely clean earth. It was an atavistically thrilling sight and, despite the high-tech equipment, it was a process almost as old as mankind.

I then let the elements have a go at breaking down the soil before tackling the next stage. These days there are power harrows which atomise the soil in minutes, but they are designed for big fields. Unfortunately, these devices are three metres wide and our old gates were made for horse-drawn implements, so that was the end of my high-tech assistance.

The previous owners of Carrigeen Hill, however, had very kindly left behind a venerable machine called a Wolseley Merry Tiller, almost forty years old and still going strong. Well, it performed strongly for about fifteen minutes and then required a rest, which suited me just fine. Its big steel tines revolve with great determination and torque, but if you simply let it run it just trots along on the surface of the soil at a brisk pace. The secret is to resist the machine's inclination to travel; as it tries to move forward you pull back and the tines then dig the soil. It takes some time to get the hang of it, and although it is a powered machine you get plenty of aerobic exercise working with it.

The Merry Tiller digs to a depth of between six and eight inches, which is not bad when you compare it to a spade. Sometimes, if it hits a stubborn furrow, it wants to keep digging downwards and heads for Australia, but generally it does the job. After a few days working with it I figured out that its tendency to conk out every quarter-of-an-hour or so was due to the ancient and rather leaky exhaust pipe overheating the carburettor. Now I insulate the carb with aluminium foil and it will work for half-an-hour. In other words, it now works longer than my arms can bear.

Mechanical digging aids can be simply wonderful. You can dig a plot in a fraction of the time it would take simply using a spade, and you don't have to buy one; renting a rotavator for a day will be quite sufficient to meet the needs of most vegetable gardeners. The Mantis Tiller, on the other hand, is the sort of thing that is worth the investment in that you can use a lightweight machine like this for all sorts of jobs, from hoeing to planting potatoes, but you need something more brutal for creating the plot in the first place.

Whether or not you resort to mechanical aids, sooner or later you will need to dig and it is important, not just for your garden but for your body, to do this properly. At first, it may be tempting to use a fork, because it breaks up the soil with less effort. However, it does not really turn the soil over and this is the whole point of digging.

Choose a spade that suits you, but always bear in mind that long-handled ones are ultimately easier to use because they give you more leverage. Don't try to take too much soil on the spade at one time; be easy on yourself. Slice into the soil, lift the sod of earth, throw it forward a little and take your next slice. Try to hold the spade fairly low on its handle to make this action easier. And do remember to stand up straight every few minutes and stretch. Your spine prefers to lie back rather than to lean forward, so take the pressure off your vertebrae by throwing your shoulders back every now and then.

Forking comes after digging. Use the fork to break up the

sods and to remove weed roots. This part of the process may be excruciatingly tedious, and if there are lots of weeds to come out – particularly if you are dealing with bindweed or scutch – I prefer to do this on my knees.

Incidentally, once you have cleared your plot of weeds and got a few crops planted, you will be amazed at how quickly weeds will attempt to re-colonise the area. This is because you will have exposed lots of wild seeds, many of which have lain dormant for years, to light, air and moisture. But the solution is simple and natural. As they germinate, all you have to do is wield your hoe every week or so. The idea with hoeing is that you scrape the weed seedlings off the surface as they start life, something that is highly effective during dry weather; they just shrivel up, die and feed the soil. But most of us think that hoeing is just about removal of weeds; done properly and regularly it means that the soil is constantly disturbed to a depth of an inch or two. Nothing will take root in those conditions so it's worth remembering that hoeing, the most effective form of weed control, needs to be done very regularly indeed. The great John Seymour, prophet of self-sufficiency, has described the hoe as 'the herbicide of the future'. And considering that hoes range from the little domestic implements with which we are familiar to big, industrial ones that are towed by tractors, I have no doubt that he is right. What would you prefer to use, selective weedkiller or a piece of metal?

Clearing a plot invariably produces lots of organic matter that can be recycled. All gardens need compost and if you are trying to reduce the amount of waste your household sends off every week to go into landfill dumps, composting can take a lot of the bulk out of your bin or your bonfire.

Compost is, for most gardeners, the Holy Grail, remaining forever just out of reach in its perfect form. I will confess that I still find the making of compost a kind of sacred mystery and if you have tried and tried, time and time again, only to find yourself with a slimy, brown heap of evil-smelling mess, let me reassure you that this is an experience with which I am all too familiar. And if you approach your compost heap with a degree of fear, having occasionally been greeted by a plump rat chewing its way through your potato peelings, I know exactly how you feel.

With rodents in mind, you would be well advised to site your compost heap as far from the house as possible, on the basis that the goodies with which you feed it on a daily basis are their idea of a running buffet. If even the furthest reaches of your domain are uncomfortably close to where you live, consider investing in a sealed, sturdy compost bin, some of which offer the further advantage of being turnable so as to help the process of aeration.

First things first. What can go into your compost? All uncooked vegetable matter, dead flowers, annual weeds, shredded paper, even the contents of your vacuum cleaner bag (within reason – it does rather depend on what ends up on the carpet). Grass clippings, in moderation, are good too, but if they are not sufficiently mixed with rougher material they will probably form a dense mat that will take ages to break down. Twiggy material will decompose too slowly for good compost, but if you have a mechanical shredder such material can be reduced to fibre and added to the heap. Wood ash adds valuable potash.

The best compost, in my experience, is made in a heap five feet square by four feet high, but you can go bigger if you have the material. The best compost also tends to be made during the summer months when there is an abundance of suitable material knocking around. The absolutely best compost, contrary to what some of the gardening books will tell you, is produced when you make a big heap all in one go, mixing vegetable waste, shredded paper, weeds, grass clippings and what have you together with some animal manure and – forgive me here – a dousing of human urine, if you can bring yourself to get into such an intimate relationship with the garden. Men, naturally, find this more convenient than even the most broadminded and athletic women; many keen compost-makers hoard the stuff in plastic bottles. Honestly. Urine is just about the best activator you can get for a compost heap, although you can buy a substitute in the garden centre. But then, why pay good money for something you can ... er ... make at home for free?

Your heap should be enclosed in a chicken-wire frame, or you can fashion a really durable container from old wooden pallets. Ensure that the bottom of the heap is in contact with the earth – this will allow earthworms to aid the process of decomposition – but place a few bricks on the soil surface to help with ventilation. Place a cover of some sort – wood, old carpet or, at a pinch, some PVC film – on the top to keep the rain out and the heat in.

Heat is produced spontaneously as the bacteria start the process of rotting down. Indeed, after twenty-four hours the temperature of a newly made, all-in-one-go compost heap will be distinctly uncomfortable if you thrust your hand into the centre. Whether or not you want to try this will probably depend on what sort of activator you have used, but don't be surprised if you see steam emanating from your compost bin within the first few days.

After a month it is a good idea to take a garden fork and turn the decomposing material over a few times so as to get plenty of air into the mix. Repeat this every six weeks or so, and after six to nine months your heap of plant material will, with luck, have turned into dark brown, crumbly, sweet-smelling material that looks vaguely like moss peat. If this is what comes out the other end, you will have the most nutritious feed that a plant could hope for – far more valuable than rotted animal manure. Don't be surprised if the final product amounts, in terms of volume, to a quarter or less of what you put in at the start. That's what happens when organic material is turned into plant food.

Most of us have to be content with building our compost heap much more slowly – adding kitchen peelings to the contents of the weeding bucket and the odd load of grass clippings. If you are building your compost heap in this way, it is even more important to keep it turned and aerated. I approach mine with my trousers tucked into my gumboots and bang the wooden sides with the fork a few times to make sure that any rats who are on safari in there have time to slink away. Add a layer of garden soil every few weeks and try to include plenty of fairly dry material, like shredded newspaper, in order to keep a good open texture. Remember that air is essential to the bacteria that do the key job of decomposition.

After the winter you may find that your compost heap, despite your best efforts, will be dense, sour-smelling and a bit slimy. Don't worry. As soon as you have enough material to build a big heap in one fell swoop, simply mix in this unprepossessing stuff and it will be transformed in the fulness of time. Do remember to wear gloves when dealing with any compost that may have provided a recreational facility for rodents.

Use compost as you would good manure, but more sparingly, as it is more concentrated in terms of nutrients and its potential for building good soil texture. You can also use it as a mulch – a layer of about one to two inches deep – in order to keep down weeds while also delivering a gourmet treat for your crops.

When you consider how much vegetable material goes into landfill sites – kitchen waste, weeds, all the grass in public parks, the fruit and vegetables that the supermarkets don't sell in time, even certain kinds of waste paper – you realise that we, as a nation, could produce thousands of tonnes of compost every year. It is a shocking waste and future generations will rightly judge us harshly for our lack of vision. Organic gardeners – and even many less naturally inclined ones – regard compost as brown gold.

When you are initially clearing the ground you have a great opportunity to make compost. Most weeds can go into your heap, but exclude docks, dandelions and bindweed as these are tenacious perennials. Extreme compost-makers – the sort of people who would take an Olympic gold medal for their heaps – use perennial weeds because they can get the temperature to rise so high as to kill them off. Mere mortals like you and me would be ill-advised to try it at home.

As you are clearing the plot you will be thinking about all the stuff that you will soon be growing. It's important to focus on this. Let's consider, then, the vegetables which are really tricky. They are few, but they can cause a great deal of grief. It's much better to start with something that is almost certainly going to perform well and leave you with a warm glow of satisfaction and a sated appetite.

I have tried celery many times and am not yet sure that I've cracked it. Celery from seed needs a heated greenhouse because, due to its long growing season, it has to have an early start. When I tried it from seed it simply stopped growing once it was planted out and then the slugs finished it off. Likewise, when I bought celery plants and gave them a sunny bed with lots of manure they just sulked all summer long and produced a few leaves (which we used in soup). Only when I gave it lavish attention, like an over-anxious parent wielding flash cards, did I get anywhere with it.

Much as I like the stuff (it is an essential, along with onion and carrot, for making the mixture of finely diced vegetables that should be the starting point of all proper risotto), I think it may be just too much trouble for most relatively normal human beings. Anyway, how much celery does one really want? Can you imagine a *glut* of celery?

I have had better luck with carrots, but the pleasure of lifting long, tapering roots of bright orange from the dark earth has been pretty elusive because I garden on stones loosely held together with soil. Carrots hate stones and they fork like mad as soon as they meet one. The sight of a long, perfect carrot is so wholesome, so wonderful, so downright tasty, with its mop of green, ferny foliage forming a glorious contrast to the soil-streaked orange beneath, it seems to represent all that is good about growing your own. In stony soil like mine the short, stumpy carrots and the round variety known as Parmex do well. But even if you have fine, stoneless soil, we must reckon with the carrot fly.

Now, you may think that carrot flies are nowhere near your nascent vegetable plot because nobody within ten miles of you grows carrots. Carrot flies are bloody everywhere because they are not choosy; they feast on most members of the carrot family. If you have cow parsley, for example, somewhere within flying distance, it will be supporting a whole dynasty of the little buggers. However, once they get a sniff of a real carrot (and they do sniff because they navigate by smell), they will descend upon it and lay their eggs. These soon hatch and your carrot plants, which have looked so healthy and vigorous, start fading. Lift the root and they will be riddled with little tunnels.

Such success as I have had with carrots has been confined to very early or late crops that somehow manage to survive in the open with minimal fly damage. I have tried newly introduced carrots, which have been bred to be resistant to this scourge, but my local carrot flies were undeterred. I have tried growing them under fleece, but I must have left a gap and the flies found their way in. I have grown them, with a mulch of grass-clippings, between rows of onions and garlic in a vain attempt to confuse their sense of smell, but the carrot flies still sniffed them out.

But I still have one trick up my sleeve for normal, maincrop sowings. It seems that carrot flies are not the brightest of creatures; they fly at an altitude of not more than two feet and when they encounter anything higher than this they take the long way around. If you surround your carrots with a barrier of fine mesh – very fine, because the flies are very small – the predators will not be bothered to fly up and over. It sounds very simple, and I have known lots of people to succeed with this approach.

So much for the problem crops – although honesty compels me to admit that I have also had problems with celeriac and Florence fennel. There are lots of easy crops which will thrive even under a regime of benign neglect.

Let me digress for a moment. Read the general run of

gardening books and you will find that vegetables are conventionally divided into two broad categories: those that are sown in pots or seedboxes indoors, and those that are sown direct into the ground. Now, through a process of bitter experience and a tendency to experiment at the drop of a hat, I have discovered that virtually everything can be sown, indoors or out, in pots or modules. Modules are those plastic trays which are divided into little compartments; you may well have bought bedding plants (God forgive you!) in them. My local garden centre throws out hundreds of them every week, and I have persuaded them to pass on a few to me. They comprise twelve slots for seedlings, each a little over an inch deep.

I have come to the conclusion that you can sow virtually anything in modules; the only crop about which I'm not entirely sure is carrots, and only because I have never tried them. Even beetroot will start life satisfactorily in modules, but I have to say that root crops are probably best sown direct. Modules are very economical. Sow four seeds of anything you like in each compartment and you will end up with at least a couple of seedlings. Modules will, in the fulness of time, give you seedlings with a well-developed root system in the form of a little plug that can be easily planted out, perfectly spaced. You have to thin down to one seedling, of course, but it's a simple matter to choose the strongest one.

I find that modules are particularly effective for brassicas, which hate root disturbance, and for lettuces. Using modules, a single packet of Little Gem seeds will keep us in salad for three years. French beans – one seed in each compartment –

can be germinated in modules indoors in March and then planted out as soon as the danger of serious frost has passed.

Beans and peas are nitrogen fixers. Little nodules on their roots contain the bacteria that does this valuable job so, when the crop is over, don't dig up the plants. Instead, cut them off at soil level and leave the roots to rot and enrich the soil. You can still use the area for other vegetables, such as sprouting broccoli, which can go in in late summer, having been started in a seedbed.

Peas may be a little more trouble than broad beans (see 'The Concise Veg Plot'), but they are not exactly rocket science. Most of the common varieties, like Kelvedon Wonder, are fairly dwarf in their growing habits and they do not require elaborate support. I use beech and birch twigs stuck into the soil every few inches and the peas' tendrils twine around them as the plants grow.

Advice as to sowing peas varies. I space them four inches apart in a triple row, zigzagged like broad beans. Pigeons will devour the young shoots (and mice may eat the seeds even before they break the surface of the soil), so it is usually a good idea to use netting for protection. Mice can be deterred, so they say, by burying twigs of prickly gorse over the seeds. Peas are at their very best when they are really tiny, so you need a lot of them to make a serving for even two people. The time spent shelling young peas is considerable, but there is nothing to equal their flavour – simply steamed for a few moments, then tossed with a little butter and black pepper and served as a first course. If you have a guest who turns up his nose at the notion of this kind of starter, you are keeping the wrong kind of company.

Mangetout peas are as easy to grow as it is to get bored with a bumper crop of them. I prefer the weird and wonderful asparagus pea with its beautiful deep-red flower and leaves like the wild vetch. This is a low-growing, bushy little pea plant and the fruits are strange winged pods with frilly edges. You need to pick them when they are less than an inch long, otherwise they tend to go stringy. The flavour has been compared to asparagus, which I don't think is really the case. It's a very subtle, elusive taste with a hint of raspberry, odd as it may seem. Steam them for a few minutes until tender and then toss with a little butter and pepper.

French beans, as I say, are quite sensitive to our Irish climate, so don't consider sowing them outside until mid-May at the earliest; otherwise they will sulk or die. A dwarf variety, like Purple Queen, has two advantages: it doesn't need support and the deep purple colour changes to an equally deep green on cooking. I sow two or three seeds every eight inches and then thin to the strongest seedling. As with most vegetables, steaming is the best form of cooking in that it retains most flavour.

No matter how you cook them, and no matter how pretty are the flowers, I can't work up any enthusiasm for runner beans. If you like them, by all means sow them and train the plants up wigwams made of tall bamboos. Personally, I think steamed grass would taste better.

Peas and beans may seem rather wasteful in that they

produce a lot of stalks and foliage to support a small quantity of edible parts, but do remember that all this material is a valuable addition to the compost heap. You are growing not just food for yourself but also food for the soil.

Beetroot, on the other hand, is edible from top to tail. Young beet leaves are terrific in a salad; they have a beety taste and a lovely crunchy texture, while their deep-red veins add colour. One of the best varieties is Forono, a small, cylindrical sort, rather than the more familiar round kinds, like Boltardy. Beetroot likes deep, fairly loose soil and is unusual in that each 'seed' that you sow is actually a capsule containing several seeds. This means that you can sow one every four inches and then thin down to the most vigorous-looking seedling. I like to do a further thinning when the little beets are about the size of an overgrown radish. Simply take out every second one – they are utterly delicious when they are this young and tender – and let the remaining plants bulk up. This approach means efficient use of space.

In Ireland we tend to refer to swedes as turnips and while the two are related, they are very different creatures. True turnips are much smaller and either snow-white or white with a shading of pink/purple around the shoulders. They grow very rapidly, are very hardy, and are best picked when they are no more than the size of a golf ball. At this stage they are tender and peppery; allow them to grow on and they will be woody and horrible. Sow them thinly in rows a foot apart and thin to about six inches. Sowing a very short row every three weeks will give you a constant supply of tender little roots. Swedes need to be sown, ideally in modules, in April, and then planted out a foot apart in May or June. Keep them hoed and they will swell to the size of a small football by October.

Parsnips divide opinion very sharply. You either love them or hate them. While I would rather eat my own hair than a dish of swedes (unless they are cooked by Denis Cotter of Café Paradiso), I do like the odd bit of parsnip. My favoured form is roasted in olive oil, but I have had a most delicious parsnip *rosti* in Roly@The Pavilion in Dún Laoghaire. They are easy to grow, but the mistake most of us make is to sow them too early. As they have a lot of growing to do – they are a big root – it has been traditional to sow them in February. It's no wonder that they are often accused of being patchy germinators; most self-respecting plants would hesitate before breaking the ground in an Irish February. The latter half of March is a much better idea, and while they are sometimes slow to come up, they will triumph in the end. I station-sow a variety, like Hollow Crown, The Student or Tender and True, placing three or four seeds every eight or nine inches, and then sow some radishes in between. The radishes will be all harvested by the time the parsnip plants are starting to put out big leaves.

Needless to say you need deep soil for good, long, tapering parsnips, but even shallow soil will produce perfectly tasty stumpy ones. You can leave parsnips in the ground until you are ready to eat them; indeed they tend to taste rather starchy when they are first ready in late September. Exposure to frost encourages the roots to produce sugar and I have known parsnip fans to place their crop in the freezer for an hour or so if the weather has been too mild to produce the true flavour that they love.

Salsify and scorzonera are rarely seen in the shops and never, in my experience, in an Irish restaurant. They are very old vegetables and quite distinctive in flavour. I first encountered scorzonera (which differs from salsify purely in the dark colour of its skin) at Downside Abbey, the Benedictine monastery in Somerset. I had no idea what the stuff was, but quite liked its subtle, slightly sweet taste, like a cross between artichoke and parsnip. As meals are taken in silence at Downside, I was unable to ask what it was and had to wait until I grew it myself to find out.

I have not had great success with either of these unusual roots, perhaps through lack of feeding, and I have ended up with rather spindly things which have to be washed, steamed, skinned and then stewed in butter. Frankly, parsnips give a lot more for less effort and I can assure anybody who has been intrigued by salsify's claim to be 'the vegetable oyster' that any similarity is so slight as to be undetectable.

In general, it's best to grow root vegetables in soil that has not been recently manured. Wait three months or so until the manure has been fully broken down – otherwise the roots tend to fork. This problem has been exaggerated by garden writers, but there is an element of potentially frustrating truth in it.

I don't grow much in the way of cabbage. Perhaps it has something to do with childhood memories. Corned beef and cabbage was a great favourite of my parents and I have been left with an abiding dislike of the former and a limited enthusiasm for the latter. Having said that, I have been converted to bacon and cabbage with parsley sauce, thanks to the gentle encouragement of Johann. A good German Riesling kabinett or a bottle of Guinness is the perfect compliment – along with some of your own floury spuds, of course.

The two types of cabbage which I grow for this very purpose differ greatly, the one from the other. Summer cabbage, sown in March where it is to grow and harvested young and tender in June, is probably the better in terms of flavour, but it suffers from the fact that there are so many other vegetables ready at the same time. The other is the very hardy savoy cabbage, our favourite in Ireland, with its dark, crinkly leaves which look remarkably beautiful on a frosty or dewy morning. I sow savoys in a seedbed in April and plant them out, two feet apart each way, in July. They are ready in late winter or early spring.

Brassicas, as members of the cabbage tribe are called, are very valuable in terms of nutrition and fibre. They have lots of folic acid and are supposed to be helpful in avoiding cancers. My favourite is sprouting broccoli, which, in addition to being often the first vegetable I harvest in the spring, is also one of the finest-tasting things that grow. It is certainly on a par with asparagus and young peas and there is no praise higher than that. It is sown in a seedbed in March and transplanted to its final position in July – although I've sometimes been as late as August and even September – four feet apart each way. With a bit of luck they will be the first new crop that you harvest the following spring. Don't harvest just the tips; the young leaves are excellent, too. Steamed and served with a little butter or – if you want to be really decadent – Béarnaise sauce they are one of the real treats of the gardening year. You can occasionally buy purple sprouting broccoli in the supermarket, but I can assure you that it tastes quite different from the sort you pick straight into the steamer.

Brussels sprouts are not, in my view, one of the most attractive vegetables, but I can live with them if they are tossed with ginger, chilli, soy sauce and a dash of roasted sesame oil. Not very traditional, then. They are quite easy to grow, however, and they do have the merit of providing you with fresh green stuff when there is little else in the garden. Sow them as you would savoy cabbage and plant them out in July or August, three feet apart each way. Four is enough for our needs and I buy the plants from Hackett's in Liffey Street in Dublin. Make sure the soil is very firm: tread it well down until it is quite compacted and don't be tempted to take off the top leaves to encourage sprouting – it doesn't.

Kales are very hardy, loose-leaf cabbages of a sort. The one traditionally grown in Ireland (and now a heritage vegetable) is known as Hungry Gap. As Christopher Lloyd, the garden writer and vegetable enthusiast, has said, you would need a very hungry gap indeed to want to eat it. The less coarse kales are, of course, a central ingredient in colcannon, but I have a feeling that traditionally it was often replaced by the outer leaves of savoy cabbage. It certainly works.

We grow cavolo nero, or Tuscan cabbage, for its long,

dark-green leaves (which have something of the texture of a savoy) and deep flavour. We even make very untraditional colcannon with this highly unusual vegetable, which looks so good in a flowerbed. We also use it to make the wonderful *caldo verde* soup from Portugal, where this very noble brassica is known as *couve tronchuda*.

Onions are essential to civilised food and, thankfully, they are easy to grow. Keen gardeners grow them from seed, sowing very thinly as early as February and then thinning them to six or eight inches apart with a foot or so between the rows. I have usually taken a shortcut and planted onion sets instead. Onion sets are little, immature bulbs not much bigger than a marble. When you plant them in early spring they start growing again. Onions need rich soil, otherwise they will be rather weedy and fail to store over the winter. Into such a medium simply press each onion set until just the very tip is showing. Planting can be done in either November, for an early start, or in March. Space them as you would onions grown from seed (but they will also do well as little as four inches apart each way), and check after a few days that the birds have not been pulling them up. Birds are curious creatures and will yank out the sets just to see what they are; unfortunately, they can remove several dozen sets before they finally realise that it's not going to get any more exciting.

There are two aspects of onions to bear in mind. First, make sure that the sets have been heat-treated; onions are biennial in that they bulk up in their first year of growth and produce flowers and seed the following year. An untreated onion set's instinct is to run to flower rather than flesh. The second point about onions, and one that is very often forgotten simply because they seem to grow very easily, is that they hate competition from weeds. Fail to keep the bed regularly hoed and you will be losing quite a lot of onion flesh.

Onions should be harvested when the foliage starts to turn yellow, in late July or August. Let the skins dry off before either plaiting them or simply tipping them into net bags, which can be hung up in a cool, dry place for storage.

Courgettes are for eating young and their close relatives, the squashes, store well during the winter. Despite their vaguely exotic character, these vegetable cousins are a doddle to grow provided you remember that they are tender and will be annihilated by frost. Sow them indoors in late April and don't plant out until there is no fear of temperatures dipping to zero. Effectively that means mid-May for us in the south, but if you live in a frost pocket it's best to wait until June.

For each courgette or squash plant dig a hole a foot deep and a foot square and almost fill it with well-rotted manure or compost. Put the soil back so you have a little mound over each hole, and this is where you carefully plant your seedling. These closely related plants like lots of water, so give regular soakings if the weather fails to oblige.

Squashes come in all shapes, sizes and colours and most of them are quite delicious. My favourites are Little Gem, or its relative, Gem Store, which are dark green with creamy flesh, about the size of a cricket ball, and the fashionable butternut with its creamy-yellow skin and delicious, nutty flesh. The great advantage of these vegetables is that they will keep, in a cool and well-ventilated place, right through until the following spring. Most of them are produced on trailing plants so although you need a fair amount of space, you will get quite a lot of fruit from just one. You might like to consider training the shoots to grow up over trellises (I've seen a garden shed festooned with Little Gems) so as to save ground space.

The Hallowe'en pumpkin is simply a big squash of a particular variety, but if you want to grow really big ones you will have to limit the growth to one fruit per plant, apply vast amounts of manure and water liberally, morning and evening. It can be fun, though, and children seem to relish the challenge of achieving a monster.

City-dwellers are often amazed to see our sweetcorn plants in full spate, planted amongst the squashes in a traditional combination that not only saves space (corn is tall, squashes low) but also seems to encourage both plants to do their best. People tend to think that sweetcorn is grown only in the land of the Jolly Green Giant, but, as country residents know, maize is now very widely grown in Ireland for cattle feed. Mind you, although it may look similar to the stuff we eat, it tastes very different.

The plant-breeders have been making it very easy for amateur growers to succeed with sweetcorn in our climate. There are now hardy varieties which require relatively low temperatures to ripen, and I have had great success with them over several seasons. It pays to start the plants off under cover in April; sow seeds individually in small pots and plant them out in late May when they have reached four to six inches. Because maize produces its pollen at the top of the plant, from where it drops onto the silky tassels of the immature cobs below, a lot can go wrong. If the pollen fails to hit the right spot, you get no corn. This is why plants are placed quite close together – eighteen inches apart each way is my usual pattern – in a block of at least thirty plants. This will maximise the chances of pollination. Sweetcorn is a thirsty plant and will thrive only if you give it plenty of water.

Before you go out to the garden to pick your corn on the cob, have a large saucepan of water already boiling. Harvest the cobs when the tassels have turned brown; pull back the husk and the strands to reveal the corn and press your thumb-nail into the flesh. If it produces a creamy liquid, you're in business. Now run back to the kitchen, peeling off the husk and silky strands as you go, and plunge your cob into that boiling water. After five minutes it will be ready.

You can, of course, take your time about it, but the taste will simply not be the same. Speed is of the essence and why spoil something wonderful by dawdling? Simply smear the cob with butter and eat it in your hands; there is no polite way to do this and corn-eaters never look dignified.

Barbecued corn can be quite pleasant but, in my experience, it doesn't really rival the boiled version. Simply soak the corn, sheath and all, in cold water for five or ten minutes and then place it on the barbecue. It will produce plenty of steam at first; when the outer sheath is well blackened the corn will be done and can be revealed. Again, an anointing with butter and black pepper is the only addition to be countenanced by right-minded folk.

If you have a glut of corn and simply can't face the idea of eating any more of it, you can cream it and put it in serving portions into the freezer. Simply take a very sharp knife and slice off the corn kernels from the cob, put them in a saucepan with a large knob of butter and simmer for five or six minutes. The creamy juices will emulsify with the butter and the flavour is beyond words. Before serving, add lots of black pepper; it doesn't need salt.

It annoys me how often what you see in the supermarket being sold as 'spinach' is actually Swiss chard. First, it's deliberate mislabelling and secondly it rather implies that chard is an inferior vegetable. Perhaps it is in the Irish mind, but chard has the edge in France where the broad white mid-ribs of the leaves are cooked separately and form the basis of a celebrated tart. Actually, I prefer chard. I like its earthy, rather beetroot-like taste and the fact that, unlike spinach, it rarely bolts into flower. Ruby chard, with bright red stems, is such an attractive plant that some people grow it in the flower garden. I sow a row of chard in early April and thin the plants to about a foot apart, giving them plenty of water as they will run to flower if the going gets dry for a few days.

Asparagus is arguably the king of vegetables and must remain in the same place – sometimes for thirty years or more. It is such a great delicacy that it is well worth growing if you have room, and because it will remain with you for so long it is worth both preparing the ground well and having patience.

Dig in lots of organic matter the autumn before planting and make sure there are absolutely no perennial weeds lurking in the soil; they will wreak havoc when they get entangled with the roots of the asparagus plant and will be well-nigh impossible to eradicate at a later stage.

In March, plant three-year-old asparagus crowns three inches deep and two feet apart. In summer, let the asparagus shoots grow away to their hearts' content; you must not pick any, nor the year after that. In their third season pick lightly and don't be greedy. Thereafter, the plants will be well established and you can go wild – until the middle of June. You have to allow all of the spears that appear from then on to grow into foliage so as to replenish the plant's food supply. The restraint you exercise in the early years will be well rewarded. It's best to choose an all-male F1 hybrid variety because otherwise you will spend hours trying to weed out little asparagus seedlings every autumn. Put a generous mulch of compost or manure on the asparagus bed – an inch or so deep – every spring so as to give it plenty of energy for shoot production.

Asparagus is best cooked by steaming until it is just tender – three minutes may be enough, but keep testing it – and there is no finer dish than asparagus simply served with melted butter. As to etiquette, eat it any way you like; after all, you have grown it. But the traditional way to consume this choice vegetable is by using your fingers – even at the poshest dinner table. The tenderest little tips can be briefly steamed and then mixed into creamy scrambled eggs. This is a dish which I first encountered in Portugal, where it was served as a starter. I ate so much that I couldn't touch my main course.

In the early winter, when your vegetable plot is looking rather bedraggled and the chilly air is infused with the delicious scent of burning leaves (if you have not decided to produce leaf-mould by simply bagging them and leaving them to rot for a year), it is worth clearing a patch for a vitally important crop. Vitally important to me, anyway. Every November I plant as much garlic as I can. I clear a fertile area, perhaps where the potatoes had been liberally fed with manure, and plant cloves of garlic three inches deep and four to six inches apart. In January the green tips will have appeared and then all you have to do is some hoeing until the crop is ready to lift in July or early August. There are few more satisfying sights in the garden shed than plaits of your own garlic hanging like garlands from the rafters.

Finally, there is one crop which is expressly used to feed the soil and not yourself. This is the so-called 'green manure', which can be one, or several of many plants which are sown thickly on bare ground and eventually dug into the soil where they rot down and enrich the soil both in terms of nutrients and texture. Lupins, clovers and mustards are all used for this purpose and there seems to be evidence that a combination of several plants gives the best results. They are simply sown broadcast in September, after you have cleared the ground, and then dug in during the Spring. This is the easiest way to get organic matter into the soil, but do bear in mind that the decomposition process will use nitrogen. Before you dig or rotavate the green manure crop into the soil, scatter a dressing of fish or seaweed manure on top to make up for this demand.

Green manures don't just feed the soil, and ultimately your-self in the form of fresh produce, they also keep down weeds. Essentially they are a growing mulch and a labour-saving one to boot. It is a good rule of thumb to avoid, wherever possible, leaving soil bare. If it's not covered by a crop or a mulch it will soon be covered by weeds, which will, in turn, require digging out. Green manuring makes a great deal of sense.

Faith and
Fatherland

We Irish have often been accused of being unable to discuss anything without dragging religion into it. It may not be as true as it once was, of course. I can't imagine that people born in the last twenty-five years are so afflicted, but they are the fortunate ones, growing up in a world where religion, as distinct from spirituality, is on the wane. In this respect it resembles the restoration of the Irish language: a good idea in theory, not so great in practice and certainly not something that we are keen to embrace with anything resembling real enthusiasm.

And here I am, true to my nationality, dragging religion into a book about food, wine and gardening. Put it down to the fact that the impetus behind religion, insofar as it reflects our interest in certain mysteries, touches on every aspect of life. And, of course, I believe that very few real gardeners are truly atheist. Agnostic, maybe. But we don't tend to exclude the possibility – probability? – of there being Something at the heart of Creation.

For many centuries religion has determined, to a significant degree, how we live our lives and create societies. Indeed, religion has had much more to do with structures than with true *savoir vivre*. Religious denomination in Ireland, sadly, has had much to do with our sense of identity.

There are many gloomy aspects of organised religion, especially in the Christian Church, of which I've been a member since birth – first as a Roman Catholic and later as an Anglican. One of them is the reluctance of clergy in general to talk about our responsibility to the small planet on which we live. I suppose it is progress when we see priests condemning corruption in high places rather than banging on – no pun intended – about the so-called sins of the flesh. However, it would be good to see the ordained ministers of the Christian Churches drawing attention to the debasement of nature through corporate greed, governmental indolence and personal carelessness. It is an area in which we have a spectacularly poor record in this land of ours.

Some people claim to be closer to God – whoever He, She or It may be – on the golf course than in church, and while I regard the pursuit of little white balls across manicured acres of grass with a genuine sense of bewilderment, I can see what they are ... er ... driving at. I am certainly closer to whatever may lie at the centre of Creation when I'm planting potatoes, hoeing the onion bed or hacking ivy off the trees in the wood on a winter afternoon. It bothers me, however, that when one starts talking in these terms we tend to express ourselves in platitudes and cloying epithets that make even the *Readers' Digest* sound profound. You know the sort of thing: the marvels of creation in a groundsel plant; the mind of God behind the spiral of a snail's shell; eternity in a grain of sand. No wonder old-fashioned gardeners tended to be the strong, silent type.

I once chatted over a cup of tea with a particularly straightforward rector in the Church of Ireland. 'Sometimes I find myself on the altar on a Sunday morning,' he said, 'and I look down at the congregation and wonder what on Earth they are doing there. It's my job. But why are they there?'

Some might imagine that such candour is par for the course (golf again) in the Church of Ireland, given its relatively liberal tradition, but I'm quite sure that the public expression of such thoughts would be met not with a belt – this being the C of I – but with a fairly sharp clip on the ear with an Anglican crozier. Andrew Furlong, the former Dean of Clonmacnoise, was actually tried for heresy in recent years because he denied the 'divinity' of Jesus.

Considering where I am now, my religious history may, at first sight, seem a little strange. On closer examination, however, there may be a curious logic to it.

I suppose if I were to define where I am now, in the context of world religions, I would be mildly Quaker with a seasoning of Buddhism and a liberal dash of scepticism. Quakers have no clergy or bishops for the perfectly sound reason that they consider them unnecessary. I have to say that I find this idea curiously compelling. Nor do they have fixed doctrines, as such, because they believe that these can be divisive. Now I wonder where they got that idea? Buddhists have a keen sense of our place in the universe and there are aspects of reincarnation which I find both attractive and scary.

It may be a somewhat facile view of Church history, but it bothers me that as soon as Christianity was established as an organisation, it became concerned with power and, to a very large extent, forgot the inconvenient aspects of Jesus Christ's pretty simple, if challenging, message to the world. Christian clergy have been responsible for a great deal of evil. To take just one extreme example, there was a Serbian Franciscan who, during the Second World War, would declare, 'see how I baptise these infidel bastards', as he slit the throats of the Muslim children who had been unfortunate enough to be born in the vicinity of his monastery; it still stands and functions as a place of prayer. Closer to home, the indiscriminate carnage of the Claudy bomb in Northern Ireland seems to have been the work of a Roman Catholic priest. General Dyer, an Irish Anglican responsible for the unspeakable Amritsar Massacre, was said to have been a very devout man. All in all, Christianity has not been a great success and has tended to encourage people to believe that they have a monopoly on Truth. Christianity, broadly speaking, has not yet been tried; its core teaching, that we should love each other, tends to be forgotten. I don't think Christ himself would recognise the so-called Christian Churches, their obsession with trivia and legalistic regulations;

and we've had two thousand years to get it right.

I object to the notion of any Church considering itself to be Catholic. (I should explain that Anglicans believe that the Roman Church and their own Communion form the unfortunately divided Catholic Church: this is why we tend to use the phrase 'Roman Catholic' and object strenuously when we are described, carelessly, as 'non-Catholics'.) It is very dangerous when you start describing your Church as universal. Where does that leave the other great religions? Are we to dismiss Islam, for example, as a mere superstition? Are we seriously to believe that Divine Providence has let billions of Buddhists bark up the wrong tree for centuries? I seem to remember that Christ himself said, 'forbear to judge'. Forbear to judge? The most vociferous Christians, of whatever hue, seem to do little else.

I suppose one of my biggest problems with modern Christianity is the insistence that we couch our beliefs in the language and imagery of ancient Palestine. I am not at all sure that this is helpful in relating our faith to the world in which we live everyday. And does the divinity or otherwise of Jesus Christ really matter? Does the Father, Son and the Holy Ghost mean that there is nothing feminine in the source of Creation? Should we rewrite it all? Do we not all share in divinity? As Quakers say, there is 'that of God' in everyone. Hilary Wakeman, an English Anglican priest living in West Cork, has written a very challenging book on issues such as these. Her *Saving Christianity* is a passionate plea for a sincere exchange of views about how tradition can stretch the credibility of

Christian doctrine to breaking point.

I suppose it would be best if we went on using the imagery and language of antiquity but were encouraged, at the same time, to have the freedom to interpret in such a way as creates, for each of us, a system of belief that makes sense. Churches, including the Anglican one, are wary of individualistic interpretations of religion; give the faithful an inch and soon they will be all over the place. Thinking for ourselves is not something that institutional Churches believe to be A Good Thing. And, of course, conservative elements within the Churches seek the comfort of certainty, of firm teaching and leadership; they seem to be deeply afraid of thought and reflection.

Despite all my reservations about organised religion of whatever kind, I do occasionally go to church, and when I do I put another much-needed bum on a Church of Ireland pew. Indeed, the relatively small numbers in the average C of I congregation give, I think, a sense of community; when, at the Holy Communion, we are enjoined to be in peace and charity with our neighbours before taking the bread and wine, we are usually surrounded by actual neighbours whom we see everyday.

My occasional attendance at Church of Ireland services may seem strange when you consider that I was brought up in a deeply devout and conservative Roman Catholic home, educated – up to a point – by the Jesuits, and even did a stint as an altar boy in an enclosed Carmelite convent which, odd as it may seem, was great fun. I still have great respect for those who devote their lives, selflessly, to prayer. At Hampton, the convent in question, we altar boys were always entertained lavishly by the nuns after working on the highly complicated and somewhat intimidating Easter services. I can still remember the smell of strong tea and the satisfying munch of dainty ham sandwiches after Midnight Mass. One rather eccentric chaplain surprised us all by leaving the priesthood to become a Moonie. Before he left, and with his mind obviously on other things, I overheard the sacristan offering him a fresh alb. 'Oh, no thank you, sister,' he replied, 'I never drink anything in the morning.'

My decision to become an Anglican at the age of twenty-one was, oddly enough, a very easy one to make. I was still sufficiently convinced by organised Christianity, as it had evolved over the centuries, to stay within the fold, but I had developed a deep distaste for both the authoritarian 'we know best' character of the traditional Roman Church and some of its more bizarre rulings, such as the ban on contraception. At the time, Anglicanism, that very broad Church, seemed like a good place to be, and I have to say that it remains so, despite the fact that I am, even by the slightly woolly standards of the Church of Ireland, a bit of a heretic.

As a matter of fact, I've always had a bit of a soft spot for heretics. Luther seems to have been a troubled sort of bloke, but quite sound on many issues; Zwingli was quite challenging; Calvin was not a bundle of laughs but you have to give him marks for zeal; even the Cathars had their own strange charm. The word 'heretic' derives, I believe, from a Greek word meaning 'to pick and choose'. Well, I've always been more inclined to go for the *à la carte* than the *table d'hôte*.

I fell under the spell of Archbishop Cranmer's *Book of Common Prayer* when I was teaching at St Columba's. In the prospectus of the typical public school – and St Columba's belongs to that tradition – it is always stated robustly that 'the chapel is the centre of school life'. This is bunkum, of course. As John Betjeman memorably explained in his hilarious poem 'Cricket Master', the centre of school life is the crease. That was probably the case at St Columba's, but chapel was compulsory every morning and on Sundays; being quite keen to impress the Head with my zeal for school life I attended chapel, well, religiously.

Intellectually, for want of a much better word, I was already quite in sympathy with Anglicanism, its emphasis on freedom of conscience and commitment to keeping the clergy in their place. However, it was the beauty of the liturgy that really swayed me. In the meantime, the Church of Ireland seems determined to modernise the liturgy, doubtless to make it more 'relevant' to everyday life. It never ceases to amaze me how clergy, of all denominations, are so inclined to dismiss the mystique, the indefinable magic of the old services, in a vain attempt to be more in tune with the spirit of the age. Have they never paused to consider that the spirit of the age is precisely what people want to avoid in church? I suppose the problem may well be that a large proportion of clergy are either a bit thick or personally rather screwed up. Many, but by no means all, of course.

I have a very clear memory – a kind of personal epiphany –

of singing the '*Nunc Dimitis*' (very traditional stuff) at the end of evensong one frosty December evening at St Columba's. And then we emerged from the bright chapel into the dark, all of us – staff and students – in the white surplices worn on Sundays. As the lights of Dublin twinkled far below in the night, I decided that it was time to take seriously something that I found so personally uplifting. Subtracting the place, the atmosphere, even the sense of community that St Columba's enjoyed, it seemed that Anglicanism had an intrinsic appeal for me. I knew that I would not be the equivalent, so to speak, of those people who convert to Rome largely because of 'the bells and smells'.

It also struck me that if I remained as I was, I would be considered ever afterwards to be 'a lapsed Catholic'. And it really annoyed me. This probably does not count as one of the highest of motives for conversion, and I will confess that I didn't bring it up when I approached the Chaplain of St Columba's, the Reverend Bertie Walsh, and declared that I wanted to join up.

I can't remember what Bertie said, but I do know that I had to remind him of my decision a few months later. 'Ah yes,' he said, 'I thought you should have a cooling-off period.' I arranged to see him in his study with a view to setting up a course of instruction. 'Tell me why you are attracted to Anglicanism,' he said. And I did. Leaving out the bit about avoiding lapsed Catholicism. When I finished he said, 'Well, that all seems very sensible and I think we can dispense with any instruction,' which was, I have to say, a great relief. But he presented me with a fascinating book, called simply *The Faith of an Anglican*, written by a former Dean of Connor.

A few weeks later I was in the Archbishop of Dublin's private chapel being officially received into the Anglican Church. More accurately, I was kneeling on an orthopaedically excruciating *prie dieu*, my knees considerably forward of my chin, with the result that I could not quite see the 'script' of the short service, which was somewhere under my nose. The result of this was that, when the Archbishop asked me if, in effect, all was gameball for joining up, I was not sure whether the correct response was 'I do', 'I will', or even a bald 'yes'. As I paused, the congregation of two (Bertie and another colleague from the school) gazed in suspense at the back of my head, convinced that I had got cold feet at the last moment. Eventually I made some sort of noise of assent and Dr Henry McAdoo shook me warmly by the hand. Ever since I have retained a considerable affection and active interest in the Church of Ireland, despite its flaws.

And the Anglican Communion certainly has flaws. As I write this, it is trying to tear itself apart over the issue of gay bishops and clergy, something which I cannot imagine the Founder regarding as being anything of consequence. And having been traditionally – in England, at any rate – the Tory party at prayer, much of its language concerns conquest and king-doms. Tony Benn, a spiritual man but not keen on organised religion, was once berated by a Born Again Christian. 'Do you accept the Lord your God?' demanded the BAC. 'Will you enter into the kingdom of Heaven?' Benn, who disclaimed his hereditary peerage, replied that he had no time for lords and couldn't countenance kingdoms, being a convinced democrat. He also once famously said that, 'Just as there are still some Christians in the Church of England, there are still a few social-ists in the Labour party.'

Explaining my move to people who don't know the Church of Ireland from within was not easy. 'I can understand you wanting to leave the Roman Catholic Church,' they said, 'but the Church of Ireland, for God's sake!' – not quite aware of how this sounds when you analyse the words. In circum-stances like this I have tended to mention a certain genetic weakness – there's more than a drop of Protestant blood in the family – and at least this usually gets a laugh.

My parents were sorely disappointed by my decision to roam in pastures new, but my mother, one of the most truly Christian people I have ever known, came to believe that if this was my path to God – as she put it – well and good. My father was bemused, to such an extent that he quoted James Joyce, a writer whom he considered to be a talented pedlar of smut. When Joyce was taken to task about his religious doubts, he was asked if he had considered becoming a Protes-tant. He replied that he may have lost his faith, but he had not yet lost his reason.

Despite my parents' conservatism, they didn't suppress debate; they were the sort of Catholics who read *The Tablet* while never wavering from the path of orthodoxy for one moment. They had vast numbers of clerical friends: not red-faced, sporting curates, but thoughtful priests with an interest in Sanskrit or liberation theology, and indefatigable nuns who devoted their lives to the poorest of the poor. My mother went occasionally to Lourdes; my father thought Marian apparitions highly dubious, nor did he enjoy exchanging the sign of peace. In the last few weeks of his life he managed to attend Mass in hospital. I asked if it had been the sort of happy-clappy service that he loathed. 'Yes,' he said. 'You know, I think I would have made a good Protestant.'

I think I began to react against the monolithic nature of Roman Catholicism quite early on. I was certainly not very good at taking anything for granted, apart, of course, from regular meals, laundry and pocket money. On one occasion when I was a teenager, my mother, exasperated by my reluctance to swallow 'the teaching of the Magisterium of the Church', accused me of being a sponge, all too ready to soak up new ideas. It was not true, of course; I wanted to subject all ideas, values and received wisdom to scrutiny. And to soak up the ones that made sense. One Jesuit at Belvedere, charged with the task of teaching us 'religion', exploded with annoyance when I challenged him once too often. 'Why must you always disagree with me?' he roared. 'Because it's more fun that way, Father,' I managed to retort, being in my last few weeks at school. (A less cerebral Jesuit at Belvedere once asked his religion class what they thought about sex on the television. One boy replied, 'I don't know about you, Father, but I find it very uncomfortable.')

My mother died in 1991, well before the avalanche of clerical child abuse cases and the exposure of the Church authorities as being, at best, highly irresponsible in their handling of such atrocities. I am glad she never knew that a shocking number of priests were raping children and being protected by the institution which she loved so profoundly.

I was one of the majority of altar boys who never experienced any sexual advances from the men in black, although I was once, in a different context, groped by a clerical student upon whom I managed to land quite a deft kick in the genital area, pretty neat work for an embarrassed eleven-year-old and I'm still rather proud of it. Needless to say, I didn't tell my parents, but I sometimes wonder how this repellent young man's career developed.

The extraordinary thing is that we, as a people, let the Church get away with so much for so long. It is only natural that we should find it impossible to understand how some nuns, priests and brothers (admittedly a small minority) could listen to the Gospel every morning and then go about crushing the spirits and the bodies of those who Christ called 'my least little ones'. But the unsavoury fact remains that we, as a people, let them.

I remember studying the Home Rule movement for the Inter. Cert. and, like everyone else in my class at Belvedere, thinking how strange it was that the unionist community feared that it would amount to Rome Rule. This was 1975: contraceptives were banned, divorce had been abolished since the early years of the State and abortion was not even debated. Rome Rule it most certainly was.

Why a revolutionary movement aimed at securing independence from the United Kingdom should have created a State that was, in effect, run by the unelected clergy of the Roman Catholic Church is a complex question, with many possible answers. However, one thing is certain: Irish identity somehow came to be linked to religion and being truly Irish meant being Roman Catholic. To be Protestant in Ireland, even today, is thought by some to suggest that one's Irishness is in some way diluted.

The Protestant community has been, of course, to some extent culpable for this sorry state of affairs. The Church of Ireland cannot see a parapet without immediately ducking its collective head below it for fear of offending the majority. At the dawn of the Irish Free State, a delegation from the Synod of the Church of Ireland went to see Michael Collins to ask if their people could stay in their own country. Collins, to his credit, was amazed that they felt the need to ask.

The society that emerged in the new and aggressively Roman Catholic Ireland became increasingly isolated. De Valera's fundamentally daft ideal of a nation of small farmers enjoying – if that's the word – a frugal existence and his pursuit of the Economic War retarded the fragile economy by decades. Our neutrality during the Second World War, however justified in terms of pragmatism, further isolated the

Republic so that by the 1950s we were even less significant in the world than when we were part of the United Kingdom. The ideal of reviving the Irish language – largely initiated by Protestants during the nineteenth century – became, and still to some extent remains, the great Sacred Cow. However noble the aspiration, this meant that huge resources which could have been used to teach science and modern languages were, instead, deployed in the hopeless task of turning us into a nation of *Gaelgoirí,* talking to ourselves. The Catholic triumphalism of the 1950s further served to isolate us at a time when secularism was sweeping through the Western World and zealots – most of them lay people encouraged by the clergy – insisted on a censorship so severe that most Irish writers had at least one book on the banned list. And if they didn't, they wondered what was wrong with their work.

A friend of mine recalls returning to Dublin, this was in the 1960s, after a few weeks on the Continent and having his suitcase searched by Customs at Dún Laoghaire. The officer retrieved a well-thumbed copy of Joyce's *Ulysses* with all the obvious distaste of a sensitive soul trying to empty a rat trap. 'Foreign filth!' he declared, and promptly confiscated the book that had changed the face of English literature forever.

So, the struggle for Irish freedom left us poor and isolated in a country with the worst public services and infrastructure in Europe. An old schoolfriend of mine, of a fairly nationalist bent, went to work in the health service in Northern Ireland ten years or so ago. He came back amazed at how the NHS and social services there were so much more efficient and extensive than our own equivalents in the south and concluded, with a bitter laugh, 'This is what we fought against in 1916?'

Social policy was, until very recently, dictated by the Roman Catholic Church, a scandalous enslavement of an ostensibly free people. It retarded our development as a society for the better part of a century. I have a theory that we, as a people, have not yet grown up. A relation of mine, who had just split up from her increasingly intolerable husband, told me that he had been very strictly brought up in a repressively religious Protestant home. 'He never had an adolescence,' she said, 'and the problem is, he's having it now.'

Now, I know that this is rather unfair to the average adolescent, but compare Ireland with the stereotypical sulky teenager. Everything is somebody else's fault: the Brits, the politicians, the EU. And there is a need to rebel: laws in Ireland are, at best, aspirations, nobody is meant to take them seriously. Then there is the parallel need to conform: we don't want to rock the boat or get above ourselves (think of our government's attitude to the Gulf War). And there's the desperate need to be loved and appreciated in spite of being unreasonable: sure, everybody loves the Irish!

Like many adolescents, we are unsure of our identity. Just as many kids define themselves by what they are not – I'm not a culchie, I'm not a rugger-bugger, I'm not a Goth – we tend to define ourselves as English-speaking exponents of American/ British culture who are not British. As Mary Harney once correctly pointed out, we are closer to Boston than Berlin. That, I suspect, is because the culture of the USA is one that we know and understand and, praise the Lord, it's not British. In the weeks preceding the last Gulf War, Bertie Ahern spoke of our ties of kinship and economics with the United States, something that I have never heard being invoked in relation to the United Kingdom, although it has equal if not greater validity.

Collective amnesia is another national characteristic, not least in our ability to dismiss the disastrous first seventy years or so of Independence as having been worth the sacrifice. We have also largely written out of our national consciousness our participation in creating, for better or worse, the British Empire. I am not a fan of empires, but I feel that the truth should be acknowledged.

I once heard a distinguished Irish journalist talk complete cobblers about this issue. She explained that the great Imperialist front entrance of the British Museum made her feel alienated and that she always used the more functional side door. She went on to say that it had always been a pleasure to work with English colleagues because they were so reliable and efficient. You have to be like that when you have an Empire, she said. But we Irish were too poor to have an Empire and so we are ... well, pretty hopeless at getting things done. Now, I don't think that having an Empire should be a source of pride. My grandfather, who had distinctly unionist sympathies (although, with characteristic Irish schizophrenia, he had a soft spot for Parnell), used to claim that the reason why the British had an Empire so extensive that the sun never set on the whole of it was because God wouldn't trust the buggers in the dark.

The British Empire evolved as a source of raw materia
a manufacturing nation and as a market for its goods; the m
vation was commercial and there was much greed, but the
Empire brought benefits, too, in terms of education, healthcare
and infrastructure. Its legacy in India is an impressive tradition
of parliamentary democracy. The Empire was a curate's egg –
not so bad in parts.

We helped to build it. Through the port of Cork poured the
provisions that fed the Royal Navy. Ireland helped to provide
not just the foot soldiers, the sailors and a great deal of
unskilled labour, we also provided doctors, lawyers, engi-
neers, administrators, missionaries and officers. Most of them
Catholic. We were, after all, whether we like it or not, part of
the home nation of the Empire and it is patently dishonest to
claim that it had nothing to do with us. Many of the Irish
Empire-builders, it can be argued, pursued their task with less
sympathy for the Imperial ideal than their English counterparts, but they enjoyed the benefits of participation. They are
now, at best, written out of our own sense of history and, at
worst, regarded as less than truly Irish.

This is not just amnesia. I believe it's the fruit born of a
deliberate policy. It is the legacy of decades of education
predicated on Dev's ideal of the Irish-speaking noble peasant
toiling away in a Paul Henry landscape, content with his frugal
existence, whose sense of culture is confined to fireside tales
and traditional Irish music and whose soul is unsullied by anything that may have sprung from the eighteenth-century European Enlightenment. Just as the British upper classes have

always mistrusted intellectuals (probably because intellectuals, being thoughtful, often question the status quo), the twentieth-century Irish ideal was based on a romantic notion of peasant culture. We can't deliver economic prosperity? Peasant culture doesn't seek such delights. We have handed over the minds – and, all too often, the vulnerable young bodies – of the people to the Roman Catholic Church? Never mind, peasant culture does not rock the boat – it's too concerned with subsistence.

Throughout the 1950s and 1960s thousands of Irish people were forced to leave their own country and seek work abroad. In the decade before I was born, in 1959, almost half-a-million people emigrated. Every day, the Holyhead boat and the tenders in Cobh were full of people, a visible manifestation of the miserable failure of independent Ireland. And at the same time, the seminaries were full, feeding the voracious appetite of the institutional Roman Catholic Church, both here and abroad, for priests.

It is tempting to see the Ireland of the twenty-first century as something quite different, as a country where we have learned from our past. I hope that is becoming true. One of the worst legacies of the Celtic Tiger is a smug tendency to engage in self-congratulation, which ignores the glaring shortcomings in how the country is run.

We undertake, in the Constitution, to cherish all the children of the nation equally, yet national schools are so poorly funded that they have to be propped up with 'voluntary' contributions from parents. Schools in poor areas don't have that support. Tesco provides more computers for schools than the State; maybe they should be asked to run our education system.

It was a Labour party Minister for Education who abolished third-level fees for all students, regardless of means, while primary schools had to raise funds just to survive. Attempts to reverse that provision have proved to be a political hot potato. What does that tell us about our priorities?

We allow doctors to practice private medicine using buildings and equipment funded by the taxpayer. I have nothing against private healthcare provided it is exactly that. Having the State subsidise the fat incomes of the top-earning consultants is an insult to the electorate. We allow religious Orders to own and run hospitals and schools although we, the people, have paid for them many times over at this stage. It means that devout atheists have to breathe their last with a crucifix over their heads and Jews and Muslims are watched over by statues of the Virgin Mary.

We have the worst environmental record in the EU, have no intention of meeting carbon emission limits and most recycling initiatives lag well behind those in other European countries. We promote Ireland as being a clean, green land but do very little to make the reality match the hype. Planning authorities continue to allow houses of breathtaking ugliness to be built throughout rural Ireland, while our road structure is completely inadequate.

We have a railway system – if that is not too strong a word – that is still underfunded, dirty, inefficient and allegedly 'getting there'. There is not yet a motorway link between any of our cities, and it will be a very long time indeed before there is. It took one Minister, after years of complete complacency, to halve road deaths in a stroke, by doing what? Insisting that the Gardaí enforce the law. And still, driving in Ireland is not something that any sane person would do just for the sheer fun of it.

We live in a country where we have to aspire to a United Ireland although we know that it is virtually impossible. There are diehard unionists, of course, who would not want to join with the Republic even if we suddenly found that we had more oil than Saudi Arabia. And there are some whose sense of identity is deeply odd. John Taylor MP, now known some-what implausibly as Lord Kilclooney, was once asked if he was Irish. 'Certainly not,' he spluttered in tones that combined Ulster refainement with a poor take on High Tory. 'I'm British.' No point in telling him that 'British' cannot exist independently of nationality. Britons are English, Scots, Welsh and, possibly, (Northern) Irish.

Of course, there are many unionists who would have no truck with such silly posturing, but who still don't want to join the Republic of Ireland as it now exists. And who can really blame them?

We need to accept that many strands of nationalities and traditions have gone to make Ireland the country that it is. We have to get away from any notion that Irishness can be neatly defined. We have to broaden our sense of who we are and to accept that very soon a whole generation of black and Asian children will be talking with Irish accents and cheering for our national teams. It's going to be one of the best things that ever happened to us – but only if we welcome it with open arms and lots of pride. Having colonised much of the English-speaking world ourselves, we must be open to those who want and need to come to our country. Racism is a deep-rooted problem with the Irish, not just here but wherever we have gone throughout the world. It is by far our most unattractive feature and we all, myself included, harbour some racist attitudes.

I like living in Ireland, but I do believe that successful survival in this country involves learning to deal with a kind of national madness, a sort of collective dysfunction. It is challenging, but the country is beautiful, most of the people are pleasant, we have a quirky sense of humour (because we have to) and it's where I belong. This is where my roots are. For better, for worse, I love this land of ours. And, as a friend of mine says when he has had it up to his tonsils with Irish life, 'Sure, aren't we a great little nation all the same!'

Spuds and Apples

Gardens have changed and I don't mean just because people now use TV make-over programmes as their point of reference when they are planning what to do. I am not alone in finding this a rather scary prospect; the august pages of the Royal Horticultural Society's magazine, *The Garden,* has seen a vigorous exchange of letters between the conservative and modernising tendencies. Most bizarre of all was a letter claiming that the anti-gnome group was motivated by class hatred. It could only happen in England.

However, the fact remains that town and city gardens are now very small indeed and this is not just because the price of development land is extortionate. The average householder these days does not want the bother of tending to a patch much bigger than a handkerchief. And a machine-washable hankie at that.

Most of the houses built in Dublin in the years immediately after the war had enough space for a few apple trees – invariably Cox's Orange Pippin for eating and Bramley Seedlings for cooking. That's what we had when I was a child, and the neighbours even stretched to a couple of pear trees. It was explained to me that you needed two trees to pollinate each other and for years after I thought of the mysteries of sex (not that I had a name for it) in terms of pollen. Such sweet innocence, of course, but not much preparation for reality.

In such suburban gardens it was possible to grow a few rows of spuds and it was common for the new arrivals in Dublin to try to recreate a memory of their rural homes with the lush foliage of Home Guards, or British Queens. Indeed, Myles na gCopaleen described the New Potato Bore: the man who looks at you pityingly when you enthuse about the first new spuds and then tells how they have had them at home for weeks. I think I have met his descendants.

Anyway, spuds and apples are so central to my idea of food that I cannot conceive of civilised living without them. If you have the space, they are the essential crops. Apples essentially grow themselves, of course, while potatoes require time, effort and planning. But the rewards are bountiful and the sight of potato foliage pushing through the earth and the scent of faintly pink apple blossom are infinitely more exciting than garden centre exotics surrounded by bark-chip mulch.

Why the French should refer to potatoes as the apples of the earth I don't know, but I have a shrewd suspicion that it reflects their care for food. That they give a starchy South American tuber this name implies a respect and an understanding of the vegetable that goes way beyond the staple status that it enjoys in Ireland.

Potatoes are taken for granted, an almost invariable

constituent of the meat-and-three-veg to which most of us still sit down once a day. Yet potatoes are so ingrained in our idea of ourselves that we retain an awareness of varieties: Duke of York, Queens, Kerrs Pinks. We know what we like, despite the fact that the supermarkets sell 'new' potatoes – unspecified and grown in Cyprus or Italy – throughout the year.

The Irish and the Scots favour floury spuds, while the English prefer the waxy varieties that many of us dismiss – far too lightly, if you ask me – as 'soapy'. Some floury potatoes, such as Golden Wonders, don't grow well in southern Britain and this may explain the national preference. One British supermarket, I hear, insists that all their Golden Wonders come from north of Aberdeen.

I believe that there is a potato for every culinary purpose: our beloved 'balls of flour' soak up the gravy of winter casseroles, while a waxier early spud, like Home Guard, retains its shape and delivers a dense, chestnut-like flavour, especially if bathed in melted butter. New potatoes cooked with a bloom of salt on their thin skins, whether floury or soapy, is one of the best things you can eat.

Potato experts talk about such features as the 'dry matter' content, the levels of starch, yield, disease resistance and what have you. For most of us we are content to know that a particular variety is good for mash or baking, chips or roasting. And the true food enthusiast will have a keen idea as to what sorts make a good potato salad (namely the non-floury kind of which the French, predictably enough, have bred several: like the unfortunately named Ratte and the confusingly named

Pink Fir Apple, which does not look like an apple or a fir cone although it does, like the overtired, have pink eyes).

Interest in potato varieties amongst gardeners has never been higher. Unwins, the seed company, even sell little packets of five tubers from a wide range of spuds so that you can grow as many sorts as you like – which is fun albeit rather more expensive than buying by the usual 5kg bag.

If you have the kind of garden that comprises a small patio, a tiny lawn and a few shrubs around the edge you may well decide that growing your own spuds is not for you. Personally, I would dig the whole lot up and turn it into a productive plot, potatoes included, but I realise that this may not suit everybody's needs nor, indeed, sense of aesthetic. But why not grow five or six potato plants in buckets (you can even use fancy planters if you're worried about appearances)? All you have to do is plant a tuber in each bucket, about four to five inches deep, in a general potting compost, and once the leaves have poked through give a liquid seaweed feed every week. If you plant them on St Patrick's Day, in keeping with the national tradition, you will have lovely new potatoes in June. Just keep an eye on the weather forecast and make sure to protect the young shoots with newspaper or fleece if frost threatens.

My only reservation about encouraging

people to do this is because I believe it will undoubtedly lead to annoyance. The joy, the sheer sensual bliss of unearthing the new potatoes – each one plump and fresh and magically made flesh, and having them with a little butter, salt and a twist of black pepper – may turn into bitter frustration. If the frustration, in turn, prompts you to dig up the lawn, well and good. All I'm saying is that those few potato plants, which seemed like just a bit of innocent fun, may change your life forever. You will want more. And more. So be careful.

The traditional advice to gardeners has been to concentrate on growing early potatoes because they taste so good fresh and because they are relatively expensive to buy in early summer. Maincrop spuds, on the other hand, take up more space and occupy the ground for longer. After you have dug all your earlies, there is still time enough to replace them with leeks and broccoli for the autumn and winter and these beacons of hope during the short, dark days will hugely appreciate the manure which you will have lavished on the spuds.

Maincrop potatoes, the ones that store over the winter and keep us going when fresh vegetables are scarce, are of interest only to those who have plenty of space and who have either the equipment or the back muscles to sustain the planting programme. On the other hand, if you do have such resources it means that you can be self-sufficient in one very important food and you will know that the spuds you roast on Christmas Day have not been sprayed with chemicals to stop them sprouting in storage (and many more chemicals when they were growing). Having said that, I have the space to grow as

many maincrop spuds as I care to, but Johann and I ha\
eventually decided to concentrate almost exclusively on earlies and the mid-season ones known as second earlies. Early
potatoes not only taste wonderful but they have a lower gly-
caemic index than stored maincrops. This is a matter of academic interest for most people, but if, like a growing number
of consumers, you want to go easy on refined carbohydrates,
it's worth considering. If you are on the extreme Atkins diet, of
course, you won't be eating spuds of any kind.

The other reasons for our decision to go easy on maincrops
are the fact that they need protection from blight, harvesting
them is such time-consuming and back-breaking work, and
the availability of good local potatoes throughout the winter
months.

Most of us can well afford the space to put in a row or two
of earlies, but it is worth trying to ensure that you get the best
possible results. To quote GK Chesterton, if a thing is worth
doing, it's worth doing badly; and if you simply plant your
potato tubers a few inches deep in unprepared soil, you will
probably get some kind of a crop and it will taste good simply
because the time involved in getting the spud from the ground
to the table is about half-an-hour. But for lots and lots of delicious potatoes you need to apply a degree of elbow grease
and as much organic material as you can muster.

In an ideal world you should dig the site of your proposed
potato plot in the autumn, simply turning over the earth and
leaving it in clumps so that the frosts can break it down. Then
you need to buy your seed potatoes (don't use ones from the

vegetable rack, even if they are defying the chemical retardants and putting out shoots) and 'chit' them. Remember to choose an early variety; just read the label carefully. My favourite earlies are Duke of York, which dates from Edwardian times, and Home Guard, which was introduced during the Second World War. Older varieties give better flavour in my experience.

Now, some gardeners maintain that chitting (or sprouting) is not necessary, but, to be honest, I couldn't be bothered to do a controlled trial; I'll just stick with tradition. Chitting involves getting the tubers to put out sprouts before they get into the ground; in theory this means that the potato has started its growth cycle in advance of planting and therefore the plant will reach maturity earlier.

You need to examine each tuber and identify what spud anoraks call the 'rose end'; this is the end displaying most buds or 'eyes'. Place the tubers in trays or, better still, egg boxes, with the rose end uppermost, and store in a bright, frost-free place until you are ready to plant. Ideally, start chitting in early February so that the tubers will be sporting sturdy little shoots of perhaps half-an-inch long by the time they go into the ground. It is important to give them light because darkness encourages thin, brittle shoots.

St Patrick's Day is supposed to be the time when all of the potato growers in Ireland go out and plant, but I have doubts about this. First of all, St Patrick's Day is almost always bitterly cold with horizontal sleet in the wind threatening to decapitate anyone foolhardy enough to spend any time in the garden.

Also, in cold areas, the late frosts may well put paid to a crop that is planted so early. If you are not bothered about when the first of your new potatoes come to fruition, you can defer planting until late April; if you're a gambler, plant on 17 March and hope for the best.

I dig drills about six inches deep and put a good layer of well-rotted manure or garden compost in the bottom. Then I place a chitted tuber with two strong shoots (rubbing off the others if there are any) every twelve inches on top. Then I pour a few handfuls of soil over each one, in order to protect the shoots, and then fill in the drill without firming the soil. I end up with a ridge of soil two or three inches high marking the position of each drill. Potatoes do best in loose soil; they find it easier to do their own thing and the growing tubers don't have to struggle against compact earth.

Watch the soil surface for the first indications that the new potato plants are 'pushing'. When the first shoots emerge, hoe some soil over them to protect them from frost and keep hoeing between the rows to keep the weeds down. If a frost is forecast after the foliage is well up, simply cover the plants for the night with newspapers weighted down with stones.

By early June you may have some small new potatoes ready to eat; it depends on the weather and on the variety you have chosen. It also depends on water, which is rarely scarce in Ireland, but if you do experience a dry spell there is no harm in giving your spuds a really good soaking on a regular basis.

By mid-June you should be in business and each plant that you lift will reveal plump new potatoes, each with a skin so thin and delicate that you can rub it off with a stroke of your thumb. You can leave the potatoes in the ground until needed – they will get bigger, but by late summer they will have lost the full impact of the early potato charm, while retaining great flavour.

If you like your potatoes on the floury side, you may be a little discouraged by the very first of the tubers you take from the soil. Even Duke of York, which is generally good and floury, will start off rather waxy, but give it time. A week or two after your first haul, the new potatoes start converting plant foods into starch and the texture changes.

But what of blight? Blight is usually a problem confined to maincrop potatoes because the weather conditions which favour its spread – warm, humid, windless – are more likely in July than in June. Well, that's the theory, of course, but anyone who gardens in Ireland knows that our seasons can be terribly confused. Should your new potatoes be stricken with this horrible fungal disease, it will probably happen when the tubers are fairly well advanced in terms of growth. There is no point in spraying at this stage; instead, cut off all of that part of the potato plants which appears above the soil (this is known as the haulm) and burn them. The potatoes will be fine and may even bulk up a little further without the assistance of photosynthesis in the leaves.

Blight is the bane of the maincrops, whose growing season extends from spring (some gardeners plant theirs before the earlies on the basis that they need all the time they can get) right into early autumn. The chances of an unprotected crop surviving an Irish summer are practically nil and even the most avid organic producer has to use some kind of defence. Commercial growers will use all kinds of modern fungicides, but the organic gardener will stick to the traditional prophylaxis of Bordeaux Mixture, which combines copper sulphate in solution with a wetting agent. The reason for the unusual name is simple. In the nineteenth century the Bordelais *vignerons* used to spray the fruit on the roadside vines with a bright blue copper sulphate mixture so as to discourage pilfering, and I have no doubt that it was an effective deterrent. In time, they noticed that the vines so treated did not succumb to fungal attack. Thus was born the world's first antifungal. It is not entirely harmless – it kills soil bacteria – and so needs to be used sparingly, but it does not harm animals or insects.

Some maincrop potatoes have been bred for blight resistance and while there is no such thing as an immune variety, some put up a fiercer fight than others. A few years ago I was amazed to see a couple of rows of Golden Wonders swoon as the blight engulfed their leaves while the neighbouring Caras still stood proudly to attention. I was able to save the Caras by spraying, while I salvaged something of the Golden Wonders – a stunning old variety with a real chestnut flavour and still used in the crisp industry – by cutting down the haulms and leaving the tubers in the ground until normal harvesting time.

Cara is a modern potato, but its ancestry includes the delicious Kerrs Pink, a bloodline which comes through in the colour of its eyes (this sounds eerily human, I know), in its floury character and deep flavour. Indeed, Cara is an exception to the general rule that only the old varieties have superior taste. Cara manages to give terrific yield while keeping dense texture and proper, old-fashioned potato flavour. It does, however, have its Achilles heel: it is a prey to slug damage.

Now, people who have never grown spuds will think of slugs as voracious beasts that eat all manner of growing stuff above ground, from seedlings to horseradish. Which is reason enough, even for the most environmentally aware, to banish these revolting molluscs. Slugs have a very unsavoury habit of eating potatoes from the inside, ignoring all the lush greenery above soil level. My average Cara can be half-slug damage, half-spud, so it's just as well it's a good yielder. These awful creatures enter the potato through a small hole, which looks as if it were made with a narrow knitting needle. First-timers will look at the entry wound and conclude that this is the work of wireworms, but no, this is the calling card of the small black slug who loves nothing more than to bore slimy, brown tunnels through the snow-white flesh of the potato. And the real horror of it all is that you may not even notice until you have peeled and sliced the potato.

These days, when I read the catalogues of seed potatoes I tend to look for slug-resistance and bugger the blight. At least you can do something about blight; slugs work underground and you won't know until it's too late. This is a further reason to plant your maincrop potatoes really early – perhaps even before St Patrick's Day – and protect them with fleece. Slugs are generally too busy above ground to bother about potatoes during the summer, but as soon as autumn comes they snuggle down to a subterranean feast.

I have found that a good handful or two of wood ash sprinkled around each tuber at planting time seems to discourage slugs, but I don't have any scientific evidence for this.

Now, I know that this flies in the face of conventional wisdom, but think about it: maincrop spuds don't need chitting, but they need lots of time to produce a crop because they grow slowly. If you are determined to have maincrop potatoes, plant them six inches deep in drills, like you would use for your earlies and a little further apart, in mid-March and the shoots won't appear until late April. With a bit of luck you should be able to lift a good crop in early September. The conventional wisdom is that you should leave the potatoes lying on the soil surface for a day so that the skins harden a little and they can dry off. In our climate, then, it is wise to keep an eye on the weather forecast and try to lift your crop on a fine day.

Maincrops need to be kept in a cool, dark place and do bear in mind that a hoard of potatoes is the average rat's idea of Valhalla. Don't be tempted to keep your spuds in bin-liners unless you want to use them for compost; commercial growers use paper sacks and with good reason – they allow the potatoes to breathe. You can buy potato sacks in packs of fifty at every agricultural co-op in the country, but they are unlikely to feature on the shelves of the average suburban garden centre (which is also notably short on such useful garden items as silage film, cheap fencing posts, electric fence batteries and very, very big tubs of rat poison).

Even the best-stored maincrop potatoes will start to sprout in spring because this is what they are designed by nature to do. The ones you buy are chemically treated to retard this process – something worth remembering when next you chew a crunchy, non-organic potato skin. Because the potato is programmed to use stored energy to produce new shoots, the quality of the flesh steadily deteriorates as the new planting season approaches. This is the reason why people who grow their own are likely to turn to other root vegetables and to rice at this time of the year; it is also why they greet the first of the earlies with unconcealed delight.

Apples, too, have their seasons. In an old-fashioned kitchen garden there would have been trees whose fruit came into their own in late summer, others bearing mid-season goodies and, finally, the late apples, which take their time and are ready as the first signs of winter approach. These are the ones that will keep right into the spring if you store them carefully.

It is easy, over a few years, to become familiar with a vast range of potatoes; with apples, it takes time and while I am happy to experiment with spuds I suspect that life is too short to do the same with apples (although it all depends on your age when you start and how much space you have).

Like most people, we have inherited apples. In the old

orchard at The Hermitage we had gnarled old specimens whose branches were covered in moss and lichen – the sort of thing that would have the average gardener in paroxysms of disgust. Moss and lichen on apple trees are bad news because they harbour pests and diseases. Personally, I think they look great and I'm prepared to take my chances.

We managed to identify two of the trees there: a red-flushed early eater called Norfolk Royal, which was introduced in the 1920s – crisp and juicy in late summer, but then going rather soft and floury; and the wonderful Charles Ross, equally good as a cooker when it's very new and as an eater after it ripens a bit. Neither of these varieties are for keeping – they crop too early – and nor was any of the others planted at The Hermitage. I wonder if this was the legacy of poor planning. It is very easy to select apple varieties on the basis of appearance, flavour and even name, then plant them carefully and wait for the fruit. However, it makes sense to plant trees that will give you a succession of fruit.

We have a Worcester Pearmain at Carrigeen Hill which, at its best, is one of the greatest apples of all. It crops in early autumn and, although it dates from the 1870s, is still one of the big commercial varieties, particularly in England. Bought in the shops it varies from the dull to the perfectly acceptable; plucked straight from the tree about the middle of September and after a good growing season it is pure joy, with a flavour that some apple enthusiasts compare to strawberry (and I don't). The whole point about Worcester Pearmain is that it's wonderful for a short time. A small tree will delight a small family. We also have a Katy, or Katja, which is a cross between Worcester Pearmain and James Grieve, one of the best cookers-cum-eaters. It dates from the 1960s and is grown commercially, mainly for juicing because it has an abundance of the stuff. However, Katy needs to be eaten straight from the tree when it ripens in early September. Even a few hours will see it turn soft and flabby.

Our other established tree is a Cox's Orange Pippin, the definitive Irish and British apple which, when fully ripe, is the best thing you can eat with a slice of proper farmhouse cheddar. Ready from early to mid-October, it will keep, if you store it properly, until the following March. A lot of people object to Cox's on the basis that the fruits are often very small and therefore rather fiddly for eating, but there is a way around this problem. When the fruit has set in late spring do some thinning so that the apples have room to swell. Some commercial growers resort to a chemical spray to achieve the desired result; hand-thinning avoids residues and is a much more refined process. Cox's Orange Pippin is, I believe, somewhat despised because it is, in effect, the apple with which we all grew up. It seems a shame that familiarity should breed such contempt.

Consider what Edward Bunyard had to say in *The Anatomy of Dessert*, published in 1929 and, despite the title, a lyrical account of the pleasure of fruit: 'November, then, for apple lovers, is the Cox's month, and this fruit needs no introduction or eulogy, the Château d'Yquem of apples and, to my taste, to be similarly used.' Well, times have changed, of course, and

Château d'Yquem is used mainly these days by billionaires. Cox's Orange Pippin, even when so good that it rivals this greatest of all dessert wines, is almost free.

If you have an old apple tree in the garden and are somewhat underwhelmed by what it is producing, it may be worth reinvigorating the tree. First of all, consider the shape of the thing. The branches are probably overcrowded and your first step will be do some thinning to compensate for years of neglect. As this involves wounding the tree it is essential that

the sap is not rising; confine your pruning and thinning to the depths of winter. Cut out as many small branches (up to three inches in diameter) as seem necessary, but if you need to take out any big boughs be careful not to shock the tree. Major surgery like this should be staggered over two or three years. Remember to paint the wounds with a sealer, which can be bought in any decent garden centre.

Once you have thinned the profusion of branches (remembering to season the timber and then use it in the fire so as to enjoy its wonderful perfume), it will be time to feed the tree. It is unlikely to have been fed for decades and your first step should be to secure some well-rotted manure or some garden compost. Your tree will consider this to be three-star Michelin fare. Remove the grass from an area of about three feet around the base of the trunk and mulch it liberally to a depth of two inches with whatever organic material you are using. So much for the bulky food. Plants need potash to produce fruit and you can apply either a chemical version or the free, natural potash that every household has to hand. As the blossoms are about to burst, sprinkle plenty of wood ash (or general garden bonfire ash – provided it's all organic material) over the mulch and gently water it in. Repeat this process once a month until the end of August.

You will be amazed at the tree's gratitude for such pampering; we all perform better when we feel appreciated and there is no more forlorn garden plant than an old apple tree that has never received as much as a nod since the day it was planted in the new, bare garden. There will be cases, of course, where a tree is beyond rescue and it needs to be felled. Enjoy the scent of its wood and do make sure to plant an apple tree in its place – not in exactly the same place, of course, because apples, like roses, refuse to grow in the spot where a relation has recently been situated.

As I write I am in the process of creating a new orchard. The site augurs well in that it faces south over the Bride Valley, traditionally an area that gives good apples and produces fine horses (who, in turn, feed my apples). The ploughed earth is just about ready to receive my initial selection: some more Worcester Pearmain and Cox's, to be sure; a Bramley for traditional cooking apples that keep; Irish Peach for its amazing flavour and historical significance; Egremont Russet for the wonderful density of its delicious flesh; Newton Wonder for cooking; Charles Ross for both cooking and eating; James Grieve because everybody tells me it's wonderful; and, finally, a Peasgood Nonsuch because it has a great name and the fruits are huge. And I am leaving room for more should the humour take me. Most come from Future Forests in Bantry at the other end of the county; ten years ago the more unusual varieties would have had to come from England, so there's an example of progress.

Mr Cox, who was responsible for the Orange Pippin, must have been a man of considerable patience. When he retired from brewing he entertained himself by sowing apple pips and seeing, several years later, if they produced decent fruit. This may seem an odd pursuit, but retired people of reasonable means didn't have a great deal to do in 1825 when one of Mr Cox's seedlings yielded the first Orange Pippin to bear his name. Apples do not reproduce true from seed – one of the reasons why apple trees are always grafted. Take the seeds of one of your own Cox's, sow them, nurture the plants, and you may well find yourself responsible for a new and exciting variety. You will also find yourself with a great many very ordinary, and some downright unpleasant, new apples. But, you never know.

Apple rootstocks – the plants onto which new apple trees are grafted as cuttings from identified varieties – have been bred from the wild apples that originated and still flourish in the wild forests of Kazakhstan. These days they come in different forms, each with different characteristics, so it is possible to have your apple trees growing to different sizes. Most of us nowadays prefer to grow our apples on dwarfing rootstocks so that the trees don't shoot up beyond convenient reach: M9 and M26 are the most commonly used, but M27 will keep the tree down to a mere six feet or less, which is ideal for a small garden. Grafting also means that several varieties of apple can be grown on one small tree.

'Stay me with flagons' is the biblical quote used by Maurice Healy, an Irish barrister and wine writer who was the toast of London in the 1930s, when he wrote his first book on the pleasures of the cellar. I have been tempted to use the rest of the quotation as the title of this book: Comfort me with Apples. On reflection, though, it sounds a little limiting and I doubt there are many readers who would immediately recognise the reference. But there's no doubt that a pristine apple, picked from your own tree, is very comforting indeed. And even one suffering from scab, bitter pit and all the other diseases to which apple flesh is heir, is still pretty good.

Winking at the Brim

There's not much of a living to be made in Ireland if you confine yourself to writing about food and wine. This is not because we are totally indifferent to these issues, but because our population is too small. In the United States, and to some extent in Britain, it's possible to make a decent income out of writing about even the most obscure pursuits simply because there are enough people who want to read about them.

For me, this has been a kind of blessing in disguise in that I have ended up doing lots of different things which would have been denied to me had I ended up as editor-in-chief (food and wine) for, say, *The New York Times*, or as a kind of Robert Parker, America's most influential wine commentator. I'm not sure I would have had the stamina for such a career anyway.

Mind you, many of the world's most famous wine and cookery writers don't actually produce their own books. I'm rather surprised that this issue does not receive more attention. I know lots of people who are unsung experts and talented authors who make their living out of researching and writing books which, when they appear, are credited to a more famous name. Whether or not this is a massive con job is open to debate. The books are generally good, the people who produce them are well paid, the reader gets what he wants. But the credit bothers me.

One of the ways in which I have tried to make ends meet has been getting involved in the commercial end of wine. I am, if you like, a wine writer who gets his hands dirty. One of the advantages in working at the sharp end of the wine business is that I have to resist any temptation to hole myself up in an ivory tower. There is nothing like the business of selling to concentrate the mind on what happens in the real world.

It is now ten years since I joined Pettitt's Supermarkets as wine consultant. Pettitt's is a small, family-owned company with branches in Wexford, Enniscorthy, Gorey, Arklow and Athy, and I have had tremendous fun working with them. Pettitt's stock most of the big brands, but we have developed a huge range of interesting, quirky, good value wines sourced, in the main, from small producers. Of late, we have even ventured into direct imports, which is a big step for a small company.

I have developed a very simple wine philosophy with Pettitt's: the wines we source and promote have to taste dearer than they cost. This, needless to say, is a lot harder than it sounds and it involves tasting mountains of samples. Well over 90% are rejected. Sampling that many wines may sound like fun but, believe me, it is tough work, if ultimately satisfying.

My work with Pettitt's has given me a fairly acute sense of what consumers want and where they are going. We are still a nation of New World enthusiasts, especially for the Chileans. We now drink as much red as white and look set to drink even more red over the next few years. We want decent wine as cheap as possible, but we have at last realised that we get what we pay for. Indeed, there is now a fairly large constituency who have had so many disappointments at the budget end that it can be hard to persuade them that Pettitt's cheaper wines, imported directly from the south of France, are actually very good indeed.

The problem for everyone, even for someone like me who is choosing wine for customers, is that the wine world is very big. Where do you start? How do you cover all the bases? What should you keep at home in order to drink decent wine at fair prices and always have a bottle of something that will go with whatever you're eating? There is no simple answer, of course, but here goes.

Let's assume that you want to put together a twelve-bottle cellar that will cover all eventualities. Now the difficulty here is that a little collection like this will require very regular replenishment, but if you keep on top of it you will be more than satisfied.

First things first. *Aperitifs*. Nothing dulls the tastebuds as rapidly as a gin and tonic, so let's consider some wines that are suitable for getting the gastric juices flowing.

A bottle of dry Sherry, ideally a *fino* or a manzanilla, to be kept in the fridge, would be a must for someone like me. It may be an acquired taste, but it's worth acquiring. Get hold of some Tio Pepe, perhaps, and have it at the ready. For more conventional tastes, buy a bottle of Australian dry Riesling, ideally with a screwcap rather than a cork (because it won't contaminate the wine with that awful musty smell and taste that characterise a 'corked' wine). Screwcaps are the best closure for wines that are designed to be drunk young. You may have aesthetic objections, but, in the end, this is just a form of snobbery. Dry Riesling, with its citrus-like tang and complete absence of oak, is one of the most pleasurable drinks and it goes with pre-meal nibbles as well as it does with seafood.

And speaking of seafood, you will need a wine to go with your smoked salmon, black sole, or a few prawns. The Riesling will do the trick, of course, but let's be very conventional as, to be frank, convention often has a lot of logic behind it. I hesitate to recommend a Muscadet because most of them are downright horrible, but the best of them are pure joy in a fresh, austerely dry, zingy kind of way. Buy the dearest one you can find (none of them is expensive), make sure it's not more than two years old and that it says Muscadet de Sèvres et Maine sur Lie, not just Muscadet, on the label. If your home eating habits run to oysters and mussels, your Muscadet will put on a stellar performance.

Chablis can be glorious. It can also be very dull. At its best, Chablis (the basic version, not the *premier crus* or *grand crus*) is the purest expression of Chardonnay; it has a mineral quality, a sharp, acidic backbone and what I tend to call a grown-up style. This is no blowsy, over-oaked New World Chardonnay but a wine for people who like the way it interacts with food. Again, fish and crustaceans are its natural partners. Don't buy on price and if you can find one that comes from a single *domaine* (or estate), all the better. Make sure it's not more than three years old.

You will also want a white wine that is rather more neutral, a kind of general crowd-pleaser in a multipurpose kind of way. The albarinho grape when grown in Spain's Rias Baixas region is just the ticket; it has good, firm fruit and just enough refreshing acidity. Beyond that there is maybe a suggestion of apricots but, overall, it's a discreet and well-behaved wine that doesn't scream and shout. In this respect it's the opposite of the pungent Sauvignon Blanc wines of New Zealand and the over-ripe, oaky Chardonnays that tend to get the New World a bad name.

There is, of course, no more multipurpose wine than a good rosé. It has to be dry but fruity, prettily coloured and fairly assertive. Generally speaking, the deeper the colour the more gutsy the flavour. The great advantage of proper, dry rosé is that it will accompany seafood and rare steak equally well. In fact, I love to drink rosé with lots of different things, especially duck breast that has been just cooked through and retains a hint – just a hint – of pink. Avoid Rosé d'Anjou and Portuguese versions as these tend to be sweetish.

And now to the reds where, for most Irish people, the real interest lies. You won't find better value anywhere on the planet than in the Rhône. A good Côtes du Rhône, even from big producers like Guigal and Chapoutier, is an excellent stand-by: generous on fruit, but not too much so. Small producers (look for the word '*domaine*' as a rule) often pack a lot of character into their Côtes du Rhône and you can expect a relatively soft, fruity style that is underpinned by decent tannins. You can trade up, of course, to a Côtes du Rhône Villages, such as Cairanne and Rasteau. These wines have extra stuffing. A good Vacqueyras, for example, will always be better than the cheaper Châteauneufs.

Meaty wines – by which I mean ones that cry out for rare beef or lamb – are essential in even the smallest cellar. After many years in the doldrums, Rioja seems to be back on track and a good one will deliver that magical combination of strawberryish fruit with plenty of spicy, vanilla-scented oak. The tannins should be ripe and round, too. Ribera del Duero, at its best, is like turbocharged Rioja, often with prices to match. Bad ones are rather weedy and too dear for what they are.

No cellar would be complete without the hedonistic, if somewhat one-dimensional delights of Barossa Shiraz (although McLaren Vale and the Hunter Valley often come up with the goods too). The ripe, plummy fruit and generous oak seasoning make it the wine of choice with a rare T-bone steak served with garlic butter. Shiraz is the red grape that Australia does best and it is worth paying an extra fiver or so for a really good one. Subtlety? That's simply not what Shiraz is about.

Chianti is not a meaty wine. That is not to say that it won't work well with meat, of course. Lamb cutlets with minted new potatoes, for example, are much better eaten with a Chianti Classico than with a big, beefy New World red. The only problem is that more Chianti is sold every year than could possibly be produced in the demarcated region of that name. Again, you get what you pay for. While there are some reasonably good generic Chiantis (such as the ones from Tesco), it is generally worth trading up in order to get a wine that has real complexity. There is a kind of mild austerity to good Chianti that makes it, in a sense, the red equivalent of Chablis. The same can be said of many Bordeaux *crus bourgeois*, but that's another day's work.

South Africa's wine industry has come on by leaps and bounds since the late 1990s and the more enlightened producers tend to eschew the wholly fruit-driven style of much of the New World. South Africa these days offers not just excellent value in the middle to top end of the market, but also a kind of style that is reminiscent of European wines. In other words, the wines of the Cape often deliver a complexity and a degree of interest that in other New World countries are frequently sacrificed to high alcohol and over-extraction. A good Cape Cabernet can be spookily Claret-like and it is one of these that I would select for the mini-cellar.

Finally, we have to have a bottle of red wine that is a no-brainer, a wine that can be consumed on its own, maybe while watching television and munching a packet of crisps. It may seem slightly disrespectful to Argentina's better producers, but I have to say that a fruity, smooth, easy-drinking Malbec from that part of the world is ... well ... just rather seductive.

And speaking of seduction, I have a theory that our development as wine drinkers closely shadows – for want of a better anthropological phrase – our initiation into mating rituals. I can already hear the cries of protest: is nothing sacred? Can the media think of nothing but sex?

Most of us remember, with a shudder, what we filtered through our livers when we were on the nursery slopes, so to speak, of wine. For example, in the infantile stages of wine consumption many of us will have taken pleasure in the likes of Piat d'Or and Black Tower, perhaps even Pedrotti. In sensual terms this is simple oral gratification and only in cases of seriously delayed oenological development can it be compared to what Baden-Powell and unworldly schoolmasters used to call 'beastliness'.

This age of innocence usually passes very quickly and we are seized with a youthful sense of adventure tempered only by a lack of confidence. We start to grow up. We take comfort in labels and seek security within the herd. We are in our oenological adolescence, buffeted by surging hormones ('Last week I liked white, now I like red, I'm so confused ...') and afflicted by spots ('Blue Nun? Don't pour it. It just makes it worse ...').

In time our discovery of lithe, lissom, seductive New World white wines and our shameless enjoyment of their uncomplicated immediacy is, without doubt, paralleled by our first real encounters with the opposite sex during our teens. And then, our embrace of silky, smooth, fruity, oaky red wines from Australia is very much akin to that point which some of us remember from our early twenties: when you have got over the guilt element, discovered some of the finer points of ... um ... technique and are more interested in having a damn good time than in anything more lasting. This is no time to start a cellar.

Most of us stick in what one might call our Coonawarra or Barossa stage for some time. It involves choosing partners largely for reasons of sensual satisfaction, however much we try to persuade ourselves that we are really interested in character; intellectual engagement is regarded as distinctly dodgy; spiritual empathy is soooo scary! I'm not sure exactly what the late Cyril Ray meant when he described Tavel, the rather over-priced Rhône rosé, as a 'popsy of a wine', but one suspects that he had in mind a fun-loving young woman with broad views. Like the Tavel, her company would be conducive to uncomplicated pleasure.

However, we grow up eventually – at least most of us do. As we start to drink Claret and even dare to scale the lower slopes of Burgundy, we are looking for something more than a quick ... er ... drink. We are prepared to spend some time and effort contemplating what's in the glass. We may even – if you will forgive the expression – lay something down. This is the stable, monogamous relationship stage. We have reached vinous and personal maturity. We find wine lists arriving by post, we start to buy stuff by the case, we are happy to spend rather more and drink rather less.

Clearly, a stable and meaningful monogamous relationship offers much more in the way of profound pleasures. This is where my analogy rather falls down, of course, but the parallel here is with wines which require a bit of thought and informed understanding. The great *chenin*-based whites of the Loire, for example, or young Burgundy. The better reds of the Veneto, perhaps, and old Hunter Valley Semillons. Nobody could describe such wines as voluptuous and seductive, but a relationship with them, while providing little in the way of instant gratification, will be a very enriching experience. Except in terms of one's bank balance, of course.

In an age when the *zeitgeist* is all about dumbing-down and when many intelligent, well-read people seem to feel obliged to act stoopid, it is very unfashionable to describe these kinds of wine as 'complicated', but we have no problem in using the word 'complex', which, in wine terms, is not far removed.

Grown-up wines, monogamous wines, are complex in that they offer layers of flavour and texture, subtle balances between acidity, fruit, tannin, oak and myriad other elements. Red or white, they appreciate air. Indeed, double decanting is vaguely analogous to a good, open chat with one's partner or spouse. And the best of them, like many of the best people, improve with age; even when elderly and frail they retain a certain charm.

Such are the rewards of patience and, I suppose, fidelity. Complicated wines usually repay both. These are the wines which don't immediately bowl you over; it takes a great deal more than one sip, sometimes more than a glassful and, possibly, sometimes two before the wine reveals itself to you. Frustrating or titillating? It's all in your point of view.

Complex and expensive wines may repay contemplative drinking, but the problem is that most of them need to be kept for a few years before they are at their best. While this is a process that requires considerable patience and restraint, it means that you end up with stuff that is ready to drink at a time when it would be well-nigh impossible to buy it from a retailer.

We are talking, therefore, about a cellar that is quite different in purpose and composition compared to the twelve-bottle mini-collection mentioned above. The extent of it depends primarily on your income and your enthusiasm – and, it has to be said, on using a wine merchant who can offer sound advice. Never, ever respond to those mail-shots that encourage you to invest in wine, promising exceptional returns. In my experience they tend to come from crooks. If you do receive such an offer, you may well find some useful advice on www.drinksinvest.org, a website dedicated to busting wine scams both here and in Britain.

However, what do you do if you want to start a cellar with a view to ageing some of the good stuff? Do you need an actual wine cellar, a subterranean, vaulted space in which your precious bottles can develop slowly and silently to perfection? It would be a great advantage, of course, but it's not essential.

My cellars have always been rather makeshift. There was

the Edwardian wardrobe in an unheated bedroom, the basement corridor, the deeply unpleasant spare bathroom shared with the family gerbils. Latterly, there has been talk of insulating a stable. The point is that you don't need a cellar to keep wine. Wine will be quite happy provided it is kept in the dark in a fairly cool and constant temperature.

Of course, most wine is not bought to age. Ninety-five percent of the world's wine is made for drinking straight away and most wine is consumed within twenty-four hours of being brought home. The ageing of wine is a minority sport and most of those who indulge in it concentrate on serious and usually rather expensive stuff. The fact that there are relatively inexpensive wines which will improve over a period of a few years is usually overlooked.

Ageing is a complex process at a chemical level; new compounds are formed over time, tannins soften, sediment is sometimes formed. However, most importantly, the smell and taste of the wine develop more nuances, perhaps even new flavours and, in winespeak, it acquires greater complexity.

A wine that is worth ageing must have suitable components to feed this process of what we might call complexification. Reds will have a noticeable amount of tannin, that substance which will be familiar to anyone who has ever had a mouthful of stewed tea. It will also have a reasonable degree of concentration. White wines will have a relatively high degree of acidity; indeed, if that acidity is allied to sugar, as in some of the great Chenin Blanc wines from the Loire, so much the better.

Such wines are never cheap. You will search in vain for a

€7.99 bottle that will repay ageing in the deep delved earth. However, they are not always expensive. The Loire wines just mentioned are amongst the greatest bargains on the market. German Riesling, still deeply unfashionable, offers the best value of all, while some of the traditional Hunter Valley Semillons have a staggering ability to improve for thirty years or more. A few years ago I tasted a Rothbury Estate Semillon 1977, which was just starting to hit its stride and is probably now only on the lower slopes of middle age.

Rhône reds, even a basic Côtes du Rhône from a top producer and in a good vintage, will be more interesting after three or four years in bottle. Modest red Burgundy from a good source may be gulpable when a year old and then become a sulky adolescent for two or three years. If the vintage is good, this is the sort of wine that will repay keeping until it is five or six years old. The more expensive wines of Corbieres and Minervois (which are still highly affordable) are worth keeping for as little as twelve months; however, they are so good in extreme youth that great restraint is needed.

The French tend to regard our enthusiasm for older wines as a kind of foreign necrophilia, but I have yet to meet a French person whose eyes do not light up when I produce a bottle of something with a bit of age. The wine producers themselves tend to share our enthusiasm for aged wines, doubtless because they show their wares to greater advantage.

Ageing wine, of course, should not be an obsessional occupation; you don't really have to do everything by the book. However, a few essentials must be taken into account.

Wine that has been simmered or frozen will be destroyed. The ideal temperature range for storing wine is 10ºC to 15ºC; anything above 20ºC is courting disaster. In an ideal world, try to achieve an average relative humidity of 75% but, believe me, life is probably too short. Beware of hot water pipes, teenage children, frost and impatience. Always store bottles on their sides in order to keep the cork moist and effective as a seal.

After you have aged a red wine hold the bottle against a light and check for sediment. If some is evident, simply stand the bottle upright for a few hours, draw the cork gently and pour, with a steady hand, into a clean decanter. Some enthusiasts like to use a candle to shine through the bottle; in fact, a table lamp will give you a better idea of when to stop pouring, thus keeping the sediment in the last half-inch of wine within the bottle. Practice in private, then decanting can be your party trick.

Whatever kind of cellar you create – from a wine rack in the kitchen with stuff for immediate consumption to a dark and cobwebbed treasure trove – the best advice I can give is to taste widely. Don't get into a rut. We all have our favourite regions and styles, but it is easy to forget that the world of wine is constantly changing. Experiment, be adventurous, read about wine and be prepared for an occasional disappointment. Overall, your enjoyment of wine will be greatly enhanced. But beware one pitfall. There's no bore as tedious as a wine bore. Don't become one.

Undercover

There are lots of good reasons for having a green-house. Now, let me stress that I'm not talking about the kind of structure in which you can grow myriad tropical plants and spend a fortune on heating in the process. I mean a straightforward greenhouse that offers some protection against the rigours of our beloved Irish climate, a structure that intensifies whatever sun we get during the summer, and which extends our short growing season. In other words, the kind of thing that is described by gardening experts, rather dismissively I believe, as a cold greenhouse.

Most gardeners, even those who confine their horticultural endeavours to growing a few roses, shrubs and bedding plants, want – in their heart of hearts – a greenhouse. Many of them have only the haziest idea of what they would do with such a thing, but the desire remains. If the love of your life falls into this category you should seriously consider investing in the ultimate surprise present. But do get the professionals to erect it unless you want the surprise to be more of a shock.

Well, there are lots of things you can do in the cold

greenhouse, and not the least of them is working away while the rain and the sleet lashes against the glass. Pricking out seedlings or scrubbing flower pots in the sanctuary of the greenhouse is, strange as it may seem, one of the gardener's pleasures. You can also grow a vine and get edible grapes, use it for propagation, try your hand at a few citrus bushes, get an early crop of spring bulbs. The list is extensive and one thing is sure; no matter what size of greenhouse you buy, you will forever feel that it is just a little too small.

To my mind, however, the most important thing you can do in a greenhouse is to grow food crops. A greenhouse allows you to grow prodigious quantities of tomatoes, the abundance of which can be almost shocking. You can also grow cucumbers, if you take a little care. And peppers, aubergines, even melons are a possibility.

If I could grow only one crop 'undercover', as they say, it would be tomatoes. For a start, they are essential to civilised living and the ones you grow yourself will have a much finer flavour than even the best of the organic, vine-ripened versions you can find in the supermarket. But the truly remarkable thing about growing tomatoes is how easy they are. You will end up giving away boxes of them to friends and freezing the rest in various forms. While other vegetables with an abundant habit may pall after a while – just think of courgettes – tomatoes go on delighting me through the whole growing season and, with a bit of care and planning, we can eat our own until almost Christmas.

I know, of course, that tomatoes can be grown out of doors

in Ireland. In a really good summer you can harvest a fair quantity, but the fact remains that they start fruiting very late – often in August – and the first smattering of frost will put paid to them. If you don't have a greenhouse but want to try tomatoes outdoors, choose a variety that has been bred for the purpose and put the plants in a very sheltered, sunny position, close to a south-facing wall if at all possible. Even with the best will in the world you may well end up harvesting the fruits while they are still green, but these can, of course, be ripened indoors and the flavour will still be great.

But even in a washout of a summer tomatoes will thrive in the cold greenhouse. Sow the seeds about a quarter-of-an-inch deep in a propagator towards the end of February. Alternatively, sow them in a seedtray and cover with a sheet of glass or perspex and keep it in a warm place until germination. After a few weeks, when the seedlings are large enough to handle, transplant them into individual small pots (three-inch ones are best) and keep them on a windowsill until you are ready to plant them out in the greenhouse. At this stage they should be about six inches tall.

Remember that tomatoes are tender plants; you don't want

to shock them. In most areas they can be planted out in the greenhouse around the end of March or beginning of April. You can plant them in growbags, in large (twelve-inch) pots, or straight into the soil, provided that you have enriched it by digging in some organic matter – manure, compost or even bone meal. If you plant straight into the soil, however, over several years you will need to change the soil in order to avoid a build-up of disease and a depletion of minerals.

From the time the first flowers appear, give the tomatoes a weekly feed of an organic liquid tomato fertiliser that is rich in potash. If you have wood ash, sprinkle it liberally around the base of the plants; this will provide extra potash, which is essential if the plants are to set and ripen healthy fruit.

Now, the only slightly complicated thing about growing tomatoes is the need to pinch out side-shoots and to support the plant as it gets taller. Tomato plants can reach eight feet or more in a well-sited greenhouse, so stake them well with tall bamboos and tie the plants to their supports every six inches or so.

Tomatoes are divided into two categories: the determinate or bush type, which needs little support and can be left to its own devices; and the more common, indeterminate or cordon sorts, which grow long and tall and put out a plethora of side-shoots which grow from the point where the leaves join the main stem. Your job, from the time the cordon tomato plants are only a few inches tall until they are in serious decline at the end of the growing season, will be to remove every single one of these shoots. This ensures that the plants' energy goes into producing fruit, not just more branches. It may seem wasteful, but stick to the regime. If the waste really bothers you, remember that the removed shoots can be rooted like cuttings to produce new plants. But as soon as they are independently established you will need to pinch out the shoots just the same as ever.

When I first grew tomatoes, I found it very hard to get the hang of this. I was convinced that by pinching out the side-shoots I would never get any flowers. From talking to others, I know that this is a common fear amongst tomato novices. In fact, nothing could be simpler. Every shoot that appears in the armpit of each leaf on the main stem must be removed; the flowers, on the other hand, sprout from elsewhere on the main stem, not from the leaf joints.

New plants from side-shoots are of particular interest if you want to grow tomatoes for as long as possible. If you root some in July these new plants should be producing fruit right into November, well after the originals have given up the unequal struggle. Simply stick the shoot into the soil, or into compost, and keep it reasonably moist. It will root in no time.

To ensure that your tomatoes set fruit it's a good idea, and a curiously satisfying routine, to go through the greenhouse everyday at noon (ideally) and tap each bamboo stake lightly for a few seconds. This will help the pollen to get into position to do its work. If the atmosphere is very dry in the greenhouse, pollination can be tricky, so it's always a good idea to water the path in order to create some humidity. You can also spray the plants themselves with water every couple of days.

When a tomato has set six trusses of fruit it's a good idea to pinch out the top of plant so that all the food and energy goes into the developing fruit. Having said that, I often let a few tomato plants set as much fruit as they want and I've never been disappointed by the quality.

Tomato flowers may not be much to look at, but there is something very attractive, to me at any rate, about the green pungency of the leaves when you brush against them. Together with the aroma of raspberries, meadowsweet, warm sand and the tang of generous bunches of fresh herbs, this is the essential scent of my Irish summer.

Tomato leaves and stems have millions of tiny glands that secrete a green liquid. You will be amazed at the hue of the water when you scrub your hands after tending to the tomatoes: it is brilliant, viridian green.

Tomatoes which don't ripen on the plant – the ones that come at the very end of the season – no matter how small they are, will ripen indoors if you keep them in a warm place, preferably close to some ripe bananas. The reason for this is highly scientific: fruit ripens because of warmth, not sunlight, and ripe fruit releases a gas that encourages unripe fruit to follow suit. As Michael Caine would say, not a lot of people know that.

Cucumbers are exotic, and most gardeners are somewhat scared of them. I know I was when I first tried to grow them. In fact, once you take account of the fact that cucumbers are very tender plants and you sow and grow them accordingly, they are a doddle. And prolific to boot. Two cucumber plants will provide you with an ongoing glut from the end of June until October.

There is nothing to be gained, except frustration, in sowing cucumbers too early. I thought I was being very clever one year when I got them started in February, but I had not reckoned with the fact that it was too cold to put them out into the greenhouse until April. The result was four triffid-like cucumber plants sprawling around the kitchen and basking in the glow of the Aga. They were so big by April that it was almost impossible to move them into their permanent position without wreaking havoc with the stems, to say nothing of the contents of the kitchen.

These days I sow cucumbers indoors around mid-March. The new F1 hybrid varieties seem to germinate in record time, and within six weeks they are a decent size to plant out in the polytunnel. Sow the seeds individually in three-inch pots and keep them warm. They need to be kept moist, but there is nothing surer to kill them stone dead than a dollop of cold water straight from the tap. Use tepid stuff instead and make sure the young roots don't get waterlogged or they will rot before you can say pickled gherkins.

Before planting cucumbers in the greenhouse, or polytunnel for that matter, dig a hole big enough to accommodate comfortably a bucket of well-rotted manure or garden compost; tread this down and refill the hole with soil so that you have a mound. Plant the cucumber in the top, stake it with a tall bamboo, to which it is then tied. As the plant grows, keep tying it at intervals so that it has plenty of support.

Cucumbers put out trailing shoots every few inches along the main stem. If unchecked these will head off into the wide blue yonder, producing fruit at various points along the way. Most gardeners allow each of these shoots to produce two flowers – and therefore, in time, two fruits – and snip off the tips. I hate to see such abundance thwarted and let some shoots go on for metres, supported on wires. As a result, all our friends and relations dread the cucumber season and never leave Carrigeen Hill without armfuls of the things.

Start your cucumbers by sowing four seeds in separate pots; this will allow for an attrition rate of 50%. Two cucumber plants are enough for even the most avaricious cucumber enthusiast, or large vegetarian family. And remember to choose an all-female variety. Old-fashioned cucumbers don't have a taste advantage over the new ones and they have a curious Achilles heel: they bear both male and female flowers and the male ones have to be pinched out as soon as they appear. This is because female cucumber flowers, the ones with the tiny, embryonic cucumber behind them, become unbearably bitter if fertilised with pollen from the male. This process requires constant vigilance and, believe me, there are lots of more interesting things to do.

If you have never

had a home-grown cucumber, the chances are that you will be completely unaware of its exquisite scent when freshly sliced; in my book, this heady perfume is right up there with the old-fashioned roses. And cucumber sandwiches, which must be made with Brennan's white sliced pan (one of the few useful functions for such stuff), crusts removed, according to my demanding specification, are one of the best things about summer. Especially if consumed on the lawn, just out of direct sunlight, with a cup of *lapsang souchong* tea. Fastidious? *Moi?*!

Melons, like courgettes, are, of course, a close relative of the cucumber and once I had mastered the humble cucumber I decided to have a go at this great exotic. The variety I chose was Blenheim Orange, a variety bred at Blenheim Palace (the birthplace of Winston Churchill) during the great days of the grand greenhouse. I didn't hold out much hope for the crop, planted as it was in a mere polytunnel on a hillside in County Cork. And, I am ashamed to say, my melon crop was sadly neglected; weeds grew up around them as I flitted about attending to other, more mundane plants.

However, by late summer I was harvesting a dozen or so small, green-/grey-skinned melons, each about the size of a bowling ball, with fabulously aromatic and lusciously sweet orange flesh. I had simply treated them like cucumbers until the point where I planted them out. Strictly speaking, I should have trained them on supports, pinched out each shoot as soon as a fruit was formed, fed them lavishly and pollinated them by hand. I did none of this; Heaven knows how many melons I would have harvested had I done so. These days I continue to grow them with benign neglect and the results are delicious.

I'm not convinced that it is easy to grow red peppers in an Irish greenhouse or polytunnel, but I am determined to keep trying. Peppers, in themselves, are dead easy. Sow them and plant them out as you would tomatoes, but you can space them more tightly. There is no need to pinch out any shoots, but they appreciate being staked and tied and they like plenty of feed, especially potash. Most of our crops have been green, but a few have changed, painfully slowly, to a kind of intense orange. As a result, I have become quite fond of the taste of green peppers, something which I thought would continue to elude me. Sweated in olive oil with some garlic and fresh onions, they go very well with steak.

Aubergines have been reasonably successful with me, but only since I have tried growing early-maturing varieties like Moneymaker, which have some chance of reaching maturity during our all too short summer. Again, they are sown and planted out like tomatoes. Thereafter, all you have to do is to pinch out the growing tip after they reach about eighteen inches. Mine, to date, have been much smaller than the glossy ones that you see in the shops, but they have had exquisite flavour. Rumour has it that the white-skinned varieties (the ones that gave the Americans the idea of calling them eggplant) do better in these islands and I may get around to growing them.

You can, as I mention elsewhere, grow sweetcorn outdoors in Ireland; there are several varieties which have been bred specially to take account of the fact that our summers and those of the southern United States are quite different. But if you have the space in a polytunnel or a greenhouse you get much more consistent results, with bigger cobs and, I think, more taste. I sow the seeds individually in modules in the polytunnel in late March, and have always been amazed at the speed with which they come up. Plant them when they reach four inches or so on a one-foot square grid in soil that has loads of organic matter dug in, and keep them very well watered from start to finish.

I have mentioned, in passing, our polytunnel, a structure that represents one of our best-ever investments. If you hanker after a greenhouse and have plenty of space, you may want to consider a polytunnel yourself. Ours measures eighteen feet by thirty-six feet, a much larger space than I could possibly have afforded to cover with glass. These days the hoops last for yonks and the PVC sheeting will give you at least five years before you notice any serious diminution in the light coming through.

There are pros and cons, of course. You will get lots of condensation in a polytunnel; this means that (a) you will get dripped upon when you least expect it, (b) you will have to ventilate very thoroughly so as to avoid moulds, and (c) if plants don't like being showered with drips of cold water, and there are many that don't, you have to be careful where you plant them. Polytunnels drip from the apex of the roof, so the major dripping activity is confined to the middle; otherwise, the condensation simply runs down the inside of the PVC, ensuring that anything planted along the edge of the tunnel gets a modest daily watering.

It has to be said that most people don't consider the polytunnel to be a thing of great beauty; this doesn't bother me as whenever I see one nestling amidst the fields, I know that someone is doing some serious growing. This is always a cheering thought.

Greenhouses, by comparison, can be delightful to look at; I love the old-fashioned sort where the base is built of red brick and the frame on top – the light area – is made of white-painted wood. Maintenance on these structures is crippling, both physically and financially, and while they look great you are always better going for a stainless steel- or aluminium-based greenhouse. The Rolls-Royce version comes from Hartley Botanic in England. When I asked them to quote for my dream greenhouse, in maintenance-free materials and high-performance glass, and converted the sum into euro, I realised that I could build a house – a domestic house with three bedrooms – for the price. But, if I were to win the Lotto …

You don't need a greenhouse or a polytunnel in order to grow crops under cover; it's easier, of course, because you can stand up inside these structures, and they afford you, the gardener, some shelter as well as the plants. Cloches, frames, fleece: all of these inexpensive options will help you to extend the growing season, first by warming up the soil and making it more conducive to seed germination, then by enhancing temperatures, and finally by keeping the frost out as autumn glides into winter. If you set up a simple plastic tunnel cloche (essentially a tiny polytunnel) and cover the soil surface within it with black plastic, which absorbs heat, you can get a headstart. I would suggest you do this during January. Within a month, unless the weather is highly unseasonal, you can take out the black plastic and sow crops like lettuce and carrots a good month to six weeks before you would even begin to contemplate such a move outside.

Melons do well in cloches and frames as do – perhaps surprisingly – tomatoes. Now, tomatoes grow upwards rather than outwards and you will need to encourage the plants to grow along the cloche rather than skywards, but the results are well worth it. Cucumbers are not quite so successful in this context, but remember there are good outdoor or ridge cucumbers which will fruit happily even in a damp Irish summer.

My first job in the polytunnel each January is to sow a fresh patch of rocket; by the end of the month I sow the first of the cut-and-come again lettuce and saladings; a row of peas goes in by mid-February, as does the first of the beetroot and a row of new potatoes, which have been sprouting since Christmas. With a bit of luck I'll have courgettes ready to plant by mid-March, a good six weeks before you can plant them outside. Early beet, carrots and fresh herbs are another bonus of having a space in which to grow undercover, whether it's a greenhouse, tunnel, or cloche.

There are lots of things I want to grow in the tunnel, but many of them will have to wait until my retirement: chrysanthemums with their brassy colours and intensely scented foliage, and the lush, decadent but still rather tasteful Malmaison carnations. Perhaps even cut flowers for the house, a little out of season. I may even, in the fulness of time, manage to plant some blue hyacinths and get them to flower, right on the button, at Christmas. And not with leggy stems that need support but rather short, stocky, plump florescences of impeccable colour and exquisite scent. Gardening is all about optimism and this last aspiration is about as optimistic as it gets.

The optimism involved in gardening under cover, however, is usually easily justified. It combines the always-look-on-the-bright-side and let's-give-it-a-go attitudes of the keen grower with a certain insurance. If you enjoy seeing things grow, even in a very small way, growing under cover will be hugely rewarding. Trust me. I'm a maniacal convert.

In the Kitchen

Eleanour Sinclair Rohde was one of the most prolific garden writers of the twentieth century and an expert on the ancient herbals. Books like *A Scented Garden* and *Gardens of Delight*, both published in the 1930s, made unlikely but rather formative reading during my teenage years. I was very grown-up, however, when I came upon her *Vegetables and their Cultivation,* which is one of the best and most thorough books on kitchen gardening that has yet appeared.

Like the great Gertrude Jekyll, Rohde was much given to issuing pretty tough directions and I dread to think what it must have been like to work as an under-gardener for them. They casually demand that you 'trench to a depth of three feet', for example, a process that would break both the spirit and the back of the modern gardener.

Eleanour Sinclair Rohde clearly enjoyed her vegetables and the book contains many good recipes although, being of its time, a lot of them involve boiling followed by the application of white sauce. Where things look tricky, the author stresses that the cook 'must be instructed clearly to do' ... such and such a thing. Those were the days.

By the time the formidable WE Shewell-Cooper had become a best-selling gardening author, after the Second World War, times had changed. When writing about certain vegetables he will casually remark that 'the housewife prefers' a particular variety. Clearly, cook had gone by the 1950s; or perhaps Shewell-Cooper was just less posh than Rohde!

Anyway, it amuses me in a faintly nostalgic kind of way when books like these betray the accepted notion of the day, *viz.* that men grew vegetables and women, married or employed, cooked them. It's not like that in our house.

Of course, there's nothing unusual about men cooking these days. In that respect there are certainly equal opportunities, even if women are generally more assiduous about the cleaning-up afterwards. But I'm now old enough to remember when males, other than chefs, steered clear of the saucepans. In the 1970s, the world was still a very old-fashioned place. My mother was, I think, quite pleased that I could cook reasonably competently. But when I was about sixteen and didn't go to the local disco (I really just couldn't take Donny Osmond and the Bay City Rollers), she must have assumed the worst. Cuttings from *The Catholic Herald* and *The Tablet* used to appear around the house, each of them a dire warning on the immorality of homosexuality.

Looking back, and knowing what I do now about teenagers, I am amazed that I didn't blow a fuse. I simply found it very funny. And I had an idea that an ability to cook could well be a point in my favour with the opposite sex.

My mother was an excellent cook, with a really visceral appreciation of good food. My childhood memories of the kitchen – apart from the trauma induced by my being a somewhat picky eater – are of the smell of apple pie being baked on a Sunday morning, the luxurious tang of home-made mayonnaise with rosy pink salmon (sent up by a family friend from the River Moy), and the distinctive whiff of hot flour from the underside of freshly baked brown soda bread. These are the key memories and they can set off an almost painful bout of nostalgia.

There are others, too, of course. The battered copy of *Full and Plenty* by Maura Laverty, in which the recipes are interspersed with rather folksy little stories which invariably involve good, home-made food solving all kinds of human problems, many of them romantic. The eternally comforting smell of roast beef with its honeycomb of crisp, golden fat. Or simply the wake-up call of smoked bacon grilling in the morning. But many of my most vivid childhood memories, in the area of food, concern Christmas.

My paternal grandmother was, by all accounts, a formidable lady. She was distantly related to Admiral Beatty who, as the historically minded will recall, adopted a firm line in the Battle of Jutland; it's not off the stones he licked it. The only recorded occasion on which her composure deserted her was when she ran an errand for my mother, who was making the Christmas puddings. My grandmother duly ended up entering the public bar of The Cat & Cage in search of a bottle of Guinness. It was just after opening time and the curate gave her a broad wink before opening the bottle and gently pouring it into a glass. She nearly passed away.

Guinness, you see, was an essential ingredient in the family pudding, along with Power's whiskey, a great deal of butter, an equal quantity of suet, a mountain of dried fruit, oceans of breadcrumbs and enough spices to stock an old-fashioned apothecary's shop. It was great stuff but, like the smell of Bewley's coffee roasting (those were the days), the ritual of preparation was even better than the consumption. For days (and nights) the kitchen walls dripped with condensation as the boiling was done.

The consumption was always a bit of a trial on the day. First there was the prawn cocktail with Marie Rose sauce, then the turkey and everything that went with it and, penultimately, the pudding. It was a solid pudding, the kind of pudding that came not so much in slices as in ingots. It was served before the Christmas cake, which was enrobed in a good inch of home-made marzipan, or 'almond paste' as we always called it. The pudding, however, came into its own in the days after Christmas. Thick slices would be fried gently in butter until the outside became lightly caramelised, then doused in chilled cream, or lathered with hot Bird's Custard.

The Christmas morning repast was taken after Midnight Mass, at about 1.00am. For some long-lost reason, this meal always kicked off with grapefruit, an item so exotic in those days that it usually came in a large tin. At no other time of the year did we brave the acidic tang of this austere citrus fruit, but at Christmas it was compulsory. Needless to say, it was followed by bacon, sausages, eggs and both black and white pudding. My mother was generous with love, and food was just one expression of it. Particularly at Christmas.

I was, as I say, a picky eater and I still have an unusually small appetite, but I have always enjoyed good food. Maybe I was destined to be a restaurant critic. In fact, my pickiness persisted right through adolescence and into early adulthood. Some of my nearest and dearest would argue that I have yet to shake it off.

I didn't really eat fish until I was well into my twenties; I was converted by having a taste of a black sole in the old Trudi's in Dún Laoghaire and have never looked back. Mind you, I'm not keen on mackerel and would never willingly eat herring, which suggests a distinct absence of Viking blood. It was around the same time that I suddenly discovered that nuts, fresh ones at any rate, taste great. This great truth had eluded me for years. The big cabbage revelation came when I was in Germany about ten years ago. Now I even grow the stuff. Turnips, as distinct from swedes, became acceptable fodder only in the last couple of years.

I think my poor mother was convinced that somebody who couldn't face corned beef would never grow up strong and healthy. She also believed that offal was, to a large extent, the staff of life. These I have cheerfully eschewed right up to the present and I don't plan changing now.

But, as I never cease to point out to people, I eat snails with relish (well, garlic butter, in fact). Balance this shocking revelation against the fact that I once thought Cheddar cheese (well, you know, plastic-wrapped Irish Cheddar) was too strong. Until the age of eighteen I stuck rigidly to Three Counties and Primula. Now, I have to ration myself and firmly believe that you can't beat a mature goat's cheese that you can smell in the next county.

Children need to be exposed to good food. They don't need to be forced to eat it, or even to try it. The philosophy of good food will eventually work its magic, even if it results in a very delayed explosion. Some parents maintain that JK Rowling's loving descriptions of food in the *Harry Potter* books help to whet the juvenile appetite for dietary adventure. Time, soon, for pumpkin pasties!

The point is that kids who drive you mad with their fastidious attitude to food, and even madder with their refusal even to try something new, will grow up and most of them will become more adventurous. Some of them may end up writing about food if they don't watch out ...

Food is a sensual thing and I suspect that my senses were sufficiently stimulated during childhood to encourage me to try my own hand at cooking. My first attempts involved soup, the slicing and sweating of vegetables in butter, and I can still remember the aromas being released and intensified with the cooking process. I graduated to making Mornay sauce – béchamel enriched with cheese and a little mustard powder. So besotted did I become with this stuff that I blanketed all sorts of things, from hardboiled eggs to fried sausages, topped off with crushed Tayto crisps and a sprinkling of grated cheese. It was a very 1970s thing – I think I got the idea from the *Hamlyn All Colour Cookbook* – and still relish the sight of one of these dishes bubbling and nicely browned on top. I'm not sure I'd manage to eat more than a spoonful these days, and I certainly wouldn't use sausages!

By my mid-teens I would take charge of the kitchen when my mother went to visit my sister, who was then living in Scotland. My father, very much a grilled cutlet man, would endure my experiments, which included *Boeuf bourgignonne* (my rather basic interpretation of the classic Burgundy stew with beef, bacon and red wine) and spaghetti bolognese. Both of these dishes, unknown to my father, contained a smidgin of garlic, a substance which my mother was brave enough to use in those dark culinary days, but always treated it with extreme caution as if it could cause severe physical harm. From a fairly early stage I took a shine to garlic and would use prodigious quantities, having taken stock of the fact that most garlophobes don't really notice once the stuff is cooked and combined with other flavours.

Johann and I discovered a mutual enthusiasm for good food when we met and when we were first married we used to cook complicated and extravagant dishes, sometimes taking all day to prepare dinner for friends. I suppose it was a rather

1980s thing. When children came along we changed tack and, at the same time, discovered that the best food is very often the simplest, provided that the raw materials are first rate. We traded in elaborate recipes for simply prepared but bloody good grub and I, for one, have no intention of changing. Not only is such food relatively easy to prepare, it is also surprisingly quick.

Having said that, when preparing some simply cooked fish or some marinaded and grilled meat, I like to take my time about it. I don't like to feel that I have to beat the clock. I like to have the kitchen to myself, with the radio on, and little of great import to think about. The ritual of first picking the vegetables, then the slicing and seasoning is very soothing. However, I would be the first to admit that preparing the evening meal with small children around your feet and a tight schedule (and budget) to meet is not exactly a definition of either fun or relaxation. It is a pity, though, if the preparation of food becomes just a chore. I have a theory, incidentally, that food prepared for your family with a conscious feeling of love, concern and nurturing is tastier and more nutritious. In fact, I firmly believe that science, in the fulness of time, will prove this.

Because we have our own vegetables and some fruit, these staples play an important role in the kitchen during those months of the year when they flourish. Even in the dark days of winter, in that lengthy hungry gap, having our own root vegetables, leeks, onions, shallots and salad gives us a dangerously smug feeling of satisfaction. But by the time the first of the sprouting broccoli is ready, in March if we're lucky, it tastes even better than it possibly could be in cold reality because it's different and new.

Like the first of the new potatoes, which we harvest from the polytunnel in early May, broccoli spears need only be steamed and dressed in melted butter or really good olive oil and sprinkled with a little sea salt and a few twists of the pepper mill. The same, oddly enough, can be said of many vegetables: broad beans, peas, young leeks, chard stalks, artichoke hearts, sliced spring cabbage, tender young carrots, baby beetroot, tiny courgettes, even sprouts. The simpler the better.

Our first 'fruit' of the year, a very early strain of rhubarb, is ready by the end of January when it is instantly turned into a crumble and served with Bird's Custard; no complicated homemade custard does the job quite so well. Gary Rhodes once told me that he blends some Bird's Custard into his rich, homemade version so as to evoke a kind of childhood food memory in his restaurant customers.

Currants, both black and red, go into jam as do many of the raspberries. But raspberries are at their best when fully ripe and darkening to almost purple: you sprinkle them with just a touch of caster sugar and drizzle some cream over. But they are also an essential ingredient in summer pudding. I take equal quantities of raspberries and currants (mainly black, but with some red for added tartness), place them in a saucepan with just enough sugar to take the edge off them and cook briefly over a low heat until the juices really flow and the fruit begins to break up a little.

I take the fruit off the heat and turn my attention to the pudding bowl. First, it must be lined with clingfilm, then with slices of white bread (sliced pan or batch loaf is fine). The slices are overlapped slightly and one is kept back to go over the top. The fruit and all its sweetened juices are then poured into the bread-lined pudding bowl and a final slice of bread placed on top. On top of this goes a saucer and a weight of some sort so that the contents of the bowl are under a little pressure. I stand the bowl in a dish, which will catch any drips, and leave it in a cool place overnight.

When it is time to serve the pudding I up-end it onto a deep dish and lift off the bowl with the aid of the clingfilm. At this stage the bread will have developed a mottled red appearance. I use the juice that has dripped out to even the colour by spooning it over. I serve slices of summer pudding with a jug of pouring cream. The title is deserved. This, for me, is the very essence of summer, perhaps after some poached wild salmon, or a risotto of new vegetables.

Gooseberries tend to end up being made into fool in our household. We simply stew the fruit with sugar (how much is a matter of taste, but gooseberries are very sour even when fully ripe) with a few elderflower heads. Elder blooms as the gooseberries ripen and the combination is somehow much greater than the sum of the parts. The elder imparts a very strange but delicious spiciness that reminds me a little of Gewurztraminer wines. When the fruit has cooled, we remove the elderflowers and fold it in lots of very stiffly whipped cream. We often serve this gooseberry fool with home-made buttery shortbread biscuits for dunking and dipping. If you are stewing frozen gooseberries later in the summer, you can substitute meadowsweet blossoms for elderflowers.

To get proper, old-fashioned strawberry flavour you have to grow your own, for the simple reason that modern commercial varieties are bred for shelf-life rather than taste. We eat ours, which are Cambridge Favourite, simply with cream, occasionally dressing them in a touch of orange juice, Campari, or even vodka. Bizarrely, black pepper works wonders when freshly ground over a bowl of strawberries, a trick we learned from Johann's late uncle, Telford McKeever. We don't add strawberries to summer pudding on the basis that they tend to get lost and detract from the texture.

Autumn is the time for blackberries and if we picked all of them that grow on our land the quantity would probably run into tonnes. We eat them very simply: stewed with a little sugar and served with cream or custard, or made into a fool. The colour never ceases to amaze me.

Dessert apples are best eaten, in our experience at any rate, either on their own or with a few slices of really good, hard cheese; the combination of saltiness and sweetness, crunch and cheese is marvellous. We sometimes make a *tarte tatin*, the classic French upside-down tart in which the pastry is topped with caramelised apples, but generally we like our apples raw. Bramleys are a different matter, of course, and no other cooker produces the true flavour of an Irish apple pie.

One twist on the apple pie theme, however, can be achieved by adding some slices of quince. I don't think I have ever seen this remarkable fruit for sale in Ireland, and it's not often one encounters it in a garden for that matter. This, in itself, is odd as the quince tree bears the most beautiful, delicate pink flowers in spring. It is a relative of the apple and the pear, is quite hardy, and all it asks is a reasonably fertile soil and a consistent water supply.

The fruits are pear-shaped, usually yellow and quite hard even when ripe. They add a wonderful extra dimension and a reddish hue to apple pie if added in a proportion of about one part quince, peeled and thinly sliced, to four or five parts apple. You can also make quince jelly, or even the *membrillo* quince paste of Spain, if you feel so inclined. So far, we have confined ourselves to adding quince to apples; indeed, if you leave a few ripe quinces in a box of apples the scent will infuse the whole lot.

Most pears need to be picked before they are ready to eat and will ripen fully only when they are off the tree. The perfection of a ripe Doyenne du Comice, to my mind the ultimate variety, is unsurpassable. With Conference and other rather ordinary pears we are inclined to core and slice them and then cover with a sweet batter. This is the classic French *clafoutis* and if you want to be really authentic you can sprinkle a few flaked almonds over the top.

The birds tend to get the lion's share of our plums and the few that survive are eaten greedily just as they are, the sweetness of the juice balanced by the distinctive slight bitterness of the skin. The variety we grow is Victoria, the commonest of them all, but deservedly so as its flavour is superb and you don't need a further variety for pollination.

I am looking forward with some trepidation to the first of the medlars, a very rare fruit in Ireland and pretty unusual in England, too. This small tree produces round fruit about the size of a Cox's Orange Pippin, but, curiously, they are not edible when picked in late autumn. They must be 'bletted'. This means that they are stored for several months until the inside of the fruit has gone off and starts fermenting. The medlars turn brown and expand at this stage; perhaps 'bletting' is a corruption of bloating?

Medlars are sliced open and the brown, rather aromatic flesh is scooped out with a spoon. The flavour is definitely a little strange, if sweetish, and I suspect this peculiar fruit is an acquired taste. Well, I shall do my best.

Fruit and vegetables are no problem, although they do take some effort. They are on our doorstep. Friends often ask if we intend producing our own meat as the next step, and the answer is yes. It would be great to have our own chickens (and even better to have our own eggs), but we live in a very foxy neighbourhood. The best efforts of the Conna Harriers and the West Waterford Hunt seem to have little impact on the fox population and there seems little point in providing sacrificial poultry. Besides, we have a great producer of organic chicken and eggs only a few miles away.

Bigger animals are another matter, of course. We could certainly have a pig, or rather a pair of pigs because they are sociable animals and need company. The main problem, but not an insurmountable one, is that we don't fancy eating animals with whom one has had a friendly and fairly intense relationship, as is the way with pigs. The best way around this difficulty would be to team up with other free-range pork fanciers who are in the same position. We could each raise a couple of pigs, send them off for slaughter, and then swap after the terrible deed is done. You see, we are sentimental only up to a point.

The problem with beef is different. We could buy a couple of bullocks in the spring, let them graze on our delicious grass and then send them off to their doom as winter approaches. However, frozen beef never seems to cook as well as fresh. Our butcher has a cradle to ... er ... counter operation and his beef is just about the best you can buy. So, we're not convinced that we need to go into livestock in a big way.

There was wild talk once – mainly from our fishing friends – of stocking the pond with trout, but, to be honest, we get great fish from the Ballycotton Seafood Company and at a fraction of the price we were paying in Dublin.

So, what do we do with the excellent poultry, meat and fish that is so abundant in our neck of the woods? As with our vegetables, we keep it simple.

Fish is simply baked, or floured and fried in olive oil, served with lemon and, occasionally, melted butter and capers. Pork is roasted with sage or rosemary (and belly slow-roasted with Chinese spices); chops are marinated in lemon and ginger, then grilled. Beef is roasted on the bone until still perfectly rare in the centre and served with eye-wateringly fresh horseradish cream and proper Yorkshire pudding, crisp and bulging. Fillet or T-bone steaks (rarely striploin) are smeared with olive oil, sprinkled with sea salt and very coarse black pepper, before being seared on a very hot barbecue (regardless of time of year and occasionally under an umbrella). Leg of lamb is either cooked in the conventional way or boned, opened out and marinated in lemon juice, garlic, olive oil, thyme and pepper before being sealed on the barbecue; it then goes into a hot oven for twenty minutes and is served pink.

Roast chicken is far and away the family favourite. We put a bunch of fresh herbs inside, squeeze a whole lemon over the bird, sprinkle with a little salt and then cook it in the usual way. The flavour is so good that it needs nothing else apart from the company of some fresh vegetables. Sometimes we find that friends who are used to the rather bland flavour of conventional chicken can be shocked by the intensity of taste; it can be almost gamey.

Good free-range chicken thighs are used in rich, earthy curries redolent of cardamom, cumin and ginger, served with fresh carrot chutney. During the shooting season we skin pheasants (plucking is a terrible chore), draw and joint them, then fry the pieces in olive oil before dumping them into a casserole with a bay leaf, a few chopped onions, lots of garlic and some fried, diced bacon. Then the whole lot bubbles away for hours in the Aga until tender and utterly seductive on the nose.

Free-range duck legs are always on sale in the English Market in Cork and we rarely visit the city without stocking up on them. We tend to cook them very slowly in a casserole with finely diced onion, carrot, celery, garlic and a dash of white wine for moisture. When the meat is literally falling off the bone we put them under the grill to crisp the skin and meanwhile combine what is left in the casserole with some cooked lentils. Served with a green salad this is a complete meal, and according to our calculations you can feed two for less than €5 on it.

Johann has spent years perfecting the domestic pizza, that is, the pizza you make at home without the benefit of a proper pizza oven. The dough and the toppings are vitally important, of course, but so is temperature, particularly in getting the base to cook to that crisp perfection after which we all yearn. Put a pizza, no matter how good, onto a normal baking sheet in a domestic oven and you may well end up eating something reasonably pleasant; but it will be to real pizza as Easi-Singles are to farmhouse Cheddar.

Johann's way around this problem – of getting the base hot enough to cook properly – came about when she found an off-cut of steel plate, the sort of material that is often used to cover holes in the pavement when excavations are going on. Very heavy, and several millimetres thick, it is placed at the top of the oven at gas mark 9, or in the Aga roasting oven, for half-an-hour or so. At this point it is as hot as it's going to get and the pizza can be slid onto its scorching surface. The general oven temperature, at the top of the scale, is enough to cook the topping; this fierce bottom heat is what you need to complete the picture because a pizza base is arguably even more important than its topping.

Johann makes thin pizzas – the idea being that they cook quickly and that's what pizza is all about despite newfangled notions of 'deep pan' and what have you. And the topping needs to be thin, too. We have three favourites. Firstly there is the no-tomato version which, instead, is topped solely with fresh Ardsallagh goat's cheese, caramelised onions and chopped sage; this is the best possible accompaniment to cool, pungent Sauvignon Blanc.

Then there's the perfectly conventional one with tomato, mozzarella and basil (added at the end; you don't want this delicate herb incinerated) which the Italians call *tricolore* after the colours of their flag, or *margherita* after Heaven knows who, possibly one of their queens. To this we occasionally add slices of pepperoni sausage, *kabanossi*, or, if the multicultural mood takes us, *chorizo,* which makes a surprisingly delicious pizza.

Finally, there's the rocket pizza which at first strikes guests dumb, then invariably seduces them. Very simply, you take a margherita, without the basil or the sausage, straight from the oven and top it with a mulch of young, tender rocket leaves that you have first dressed with good olive oil, a squeeze of lemon juice and a sprinkling of sea salt. Eat it quickly, before the rocket completely wilts; the contrast between the cool green top and the hot, tomatoey base is glorious.

I discovered this pizza in a little café in Milan when I was shooting a corporate video for Guinness Pubs International. During the day I was delivering carefully scripted pieces to camera about these oases of soda bread and Irish stew, but at meal times I would adjourn for rocket pizza and a few glasses of brand-new, purple Oltrepo Pavese served in a jug. Johann's version is just as good.

I mentioned that one of my early cooking experiences involved spaghetti bolognese, that staple of bedsit fare and icon of the 1970s' kitchen. Terrible crimes have been perpetrated in the form of a sauce masquerading under the name of bolognese, some of them televised, as in the case of the commercial that shows an Oxo cube being crumbled into a red, bubbling panful.

Memories of spag. bol. are so painful for many sensitive cooks that they pretend it has never existed; they airbrush it out of their personal culinary history and, if the subject ever comes up, mutter about it never being seen in Italy.

Which is a load of cobblers, of course. *Sugo al carne*, or meat sauce, is far from unknown in Italy and they make a bit of a thing about it in Emilia–Romagna, of which Bologna, hotbed of Communism and chunky food, is the regional capital. I realised pretty early on that frying off some chopped onion and minced beef, adding a can of tomatoes and some mixed herbs and hoping for the best was probably not the best way to achieve authenticity. And I hankered after authenticity having had the real thing on a school trip to Rome in 1975. One day we went to Frascati, where we ate at a very simple little restaurant; it was actually someone's living room. Our hostess produced a vast bowl of pasta dressed with something vaguely resembling bedsit bolognese. But what a flavour!

Well, it took me many years to get it right, and I have to acknowledge the assistance of Elizabeth David and Marcella Hazan, two writers who could not be more different in style: David, rather cool and aloof in a very English way; Hazan, very matey and passionate in an entirely Italian way. Anyway, I make my *sugo al carne* like this.

I take some pancetta or Continental streaky bacon, slice it finely and brown it slowly in a little olive oil. I then take it out, using a slotted spoon and lightly brown some finely chopped onions and a little celery in the remaining fat. Then I throw in the minced beef and return the bacon to the pan and stir until it has all cooked through. Then I add a good glass or two of dry white wine, a few cloves of garlic very finely chopped, and cook on a high heat until most the liquid has evaporated. Then I add a couple of cans of chopped organic tomatoes and reduce the heat to a bubbling simmer. At this stage I usually take a potato masher to the nascent sauce and use it to break up the tomato pieces and any of the mince that has clumped together. Then I season with lots of black pepper, a little salt (depending on the bacon) and a bay leaf.

Having let it simmer on the stove for half-an-hour or so, I put the saucepan, covered, in the bottom oven of the Aga (or in the cooker at gas mark S) and leave it there for at least four hours, preferably ovenight. Sometimes, if I'm feeling exceptionally decadent, I will add a knob of butter and a little milk or cream before it goes into the oven. The difference between the bedsit version, which sustained me during my Trinity days, and this one is immeasurable and yet, taking into account the ravages of inflation, I'm pretty sure it costs much the same.

A lot of nonsense is talked about pasta. It is supposed to be a terribly healthy food. Well, it's as healthy as any highly refined food. Pasta is fine now and then, but its potent payload of concentrated carbohydrate means that we should treat it with a degree of caution. The same goes for pizza, of course.

But even more nonsense is talked about forms of pasta. Glenageary gastronomes and Ballsbridge *bon viveurs* will tell you that fresh pasta is the only sort to consider serving. They then proceed to unwind reams of leaden putty and invariably end up overcooking the stuff. Frankly, there is very little fresh pasta in Ireland worthy of the name (one glorious, happy, brilliant exception being the stuff they serve at Romano's in Dublin's Capel Street; another comes from Iago in Cork, especially the ravioli). Good dry pasta is just as good as good fresh pasta, it's just different, as Marcella Hazan, to whom I defer in such matters, insists. Mind you, it's important to buy a decent brand: De Cecco is the enthusiast's choice amongst the big brands; Barilla, too, isn't bad.

As for shapes, I like *penne rigate* because these short, ridged tubes are good at taking up sauces, but my favourite are *orrechiette*, little indented discs about the size of a twenty-cent coin, which are usually hand-made (and so called because they are supposed to resemble ears). As pasta goes, *orrechiette* is fairly dear, but pasta is never an expensive food.

Johann is a much more accomplished cook than I am, and when she wrote the cookery column in the *Sunday Tribune* she developed a considerable base of fans who responded to her passion and her clear instructions. Her instinct for good food runs very deep. Partly it comes from being the daughter of a beef farmer who had great pride in his produce; partly from her knowledge of food history and a rigorous, logical discipline in the kitchen, but most of it comes from a sensual delight in good food. And that is one of the things we share. I can't imagine sharing my life with anyone who lacks an interest in food. But then again, I can't imagine sharing my life with anyone other than Johann.

Carrigeen Hill

By the time we found our new home at Carrigeen Hill in the summer of 2002, we were getting a little desperate. We had trawled through all of East Cork and much of West Waterford and found nothing we particularly liked and could also afford. There were, of course, hundreds of dormer bungalows on the standard issue half-acre (which usually turns out to be a lot smaller than that), but this would not really be enough to create the kind of garden I hankered after. It came to the point where we would have to vacate The Hermitage within a few months and let the developers get on with their scheme to turn it into a pub-cum-restaurant surrounded by hundreds of houses. And we had yet to find somewhere to live.

There were several disappointments, notably one involving a charming, newly built cottage on a few acres complete with river frontage. The very reasonable price, it soon became apparent, was because the builder had contravened as many of the building regulations as you care to mention.

Then one Saturday morning, as I sat browsing through the

property pages of *The Examiner*, I noticed an ad featuring what seemed to be a charming Victorian house with nine acres and, again, a suspiciously low price tag. Needless to say we fell for this charming semi-ruin – we have a penchant for rescuing neglected houses – and were only talked out of it when our ashen-faced surveyor suggested that half-a-million might just about save it from collapse.

And then I remembered the other house featured in the estate agent's ad. It was a bungalow on ten-and-a-half acres, with outbuildings, near Conna in the Bride Valley. We asked to see it.

Carrigeen Hill is indeed a hill and it overlooks the valley. It faces south and on a clear day you can look at the little hills undulating away into the distance towards Youghal and Bally-cotton. The view is undramatic but vast, and you can glimpse the Nagle Mountains away to the west. We looked at the view on a sunny summer's day. We also looked at the bungalow, which was built in 1950 ('Quite cute as bungalows go,' Johann remarked), and realised that it was far too small. But we also walked through the woods which came with the property and reached the conclusion that Carrigeen Hill was indeed a rather special place.

We calculated that we could just about squeeze into the bungalow if we bought a couple of prefabs for storage and office space and set about building a new, larger house else-where on the ten-and-a-half acres, which, in the end, turned out to be almost eleven acres. Most auctioneers would have called it '*circa* twelve acres of land'; in this part of the world

the word 'acres' is always followed by 'of land'.

The three-bedroomed bungalow became a four-bedroom bungalow as we sacrificed the dining room and transferred our meal consumption to the lean-to conservatory in which a Riesling vine flourishes (the house was occupied by Germans in the 1960s). We refer to this small space rather grandly as 'The Vinery' and at the time of writing are yearning for the considerably more generous dimensions of our new house, which is in the process of being built.

We gained a lot in moving to Carrigeen Hill. After many years and a few false starts, we got what most families take for granted these days – a central-heating system that works. We also gained space – not on the domestic front, of course, but in the form of the woods and the fields that surround us. Our woods and our fields. It can make you rather unhealthily pro-prietorial, but I suspect this will pass.

If you look beyond the current house you see what appears to be just a belt of trees. But if you explore properly you find that it is an actual wood with meandering paths and bluebells, wood anemones, primroses, enchanter's nightshade and ragged robin. Not only that but the trees themselves are an eclectic mixture of ash, beech, oak, birch, Scots pine and the odd chestnut. The eastern part is dominated by a phalanx of sycamores, about eighty years old. This rather unloved tree can look quite impressive given age; and this particular stand of mature specimens certainly has charm, and we are not plagued by thousands of seedling sycamores; why this should be is a mystery.

You might be forgiven for thinking that our four or five acres of woods are maintenance-free, but it is not entirely true. Where the leaf canopy is sparse the brambles run wild and threaten to take over. They need to be knocked back regularly with a brushcutter – a rather vicious machine which is like a strimmer but with a metal blade rather than mimsy nylon thread. Ivy is always trying to move up in the world from its usually prone position where it is useful in keeping down invasive weeds. The only problem is that it loves climbing trees and forming dense, heavy growth up in the branches. The trees don't seem to mind much, but the problem is that the ivy makes them top-heavy and they can snap in high winds. I spend many a winter afternoon taking counter-measures, armed with bow saw and loppers, a curiously satisfying and nurturing kind of occupation, even when your fingers lose all sensation. I know it sounds awfully New Agey, but I really do feel that we all benefit by spending time with trees, especially helping to cultivate them. I have never yet been tempted to start hugging them, however.

The wood is not just a wood, of course. It's a source of fuel. Ash can be quite brittle and after a gale there are plenty of branches down, which are sawn into suitable lengths for the fire. Ash is the greatest firewood, so they say, because it gives great heat, doesn't spit, and burns well even when 'green', or unseasoned.

Having such a source of natural, sustainable fuel has been instrumental in my graduation to true country living. Country life is not possible, it seems, without a lot of very dangerous and noisy equipment. I have yet to acquire a shotgun, without which no rural home is complete, as I'm a lousy shot and, frankly, scared stiff of the things. I make do with having an occasional pot shot at a sitting rabbit with a .22 rifle. Very carefully, I should add. Not for nothing does the owner's manual refer to a 'high-velocity weapon' and I am acutely conscious that the bullets can travel for a mile.

However, while fighting shy of the shotgun, I have acquired a machine that is potentially even more dangerous: a chainsaw. It is, of course, physically possible to manage our firewood supply and the woods themselves using manual equipment. After all, our ancestors didn't wield a Husqvarna, they used bow saws. On the other hand, modern life being what it is, speed and efficiency are pretty well essential and this is what a chainsaw delivers.

The late Richard Gordon, author of the *Doctor in the House* books, wrote an introduction to anaesthesia for medical students. At the end of the volume he says, 'If, by now, you are terrified of the very idea of anaesthetising a patient, this book will not have failed in its purpose.' Well, the manuals that go with chainsaws have a similar effect. Along with the details of all the great modern safety features, there are terrifying warnings about 'kickback' and injunctions to wear bullet-proof clothing. I've been tentatively slicing up a few logs for quite some time now, but the adrenalin still surges whenever I press the throttle and cut into the timber. I wouldn't dream, however, of felling any kind of sizeable tree. That is a job for the experts and I am delighted to leave it to them.

Maintaining the woods is, for the most part, less scary than cutting logs. I have to keep paths clear by cutting back the brambles and the elders twice or three times a year. Ivy removal goes on all the time. Sometimes I will be sitting at breakfast and notice a tree on the horizon with an ivy-choked crown. I make a note of where it is and make a point of seeking it out and cutting the stems before the day is out.

Eventually we will reinvigorate the woods by taking out some of the less happy trees and replanting. This is where the faith of the gardener is really tested; most of those trees will outlive us by a wide margin, even if we survive into our dotage (and I have a headstart on Johann in this regard). But while young trees may not have the visual impact of mature ones, there is something very satisfying about knowing that they are growing away slowly but surely and that one day, property developers permitting, they will look properly majestic.

I read somewhere that it takes about eighty years for a bluebell wood to become fully established, by which I suppose they mean to become so densely packed with bulbs that you get the breathtaking blue-carpet effect. Eighty years seems about right because most of our trees were planted between 1920 and 1930. Somebody with great foresight must have planted the bluebells at the same time and we are now the beneficiaries. When the bluebells are at their height, in the western part of the woods, there is a strange intensity in the colour, while there's also an impression of great delicacy – as if the masses of blossoms are like gossamer, about to be blown away by the slightest breeze.

The best of the woodland flora performs in the spring because by the time the leaf canopy closes over in early summer the ground becomes quite dark. I know it can be a pest of a weed, but the bright, star-like celandines, which form a carpet of dark-green sprinkled with gold, are one of the most cheerful sights in our extended garden. Which just goes to underline the fact that a weed is just a plant in the wrong place. Even the dreaded bindweed that twines through the hawthorn hedges on the woodland boundaries looks wonderful with its immaculate snow-white trumpets; but woe betide any of them that venture into the garden proper. And speaking of whiteness, the luminous blossoms of literally thousands of wood anemones scattered over the woodland floor is perhaps the loveliest sight of all.

The remains of the medieval road from Fermoy to Lismore – barely the width of a cart – can still be seen on the northern boundary of the woods. Step across that boundary, being very wary in case our neighbour's bull is hanging about, and you will pick up an old farm track that takes you over the top of the hill. Suddenly you see the vast sweep of the Knockmealdowns and the Comeraghs, with the deep groove of the Blackwater in the foreground. This is a glorious landscape, understated, undulating, with blue hills in the distance that have the distinctive blue haze about them that Elizabeth Bowen regarded as being peculiarly Irish. She was, of course, a native of North Cork. And it is virtually unknown by anyone who isn't fortunate enough to live here. Perhaps that is part of its charm.

Our little part of this landscape needs upkeep, as I say. The woods will become an impenetrable wilderness within a season or two if they are not managed – and not the kind of wilderness that wildlife likes, odd as that may seem to townies. The fields, too, need to be used, otherwise they will degenerate into scrub. Our initial solution to this problem has been to let much of the land and the stables to neighbours. The resulting horse manure, matured for a year, feeds our garden. In our first summer at Carrigeen Hill, it was good to see the sweet grass being turned into hay – several hundred bales of the stuff. Now the yield is smaller as all of the land is managed organically, but the quality is better. Nevertheless, the grazing needs to be 'topped' several times a year in order to keep down the thistles. When I lived in Dublin, I was probably convinced that the countryside looks after itself. Nowadays, I can tell at a glance if land is in good heart.

At the time of writing plans are afoot to plant lots of trees – oak, ash, larch, chestnut, plus enough Norway spruce to keep us and our friends in Christmas trees for the foreseeable future. The Norway spruce is the proper festive tree, the sort with which I grew up. Yes, I know it sheds its needles if you don't keep up the water supply, but this tree smells of Christmas, the very essence of Christmas. The Noble fir, which has virtually replaced the traditional spruce, is a very poor substitute, even if it does cause less of a mess. We could, of course, grow Noble firs and make money out of them, but that, frankly, would be giving in.

You don't hear much about coppicing these days, but I think its time will come. This is a traditional short rotation method of timber production for poles and firewood. Trees – usually young ones – are cut down to the base and allowed to sprout. After four to seven years you have a fine crop of wood, which can be cut up for the stove or the fire, or used to make fences or rustic-style furniture for the garden. Coppiced trees can be grown only a metre apart, so even a small amount of land can produce a large amount of timber. Or energy, if you want to use it for heating.

That's the great thing about trees: they have so many useful and important roles. They not only look beautiful and help to create a sense of place, they are also air-purifiers. They can lower the water table in boggy places, provide shelter for wild-life, produce building material and fuel. The only problem is that they take time, but, of course, most worthwhile enterprises are not exactly instant.

Down by the road our land tends to be waterlogged for most of the year – thanks to the fact that Carrigeen Hill is an actual hill and the land has to drain. But there is other water, too, in the form of a spring which, they say, has never dried up. As wells in the locality ceased to produce water during the remarkable summer of 2003, and our own one threatened to falter, the spring produced its consistent, sparkling flow of cool water from deep beneath the land.

When we arrived at Carrigeen Hill the previous owners kindly presented us with several closely typed sheets of essential information about the house, the land, the woods (including the great news that ravens nest here) and the locality. It mentioned the spring and gave a rough indication as to its whereabouts, which seemed to be in the middle of a huge thicket of gorse and brambles.

As soon as we had unpacked I set off with the girls on what Winnie-the-Pooh would call 'an expotition' to uncover the spring. We hacked through the dense and prickly growth with a slash-hook and revealed a muddy expanse, about forty feet square. Somewhere roughly in the centre was a few gallons of muddy water. It was, to be frank, not a very inspiring sight.

Months later, I returned, preferring, as a rule, to go for a ramble in the woods rather than sloshing around in the mire. On this occasion, however, I looked rather more closely and discovered a plastic drainpipe through which a trickle of water escaped through the bank. Lying nearby was a large, plastic, elbow-shaped joint which, in a moment of abstraction, I attached to the pipe. I had a hazy notion that this would raise the outflow level and hoped that it might produce something resembling an ambitious puddle – enough, perhaps, to encourage a few ducks to come up from the River Bride nearby.

A couple of days later I was thrilled to discover that this simple device, installed originally by the previous owners, had transformed our muddy patch into a very decently sized pond, three feet deep and even more profound in the centre. This, strange as it may seem, was a momentous experience. I have always hankered after water in the garden (or even at the bottom of a large, rather unkempt field), but I had been daunted by descriptions of how you have to buy a plastic lining, excavate the site, anchor the PVC and, basically, pray that it all works. I was determined to do it some day, but it was quite low down on my list of domestic priorities. And here I was with a ready-made pond, which had required me only to stick one pipe on top of another.

A week of hard labour with loppers, brushcutter and sheer brute force saw the pond revealed in all its glory. I slashed and burned, literally, a small forest of gorse and bramble and revealed the spring itself, tinkling out of the ground with what, to my ears at least, was sweet music, and a few metres of stream which feeds the pond.

It may not look like much – indeed, I'm quite sure that most suburban gardeners would be decidedly unimpressed – but as ponds go, this is a serious affair. For a start, it's bigger than I would ever have dared try to create from scratch (the cost of the plastic lining would be prohibitive, for a start) and, of course, it's fed by a natural spring so there is no danger of the water going stagnant.

The second phase of the pond epic came with my birthday when Johann presented me with a pair of waders. These allowed me to get up close and personal with the pond, wallowing around, trying to pull out the overgrowth of water-cress, planting the odd water lily here and there.

I quickly discovered that a natural pond is not to be trifled with. I might have waders to keep me dry, but there was no guarantee that I was not going to sink into the muddy bottom and become stuck fast. After being marooned up to my waist in very cold water (spring water is deliciously cool to run over your fingers; standing in it for an extended period is a different matter altogether) for a couple of hours waiting for help to arrive, it was difficult not to (a) panic and (b) wish that I had brought something long and rigid with me so that I could gently lever myself out of what increasingly felt like the con-crete shoes much used by the Mafia.

These days I tend not to wade in without some human com-pany, or at least my mobile phone. But working in the pond – literally in it – is a joy. There is some-thing about the smell of the water

– not unlike river water, indeed – and the distinctive plants and tiny insects that thrive there that makes an hour or so at my aquatic labours simply fly by. I realise that most gardeners of the conventional kind would far prefer to dead-head the roses or trim the edge of the lawn, but they don't know what they are missing.

Ours is not a pond for pampering. All I have done is to try to check the rampant growth of some of the more vigorous, naturally occurring plants while adding just a few exotics: very plain white or yellow water lilies and a few clumps of the deliciously scented water hawthorn. It also provides a wild harvest in the form of watercress and water mint.

As I write, phase three of the pond is about to start. The pond may be big by average standards, but it could be bigger. We have mapped out an extension and soon the JCB will be creating a small lake. And it's going to have an island, which will be reachable only by raft. I can think of nothing more fun

that you can do for a few hundred euro, and the children are inclined to agree.

With a greater expanse of water we hope to attract water fowl. A duck did nest and produced nine snow-white eggs on the bank of the existing pond, but it seems that the local fox population put paid

t

to her well-laid plans. Foxes are, as anyone who has read Beatrix Potter will know, inordinately fond of duck eggs and whatever creature stole our clutch did a very thorough job; there wasn't a shard of shell or a drip of yolk to be seen. Foxes can swim, but prefer not to, so I hope that our next duck may be persuaded that the island is a highly desirable residential area.

When our new house is built – with a bit of luck by summer 2005 – it will have a glorious view. Westwards the landscape stretches away into the hazy distance across the gentle hills of North Cork, eastwards over West Waterford towards the confluence of the Bride and the Blackwater. The house will be tucked into what we call the Barn Field, a sloping meadow of about an acre that already contains the kitchen garden, thoroughly rabbit-proofed, and the polytunnel. In the shelter of the embracing woodland stands our juvenile apple and pear orchard along with a fine young walnut tree which, in time, will bear nuts.

It will be here, God willing, that we will plant dozens of old-fashioned shrub roses and a herb garden. As I've said elsewhere, scented plants always have the edge in my book. We hope also to enrich the meadow with more native wild plants, a tricky business, but worthwhile, and somewhere or other I may achieve my ambition of planting a proper herbaceous border. Whether or not I will be able to give it the care it needs and deserves is another matter. I'm not sure that the formidable Gertrude Jekyll, champion of the herbaceous border as an art form, would approve of such a defeatist attitude. But, then again, she had a much larger income than mine.

Carrigeen Hill seems like a good place to put down roots. Admittedly it is a little too far from the sea to meet our ideal aspirations, but Whiting Bay is only half-an-hour away. The landscape around here has a comfortable, somewhat lived-in appearance. It may lack the wild, romantic, primeval appeal of West Cork, but its lush charm runs very deep if you stand and look. It needs to be contemplated.

Shortly after we moved to Carrigeen Hill, I took part in a radio discussion on life in rural Ireland. After joining in the general complaint that Dublin thinks that it's the true Ireland and that nothing beyond The Pale really matters, I was asked if I wanted my children to settle here.

I was astonished by the question, and this demonstrates my naïveté. Country people, as a rule, desperately want their off-spring to remain in what they tend to call – in a lovely phrase – 'the home place'. I'm not a real countryman, of course. I love country life and would find it well-nigh impossible to adjust to urban life again. But that sense of visceral connection with place is missing.

To employ that dreary cliché, I feel that I am a citizen of the world. It suits me to live where I do and I expect I will continue to live there. But my children will decide where they want to be. Where they need to be, indeed. If you become too attached to places and to possessions, your spirit becomes somewhat imprisoned. Attachments to people, on the other hand, and perhaps perversely, are liberating. Provided that attachment does not mean possessiveness. At least that's the way it is for me. As a Chinese philosopher, I believe, once said of children, 'You may house their bodies, but not their spirits.'

I sometimes sit, on warm evenings, above the kitchen garden, in the shade of the trees and look westwards over what must be hundreds of square miles of countryside. And I consider how lucky I am. I had parents who, for all their human frailties, believed that I could be whatever I chose to be. In Johann I have had the best partner and friend, in every sense, that I could possibly hope for. And the quiet intensity of my love for her and for my daughters is the greatest gift of all.

Everything else, however eloquently I try to wax about it – as befits a writer – is pretty trivial. All that matters, as so many others have said before me, is love.

Appendix I:
A Shopping List

This little list is just that. It's not comprehensive, but rather a short guide to where we buy various things that have to do with eating, drinking and growing things. It is worth bearing in mind that there are lots and lots of good producers throughout Ireland and that there is no substitute for local knowledge. In any case, these recommendations are born of our own experience. Yours may well overlap.

AGA

The Aga is not so much a cooker as a way of life, and we regard it as pretty well essential to our existence. Having said that, I suspect that many Agas these days are bought for appearances rather than use. This is pathetic, because the Aga is a wonderful device if you understand it. It differs from other cookers in several important respects, not least the fact that it weighs more than a tonne, is always on and cooks with a consistent, dry heat. Oil, gas, solid fuel and electric versions are available and they come in two sizes: the four-oven, which is justified only if you are cooking for a small army and which is often installed these days merely as a status symbol; and the good old two-oven version, which is good enough for us.

The top oven is for roasting and baking, the bottom one for very slow cooking or making brilliant oven-dried tomatoes. On top, there are two big plates, one for boiling and one for simmering. When not in use the heat is preserved by insulated covers which hinge down. Superb toast can be made by putting a slice of bread in an Aga toastmaker, a device that looks like a stange metallic tennis racket, which is placed on the boiling plate and the cover then placed over it.

When we graduated to our Aga we thought we would need a supplementary cooker of conventional type, but in fact we didn't. The only thing you can't do on an Aga – no matter what Aga may tell you to the contrary – is stir-frying. We are trying to get some Chinese contacts of ours to rig up a proper wok ring in our new kitchen; with that and an Aga we'll be exceptionally well equipped.

Agas are very expensive, but they are not just a piece of kitchen equipment, they are part of the house. They heat the kitchen and quite a lot of hot water. Reconditioned and second-hand Agas are available and worth considering.

The Aga agents for Ireland are: Campbell & Cooke Ltd, 16 Rutland Place, Dublin 1; Tel: 01-878 6099.

BACON

Our favourite bacon used to be the dry-cure version from Rudd's, which was never oversalted, shrank very little on cooking and was remarkably consistent. Alas, Rudd's have gone out of business. For Continental-style bacon we like to use the Campofrio brand, which is in most of the supermarkets. Fingal Ferguson's smoked bacon is a treat if you like your bacon smoky. His unsmoked bacon is superb and we buy it at the Organic Shop in the English Market, or at the Skibbereen Country

Market. There is also good ham and bacon to be had from O'Flynn's in Cork. Hugh Robson produces excellent pork and bacon in County Clare and sells them through various outlets, including the Temple Bar Market. He also supplies his son, Eric, at the Ely Wine Bar in Dublin.

Gubbeen Smokehouse, Schull, Co. Cork; Tel: 028-27824
O'Flynn's Butchers, 36 Marlborough Street, Cork; Tel: 021-427 5685
Hugh Robson/Glencarn Foods, Carron, Co. Clare; Tel: 065-89125

BEER

One of the most cheering aspects of Ireland's new enthusiasm for real food and real drink is the burgeoning micro-brewing industry, which started at Inagh in County Clare almost two decades ago. The beers of the Biddy Early Brewery are all excellent, but the Black Biddy Stout is my favourite. The Porterhouse in Temple Bar (and also in Bray, Phibsborough and London) produces world-class beers. Their Wrassler's XXXX Stout is the best I've ever tasted. The Dublin Brewing Company's range is worth seeking out, too. We also have a tremendous range of imported beers available to us these days and I'm a particular enthusiast for Budvar, the original Czech Budweiser pilsener, and for the recently arrived Krombacher lager from Germany. These, and many other unusual beers, are imported by Noreast Beers.

The Biddy Early Brewery and Pub, Inagh, Co. Clare; Tel: 065-36742
The Porterhouse, Parliament Street, Dublin 2; Tel: 01-679 8847
Dublin Brewing Company, 141–146 North King Street, Dublin 7;

Tel: 01-872 8622
Noreast Beers, Dundalk, Co. Louth; Tel: 086-258 4536

BREAD

The Doorley Diet is very light on refined carbohydrates, so bread is not eaten in vast quantities in our household. However, if you leave aside the white sliced pan which the children like for toast, we eat quality rather than quantity. Johann's brown soad bread has been honed and refined over the years and her yeast and sourdough breads (with a lot of fine wholemeal) are very similar to the rustic *pain de campagne* that you get in Europe. However, when we do buy bread we like to larrup into Declan Ryan's Arbutus Breads when we are at home, or, when in Dublin, Penny Plunkett's wonderful stuff from La Maison des Gourmets. The latter also does brilliant cakes, pastries, brioches and croissants. Another Dublin port of call, especially for croissants and scrumptious little Italian almond nibbles, is Panem. The Gallic Kitchen produces good stuff, too.

Arbutus Breads, Rathdene House, Montenotte, Cork; Tel: 021-450 1113
La Maison des Gourmets, 15 Castle Market, Dublin 2; Tel: 01-672 7258
Panem, 21 Lower Ormonde Quay, Dublin 7; Tel: 01-872 8510
The Gallic Kitchen, 49 Francis Street, Dublin 8; Tel: 01-454 4912

CHEESE

We love all kinds of cheese, but especially goat and sheep

kinds. One of our nearest cheesemakers is Jane Murphy, whose range of Ardsallagh goat's cheeses form quite a significant part of our diet. We buy our cheese mainly from the supermarket (and we quite like the oddly named Dubliner Cheddar from a co-op in West Cork), from Iago in the English Market and from Sheridan's in Dublin. Frankly, when you move beyond the supermarket you want to deal with cheesemongers who really know what they are at. Even the most pretentious supermarket cheese department (and Heaven knows there are plenty of them) knows as much about perfect ripeness and readiness as I do about the finer points of hurling. Watch out for stunning blues from Sheridan's and the weird but wonderful little *Brique de Brebis* from Iago, made from sheep's milk near Roquefort.

Ardsallagh Cheese, Woodstock, Carrigtwohill, Co. Cork; Tel: 021-488 2326
Iago, The English Market, Cork; Tel: 021-427 7047
Sheridan's Cheesemongers, 11 South Anne Street, Dublin 2; Tel: 01-679 3143

COFFEE AND TEA

These two beverages are so much part of daily life that most people don't give them a second thought. And, of course, there's a notion that being choosy about tea or coffee is just downright pretentious. Frankly, life is too short to eat bad food and drink bad drink, and there's a lot of really crap coffee out there. Personally, I never willingly drink instant coffee or tea-bag tea and I don't give two hoots if that's considered snobbery. We drink the Chinese *keemun* as our daily tea, either from Maher's in Cork (which I think is the better), or from Bewley's in Dublin. We also drink *lapsang souchong*, the smoky and highly distinctive Chinese tea, and occasionally the malty, somewhat astringent *oolong*, especially with Chinese food. It's hard to get decent Earl Grey these days, but the Fair Trade version is pretty good. Fortnum & Mason have a good one, but we have been known to make our own by pouring a few drops of oil of bergamot (the citrus fruit, not the herb) onto a strip of blotting paper and then placing it in a caddy of tea. Many Earl Greys are based on very poor tea in the hopes that the bergamot will distract attention; and, of course, as bergamot oil is volatile, Earl Grey loses its savour fairly rapidly. If you make your own, you can solve both of these problems.

We tend to drink relatively little coffee these days, so it is always something of a treat. We have an espresso machine into which we put Illy coffee pods (pre-measured for a shot of espresso and contained within a paper skin). Even Illy decaff is pretty good. Our plunger coffee, which we grind ourselves, comes from Fair Trade. We have also been impressed by the serious enthusiasm of the team behind Java Republic.

Maher's, 25 Oliver Plunkett Street, Cork; Tel: 022-427 0008
Bewley's, 78 Grafton Street, Dublin 2; Tel: 01-635 547
Fairtrade, Carmichael House, North Brunswick Street, Dublin 1; Tel: 01-475 3515
Java Republic, Unit C1, City Link Business Park, Old Naas Road, Dublin 12; Tel: 01-456 5506

COUNTRY MARKETS AND FARMERS' MARKETS

Country markets are great fun and good places to find real home-baking; in summer and autumn you may well get good vegetables and fruit, too, as stallholders sell their surplus. The most famous country markets include Kilternan in County Dublin, Blessington in County Wicklow and Carrigaline in County Cork.

Farmers' markets are a different and newer phenomenon, with examples trading very successfully in places like Skibbereen, Midleton, Westport and Galway. The Dublin markets at Meeting House Square, Leopardstown, Dún Laoghaire and Cow Lane are all, in effect, farmers' markets. In my experience you certainly get a few farmers at these events (Johann's sister, Madeline McKeever, sells her beef every Saturday at the Skibb market; our neighbour, Tim Yorke, sells his vegetables at the Midleton market), but there are plenty of other stalls, too, selling all manner of produce, from cheese and imported organic produce to dried herbs, eggs and poultry. Make enquiries locally and see what is happening. Farmers' markets are going to be big in the future and I see that Bord Bia and the IFA want to offer support. So we must be vigilant: let's make sure that most of the food sold is locally produced to excellent quality. And above all, let's ensure that farmers' markets do not become the preserve of the rich. I had the experience, recently, of buying an item by weight at a farmers' market and found that the trader rounded up the price. Not the way to go.

FISH

We've almost given up eating fish in Dublin because it has become so expensive, but we still go to Caviston's when we're in town. Otherwise we buy all our fresh fish from the Ballycotton Seafood Company in Midleton, where the hake and the Dublin Bay prawns (that's a species, not where they come from) offer outstanding value for money. The best smoked salmon in the world comes from Frank Hederman, who used to be a neighbour of ours in Cobh. His wild Irish smoked salmon is not cheap, but it is simply outstanding, melting in the mouth, quite dry and very sensitively smoked. Try this and you will never want to touch sloppy, fishy, yucky, so-called smoked salmon ever again. Frank's smoked mackerel is likewise superb, his smoked haddock (undyed, of couse) is an undiscovered delicacy, while his smoked eel, especially if eaten with horseradish, is a revelation. Fairness compels me to add that some of the smoked fish from Sally Barnes at the Woodcock Smokery in West Cork is in the same league, but smokier.

Ballycotton Seafood Company, 46 Main Street, Midleton, Co. Cork; Tel: 021-461 3122
Caviston's, 59 Glasthule Road, Glasthule, Co. Dublin; Tel: 01-280 6767
Belvelly Smokehouse, Belvelly, Cobh, Co. Cork; Tel: 021-481 1089
Woodcock Smokery, Castletownsend, Co. Cork; Tel: 028-36232

FRUIT AND VEGETABLES

We occasionally have to supplement from the supermarket (Lidl is quite good for basic, conventionally farmed produce), but a great deal of what we eat is grown by us at home. We also buy from our neighbour, Tim Yorke, at Glenribeen from time to time, and in Dublin we use either the organic selection at Bloomfield's, or go to Roy Fox's. At the Temple Bar Market, Denis Healy has a terrific range of his own organic produce from County Wicklow.

KITCHEN EQUIPMENT

It is very hard to come out of the Ballymaloe Shop without buying something: there's always a knick-knack that grabs you by the lapels. Brennan's in Cork City carries a very comprehensive range of kitchenware.

Ballymaloe Shop, Ballymaloe House, Cloyne, Midleton, Co. Cork; Tel: 021-465 2023
Brennan & Co. Cookshop, 7 Oliver Plunkett Street, Cork; Tel: 021-427 8283

MEAT

In general, we like to buy local produce as much as possible. Our beef and our lamb come from McGrath's in Lismore, just a few miles away. This small family business produces its own meat, from field to fork, and the quality is generally excellent. We also buy from Barry McSweeney in Midleton, who is a tremendous source of information on all aspects of meat. Organic chickens and eggs come from Dan and Ann Ahern who have a stall at the Midleton Farmers' Market. We occasionally get meat from Johann's sister, Madeline McKeever, who is an organic beef producer in West Cork. Pork is bought from Pettitt's in the southeast, but free-range organic pork, such a rarity in Ireland, is snapped up whenever we can get it without breaking the bank. When I'm in London, I buy free-range Gloucester Old Spot from Lidgate's in Holland Park Avenue. In Dublin we tend to buy the Ballybrado organic meats as supplied to Tesco by Josef Finke. Ballycumber Meats is another port of call for good, conventional beef and lamb sourced from their own farm in the Midlands.

Michael McGrath, Main Street, Lismore, Co. Wateford; Tel: 058 54350
McSweeney's, 28 Main Street, Midleton, Co. Cork; Tel: 021-463 1083
Madeline McKeever, Ardagh, Church Cross, Skibbereen, Co. Cork; Tel: 028-38898
Dan and Ann Ahern, Ballysimon, Midleton, Co. Cork; Tel: 021-463 1058
Pettitt's Supermarkets, St Aidan's, Wexford; Tel: 053-24055
Ballycumber Meats, Unit 114 Dún Laoghaire Shopping Centre, Co. Dublin; Tel: 01-280 3010
Ballybrado, Cahir, Co. Tipperary; Tel: 052-66206

OLIVE OIL

We buy all sorts of olive oil and bring it home from places as diverse as Australia and Portugal. Everyday stuff tends to be Tesco's own-brand Extra Virgin, but we also buy an organic Portuguese extra virgin olive from The Real Olive Company. They also, as it happens, do a brilliant range of olives.

The Real Olive Company, The English Market, Cork; Tel: 021-427 0842

ORGANISATIONS

I'm not really the joining type, but some organisations do great work, are worthy of support and give you certain benefits. Cork Consumer Choice meet monthly in the Crawford Gallery and deal with a plethora of food issues. Growing Awareness is based in Skibbereen and campaigns on food-related and environmental issues. The Henry Doubleday Research Association (HDRA) is devoted to the encouragement of organic horticulture and runs a very useful heritage seed library. Irish Seed Savers does the same, in a smaller way, here in Ireland. The Royal Horticultural Society is the largest of its kind in the world, hosts many flower shows, including Chelsea, publishes *The Garden* magazine and offers free advice to members. It's a must for serious gardeners. Slow Food Ireland is the local branch of an international organisation concerned with proper food, artisan production and the pleasures of the table. I have, in the past, accused SFI of being somewhat élitist, but their hearts are in the right place and most of its members are committed to spreading the good news to everyone in the land.

Cork Consumer Choice, c/o Ballymaloe House, Midleton, Co. Cork
Growing Awareness, c/o Madeline McKeever, Lisheen, Church Cross, Skibbereen, Co. Cork: www.westcorkweb.ie/growing
HDRA: www.hdra.org.uk
Irish Seed Savers, Scariff, Co. Clare: www.catalase.com/issa
Royal Horticultural Society: www.rhs.org.uk
Slow Food Ireland: www.slowfoodireland.com

MAGAZINES

The Kitchen Garden magazine is published in Britain and

every month provides reams of reading for anyone interested in growing their own fruit and vegetables. There is also a very useful readers' forum on their website. *Observer Food Monthly* (OFM) is published monthly with the *Observer* newspaper and is very up-to-the-minute in terms of food and food fashions. *Waitrose Food Illustrated* is published by the British supermarket chain of the same name and is available on the newsstands. Waitrose is a very ethical supermarket and was the first in Britain to stock organic food. They also stock heritage apple varieties in season. Lovely pictures, great recipes and some serious campaigning.

The Kitchen Garden: www.kitchengarden.co.uk

PLANTS

I try to grow as much from seed or cuttings as possible, but occasionally I need plants. For trees I go to Future Forests in Bantry (great collection of heritage apples and much, much more), and for roses I go to John McNamara near Midleton (but bear in mind that he's a wholesale grower who will let you know what garden centres he supplies). Carewswood Garden Centre is my usual port of call for anything else.

Future Forests: www.futureforests.net
McNamara Rose Nurseries, Dunsfort, Midleton, Co. Cork; Tel: 021-461 3733
Carewswood Garden Centre, Bridgefield, Castlemartyr, Co. Cork; Tel: 021-466 7283; www.carewswoodgardencentre.com

SEEDS

I buy most of my seeds from *The Organic Gardening Catalogue* and some from Thompson & Morgan. But I find myself getting more every year from Brown Envelope Seeds, a small West Cork operation that specialises in Irish organically grown seeds. Their list is getting bigger.

Organic Gardening Catalogue: www.organiccatalog.com
Thompson & Morgan: www.thompson-morgan.com
Brown Envelope Seeds: www.westcorkweb.ie/market

WHOLEFOODS AND SUPPLEMENTS

We are blessed with one of the best shops dealing in wholefoods, dietary supplements and alternative remedies; proprietor Jill Bell is a fund of information.

Well & Good, Coolbawn, Broderick Street, Midleton, Co. Cork; Tel: 021-463 3499.

WINE

Like everybody else, we buy some of our wine from the supermarkets, particularly from Pettitt's (because I select their range), and from Dunnes Stores, which is probably the best of the big guys. I am also seriously impressed by O'Briens who have branches throughout Dublin. But small, quality-conscious merchants have a special advantage in that their enthusiasm is often infectious. This is a list of the places where I regularly buy (obviously I occasionally stray beyond these outlets):

Berry Bros & Rudd, 4 Harry Street, Dublin 2; Tel: 01-677 3444; website: www.bbr.ie

Dublin satellite of one of London's oldest and best merchants. Exceptional range in all regions, but Burgundy and Bordeaux are really outstanding.

Cabot & Co., Valentia House, Custom House Plaza, IFSC, Dublin 1; Tel: 01-636 0616

For stunning Italians and offbeat Australians in particular.

Le Caveau, Market Yard, Kilkenny; Tel: 056-52166; website: www.lecaveau.ie

Terrific Burgundys direct from the growers at keen prices, along with many offbeat French wines sourced direct from small producers.

Greenacres, Main Street, Wexford; Tel: 053-24905; website: www.greenacres.ie

One of the best ranges of Bordeaux in the country, plus a fine picture gallery.

Mitchell & Son, Kildare Street, Dublin 2; Tel: 01-676 0766; website: www.mitchellandson.com

Terrific, eclectic range with real depth and quality in all regions.

O'Brien's

By far the best of the chains and always keen value. Spain, France and Australia are particular strengths. Branches all over Dublin, and somewhat beyond.

Oddbins

Getting back on form after changing hands . in 2002. Plenty of pleasant surprises, particularly strong in southern France and Australians. Branches in Baggot Street, Blackrock, Churchtown and Blanchardstown.

Pettitt's Supermarkets, Head Office, St Aidan's, Wexford; Tel: 053-24055; website: www.pettitts.ie

My work with Pettitt's keeps me in touch with commercial realities. Large, eclectic range with seasonal collections and some exceptionally keen value. Lots of wines from small, high-quality producers that you won't find in other supermarkets. Branches in Wexford, Enniscorthy, Gorey, Arklow and Athy.

Redmond's, 25 Ranelagh Road, Dublin 6; Tel: 01-497 1739; website: www.redmondswine.ie

Probably the best off-licence in the land. Vast range, lots of curiosities and a terrific beer selection.

Searson's, Monkstown Crescent, Monkstown, Co. Dublin; Tel: 01-280 0405

Marvellous range, especially in Bordeaux and Italians.

Wicklow Wine Company, Main Street, Wicklow Town, Co. Wicklow; Tel: 0404-66767

One of my favourite places for browsing. Virtually everything comes direct from the producers and there are some great bargains, especially from Bergerac, the south of France and Portugal.

The Wine Vault, High Street, Waterford; Tel: 051-853444; website: www.waterfordwinevault.com

Personal selection by David Dennison whose wine enthusiasm is boundless. Some exceptional Australians.

Wines Direct, Mullingar, Co. Westmeath; Tel: 1890-579579; website: www.wines-direct.ie

Ireland's leading mail-order wine merchant, offering remarkable value from the south of France but now with offbeat wines from other places, notably Australia and Italy.

Appendix II:
A Reading List

I love books and always have done. At the last, very rough, count the family collection extends to some 6,000 volumes and rising. What I have tried to do here is to select a core group of books which have either inspired and informed me, or which I consult on a regular basis.

A comprehensive list of those cookbooks which I use regularly would simply be too long to record here. Instead, I might just mention the cookery writers whose works are constant companions: Arabella Boxer, Marcella Hazan, Elizabeth David, MFK Fisher, Simon Hopkinson, Nigel Slater, Myrtle Allen, Darina Allen, Jane Grigson, Claudia Roden, Madhur Jaffrey, Alistair Little, Maureen Tatlow, Richard Olney, Julia Child, Ken Hom and Tamsin Day-Lewis. I'm sure there are some omissions.

Many of the books mentioned below are now out of print, some of them for many years. However, if you use some of the internet book search engines, such as www.abebooks.co.uk – a database of five million books for sale around the world – most of them should be easy to track down and many of them are really quite cheap.

This is an eclectic collection of books – it may seem odd that a history of family planning rubs shoulders, so to speak, with a book on rare vegetables – but I have done my best to group them under relatively logical headings. All of them are worth owning, and I hope you will glean as much enjoyment from them as I have had.

FOOD

Arabella Boxer, *Food in Vogue from Boulestin to Boxer* (Pyramid Books: London, 1988).

Alan Davidson (ed.), *The Oxford Companion to Food* (OUP: Oxford, 1999).

Edouard de Pomiane, *Cooking in Ten Minutes* (Faber & Faber: London, 1960).

Christopher Driver, *The British at Table 1940–1980* (Chatto & Windus: London, 1983).

Dorothy Hartley, *Food in England* (reprint) (Little Brown: London, 1996).

Tom Jaine, *Making Bread at Home* (Phoenix: London, 1995).

Maura Laverty, *Full and Plenty* (Irish Flour Millers Association: Dublin, 1960).

Harold McGee, *On Food and Cooking: The Science and Lore of the Kitchen* (Allen & Unwin: London, 1986).

Richard Mabey, *Food for Free* (Collins: London, 1972).

Monica Sheridan, *Monica's Kitchen* (Castle Publications: Dublin, 1963).

Maureen Tatlow, *Good Enough to Eat* (Gill & Macmillan: Dublin, 1998).

JC Vaughan and CA Geissler, *The New Oxford Book of Food Plants* (OUP: Oxford, 1997).

GARDENING

Peter Beales, *Classic Roses* (Harvill Press: London, 1992).

Judith Berisford-Ellis, *The Wild Garden* (Faber & Faber: London, 1966).

Christopher Brickell (ed.), *The Royal Horticultural Society Encyclopaedia of Gardening* (Dorling Kindersley: London, 1992).

Lawrence D Hills, *Down to Earth Gardening* (Faber & Faber: London, 1967).

Eleanour Sinclair Rohde, *The Scented Garden* (The Medici Society: London, no date).

Graham Stuart-Thomas, *The Old Shrub Roses* (Dent: London, 1957); *Shrub Roses of Today* (Dent: London, 1962).

VEGETABLES

DG Hessayon, *The Vegetable Expert* (Transworld: London, 1995).

ER James, *The Vegetable Garden* (Penguin: London, 1954).

Joy Larkcom, *Vegetables for Small Gardens* (Hamlyn: London, 1995).

Brian Organ, *Rare Vegetables for Garden and Table* (Faber & Faber: London, 1960).

WE Shewell-Cooper, *The Complete Vegetable Grower* (Faber & Faber: London, 1975).

Eleanour Sinclair Rohde, *Vegetable Cultivation and Cookery* (The Medici Society: London, 1938).

William Watson, *The Gardener's Assistant* (Volume I, Gresham Publishing: London, 1925).

FRUIT

Alan Davidson and Charlotte Knox, *Fruit: A Connoisseur's Guide and Cookbook* (Mitchell Beazley: London, 1991).

Joan Morgan and Alison Richards, *The Book of Apples* (Ebury Press: London, 1993).

GARDEN HISTORY

Susan Campbell, *Cottesbrooke, An English Garden* (Century: London, 1987).

Joan Morgan and Alison Richards, *A Paradise out of a Common Field: The Pleasures and Plenty of the Victorian Garden* (Century: London, 1990).

C Anne Wilson, *The Country House Kitchen Garden 1600–1950* (Sutton Publishing: Stroud, 1998).

Ted Humphris, *Garden Glory* (Collins: London, 1969).

THE COUNTRYSIDE

Marcel Bon, *The Mushrooms and Toadstools of Britain and Northwestern Europe* (Hodder & Stoughton: London, 1987).

Geoffrey Grigson, *The Englishman's Flora* (Phoenix House: London, 1960).

RM Lockley, *The Private Life of the Rabbit* (Andre Deutsch: London, 1964).

Niall MacCoitir and Grania Langrishe, *Irish Trees: Myths, Legends and Folklore* (The Collins Press: Cork, 2003).

Ernest Neal, *The Badger* (Collins: London, 1948).

Brian Vesey-FitzGerald, *A Country Chronicle* (Chapman & Hall: London, 1949); *Town Fox, Country Fox* (Andre Deutsch: London, 1965).

Michael Viney, *A Year's Turning* (Blackstaff Press: Belfast, 1996).

John Seymour, *The Complete Book of Self-Sufficiency* (Corgi: London, 1981).

WOODS

Ken Broad, *Caring for Small Woods* (Earthscan: London, 1998).

William Mutch, *Tall Trees and Small Woods* (Mainstream: Edinburgh, 1998).

FAITH, FATHERLAND, FERTILITY

Paul Blanshard, *The Irish and Catholic Power* (Verschoyle: London, 1954).

Terence Brown, *Ireland: A Social and Cultural History 1922–1979* (Fontana: London, 1980).

Andrew Furlong, *Tried for Heresy; A 21st Century Journey of Faith* (O Books: Winchester, 2003).

Dermot Keogh (ed.), *The Lost Decade: Ireland in the 1950s* (Mercier Press: Cork, 2004).

John Robinson, *Honest to God* (SCM Classics: London, 2001).

RL Smith, *A Quaker Book of Wisdom* (Orion: London ,1998).

Hilary Wakeman, *Saving Christianity* (Liffey Press: Dublin, 2003).

Clive Wood and Beryl Sutters, *The Fight for Acceptance: A History of Contraception* (M&T Press: Aylesbury, 1970).

W Gilbert Wilson, *The Faith of an Anglican* (Collins/Fount: London, 1980).

WINE

Andrew Barr, *Wine Snobbery* (Faber & Faber: London, 1988).

James Halliday and Hugh Johnson, *The Art and Science of Wine* (Mitchell Beazley: London, 1992).

Hugh Johnson, *Pocket Wine Book* (Mitchell Beazley: London, 2004).

Hugh Johnson, *The Story of Wine* (Mitchell Beazley: London, 1989).

Jancis Robinson (ed.), *The Oxford Companion to Wine* (OUP: Oxford, 2002).

Jancis Robinson, *Wine Course* (BBC Publications: London, 2003).